FAIR GROWTH

FAIR GROWTH

ECONOMIC POLICIES *for* LATIN AMERICA'S POOR *and* MIDDLE-INCOME MAJORITY

NANCY BIRDSALL, AUGUSTO DE LA TORRE, and RACHEL MENEZES

Center for Global Development
Inter-American Dialogue
Washington, D.C.

Copyright © 2008
CENTER FOR GLOBAL DEVELOPMENT
1776 Massachusetts Avenue, N.W.
Washington, D.C. 20036
www.cgdev.org

INTER-AMERICAN DIALOGUE
1211 Connecticut Avenue, N.W.
Washington, D.C. 20036
www.thedialogue.org

Fair Growth: Economic Policies for Latin America's Poor and Middle-Income Majority
may be ordered from:
BROOKINGS INSTITUTION PRESS
c/o HFS, P.O. Box 50370, Baltimore, MD 21211-4370
Tel.: 800/537-5487; 410/516-6956; Fax: 410/516-6998; Internet: www.brookings.edu

Library of Congress Cataloging-in-Publication data
Birdsall, Nancy.
  Fair growth : economic policies for Latin America's poor and middle-income
majority / Nancy Birdsall, Augusto de la Torre, Rachel Menezes.
    p. cm.
  Summary: "Presents 'tools' to make life in Latin America more equitable and fair
for the majority. Suggests policies and programs for making tax structures more
progressive; giving small businesses a chance; protecting labor mobility and workers'
rights; tackling corruption; and raising levels of quality, efficiency, and equity of the
education systems"—Provided by publisher.
  Includes bibliographical references and index.
  ISBN-13: 978-1-933286-16-7 (pbk. : alk. paper)
  ISBN-10: 1-933286-16-4 (pbk. : alk. paper)
  1. Latin America—Economic policy. 2. Latin America—Social policy. I. Torre,
Augusto de la. II. Menezes, Rachel. III. Title.
  HC125.B52 2007
  330.98—dc22   2007044749

1 3 5 7 9 8 6 4 2

Printed on acid-free paper

Typeset in Sabon and Ocean

Composition by Cynthia Stock
Silver Spring, Maryland

Printed by Versa Press
East Peoria, Illinois

Contents

INTER-AMERICAN
DIALOGUE

The Inter-American Dialogue is the leading U.S. center for policy analysis, exchange, and communication on issues in Western Hemisphere affairs. The Dialogue brings together public and private leaders from across the Americas to address hemispheric problems and opportunities. Together they seek to build cooperation among Western Hemisphere nations and advance a regional agenda of democratic governance, social equity, and economic growth.

The Dialogue's select membership of 100 distinguished citizens from throughout the Americas includes political, business, academic, media, and other nongovernmental leaders. Twelve Dialogue members served as presidents of their countries and more than two dozen have served at the cabinet level.

Dialogue activities are directed to generating new policy ideas and practical proposals for action, and getting these ideas and proposals to government and private decision makers. The Dialogue also offers diverse Latin American and Caribbean voices access to U.S. policy debates and discussions. Based in Washington, the Dialogue conducts its work throughout the hemisphere. A majority of our Board of Directors are from Latin American and Caribbean nations, as are more than half of the Dialogue's members and participants in our other leadership networks and task forces.

Since 1982—through successive Republican and Democratic administrations and many changes of leadership elsewhere in the hemisphere—the Dialogue has helped shape the agenda of issues and choices in inter-American relations.

Center
for Global
Development

The Center for Global Development is an independent, nonprofit policy research organization dedicated to reducing global poverty and inequality and to making globalization work for the poor. Through a combination of research and strategic outreach, the Center actively engages policymakers and the public to influence the policies of the United States, other rich countries, and such institutions as the World Bank, the IMF, and the World Trade Organization to improve the economic and social development prospects in poor countries. The Center's Board of Directors bears overall responsibility for the Center and includes distinguished leaders of nongovernmental organizations, former officials, business executives, and some of the world's leading scholars of development. The Center receives advice on its research and policy programs from the Board and from an Advisory Committee that comprises respected development specialists and advocates.

The Center's president works with the Board, the Advisory Committee, and the Center's senior staff in setting the research and program priorities and approves all formal publications. The Center is supported by an initial significant financial contribution from Edward W. Scott Jr. and by funding from philanthropic foundations and other organizations.

Preface and Acknowledgments

As a cofounder of the Center for Global Development, which was established just over five years ago, I was determined that the Center tackle the problem of inequality in the world—of income, wealth, opportunity, and access to health and education—both between and within countries. Until very recently, students of development have put much more energy into understanding the causes and consequences of absolute poverty than of inequality. But globalization, with its new opportunities for generating winners and losers and its new insecurities and competitive pressures, is changing that. Nowhere is the issue of inequality more worrying than in Latin America, the setting of many of the world's most unequal societies.

This book presents a dozen ideas, or "tools," meant to make life in Latin America more equitable and fair for the great majority of its people—not only for the rich, a small elite, but also for the rest. As a coauthor of this book and as president of the center I have been extraordinarily fortunate to have had as a partner in its conception Peter Hakim and as a partner in its production the institution that he leads, the Inter-American Dialogue. In its own work the dialogue hews to the premise that business, government, and civil society leaders in North, South, and Central America can work together to build a consensus on key economic, social, and political issues that will serve their mutual interests.

The seeds of this 2007 book were sown in the late 1990s, when Peter and I talked about the tough challenges presented by poverty and inequality in Latin America. We collaborated in setting up a group of academics, policy experts, businessmen and –women, and former officials from across the hemisphere with the objective of developing a practical and visible agenda to address those problems. A product of the resulting discussions was *Washington Contentious: Economic Policy for Social Equity in Latin America*, published in 2001 by the Carnegie Endowment for International Peace, where I was then a senior associate, and the Inter-American Dialogue. The title of the book, which was written by Augusto de la Torre, a key member of the original expert group, and me, was meant to signal the difference between the objectives of stability and efficiency, which were at the heart of the so-called Washington Consensus reforms, and our objective: social equity.

The book was sufficiently popular and useful that it was soon out of print. Although since then Latin America has enjoyed almost five years of reasonably good growth, benefiting from an unusually benign external environment, only modest progress has been made in reducing the number of poor people in the region (still upward of 200 million). In many countries, already high income inequality has risen further. Whether despite or because of globalization and the Washington Consensus reforms, the failure to achieve a breakthrough on poverty and inequality has taken a toll—in lost opportunities for better lives for millions of people and in growing political resistance to deepening critical market reforms. Voters in Venezuela, Bolivia, and Ecuador (and almost those in Mexico and Peru) have turned in frustration to leaders who have promised to finally deliver social justice—leaders with good intentions but in some cases with fundamentally counterproductive policy ideas.

Augusto and I, along with Rachel Menezes, who had worked with us on *Washington Contentious*, decided that it was time to update and deepen our analysis to put a clearer emphasis on fairness and social justice as a fundamental objective of good economic policy. We believe that fairness in economic policy can be fully consistent with growth. We do not want justice, fairness, and equity to be monopolized as political and economic ideals by one side of the ideological aisle. Thus our title, *Fair*

Growth. We also wanted to rethink our analysis to focus not only on the 40 percent of the "poor" in the region but also on the additional 30 percent of working-class and middle-income Latin Americans living in many countries on less than US$10 a day. New analysis suggests that the poor and middle-income majority has not benefited from the growth and market reforms of the last fifteen years, either because they lack skills or because they lack new job and income opportunities that could use and extend their skills. Thus our subtitle: *Economic Policies for Latin America's Poor and Middle-Income Majority*.

Our objective in this book is to encourage real change in Latin America and new understanding and support for that change in North America and the rest of the rich world. Change and reform to promote greater fairness requires not only political leadership and technical know-how on the part of the region's government officials and legislators but also support and input from the business community throughout the Americas, from an increasingly vocal and effective civil society, and from students and intellectuals. In the hope that members of all those groups will turn to our dozen equity or fairness tools, we have made an effort to write in a manner that is easily accessible as well as technically sound.

In addition, for those interested in the strong evidence that grounds our analysis, we have provided extensive endnotes that include more detail on the points that we raise and citations to the studies on which we have relied. We hope that this approach makes our book especially appealing to a new generation of students in Latin America and students of Latin American economics and politics.

I extend my personal thanks to my coauthors, Augusto and Rachel, for their intellectual energy and hard work and the spirited conversations that we have had. Together we thank William Cline and John Williamson for their close reading of an earlier draft and their careful comments on it. We are grateful to Carola Pessino and Ricardo Fenochietto for their help with our discussion of tax reform, to John Nellis for comments on privatization, and to Jeffrey Puryear and Tamara Ortega Goodspeed for answering many questions about the details of education policy in the region. We thank Vito Tanzi, Vicki Perry, Eduardo Lora, Isaias Coelho, and Michael Walton for their help during our early discussion of fairness in taxation,

Claudio Loser for his help on fiscal policy issues, Peter Timmer for his suggestions on rural and land markets, Manuel Orozco for his guidance on remittances, and Eduardo Lora and Carmen Pagés for their suggestions on labor policy. We received useful contributions from Andrei Kirilenko (on financial transaction taxes), Daniel Artana (on tax policy), Joan Caivano (on access to information and freedom of the press), and Carolina Menezes (on financial and credit markets), and we thank all of them.

In 2006 we presented an early draft of the manuscript to the members of the Inter-American Dialogue at the Sol Linowitz Forum. Their enthusiasm inspired us, and their many suggestions led to substantial revisions. We would like to thank in particular Peter Bell, Carla Hills, David De Ferranti, Guillermo Perry, Beatriz Merino, Epsy Campbell Barr, Roberto Teixeira da Costa, Peter McPherson, Joyce Chang, Yolanda Kakabadse, Darren Schemmer, Nora Lustig, Robert Hart, Jennifer McCoy, Sonia Picado, Earl Jarrett, John McCarter, Oliver Clarke, Roberto Murray-Meza, Beatriz Nofal, Jesús Silva-Herzog, Paula Stern, Jaime Zabludovsky, Claudio Loser, José Octavio Bordón, Jan Boyer, José María Dagnino Pastore, Everett Eissenstat, Thomas Mackell Jr., and Marta Lucía Ramírez de Rincón.

Eileen Hughes edited our manuscript with patience and care. At the Center for Global Development, Lawrence McDonald and Lindsay Morgan were generous with their time and suggestions and guided the manuscript to its final publication. Lawrence McDonald brought his creative genius to our struggle to find the right title. At the Inter-American Dialogue, Jeffrey Puryear was stalwart in providing comments and managerial support and in keeping us on track.

All three of us are especially grateful to Peter Hakim, who helped conceive the project that resulted in this book and who has kept us motivated with his commitment to sound analysis, to a better life for the people of Latin America, and to the agenda we here propound. Augusto thanks Guillermo Perry, the chief economist for Latin America at the World Bank, for supporting Augusto's continuing involvement in this project.

Finally, we are grateful to Ed Scott for his generous support of the Center for Global Development's work and to the Canadian International Development Agency (CIDA) and Swedish International Development

Cooperation Agency (SIDA) for their support to the Inter-American Dialogue for this project. I and my coauthors look forward eagerly to a serious round of advocacy of our fairness agenda through our many partners in the development community and in Latin America.

NANCY BIRDSALL
President

Center for Global Development
December 2007

INTRODUCTION

Giving Latin America's Majority a Fair Chance

I n the 1990s, most countries of Latin America firmly embraced the economic reform package that has come to be called the Washington Consensus.[1] The policies included in the package emphasized price stabilization and structural adjustment measures such as privatization, reduction of import tariffs, liberalization of local financial markets, and opening of economies to foreign investment—all with the objective of making the economies more efficient and competitive, in the hope that the resulting growth would trickle down. But more than a decade of such open market economic reforms in Latin America failed to deliver much in the way of growth or social progress. Per capita income growth in the region during the 1990s lagged behind that of the advanced economies and emerging economies in Asia (figure 1). That lag has led to anxiety and frustration—with market reforms, with the political process, and with the way democracy is working.

The early part of the new century did nothing to bring a new sense of promise. Latin American economies continued to suffer from the wave of financial turbulence that started in the late 1990s, with several countries falling into crippling banking and currency crises—for example, Ecuador

---

1. See Williamson (1990) for the original set of reforms associated with the Washington Consensus. General statements about Latin America in this book refer to continental Latin America excluding Belize, French Guyana, and Suriname (Argentina, Bolivia, Brazil, Chile, Colombia, Costa Rica, Ecuador, El Salvador, Guatemala, Honduras, Mexico, Nicaragua, Panama, Paraguay, Peru, Uruguay, and Venezuela), plus the Dominican Republic.

FIGURE 1. Real Per Capita Growth, Various Years

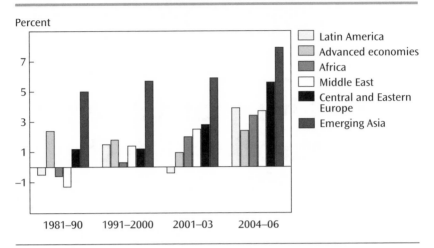

Source: IMF (2007a).

(1999–2000), Argentina (2001–02), Uruguay (2002), and the Dominican Republic (2003). Not surprisingly, during 2001–03 per capita income growth in the region was negative, even as all other regions in the world were experiencing positive growth in per capita income.

Since 2003, however, Latin America's macroeconomic performance has improved significantly relative to its performance over the past two decades or so. Per capita income rebounded while inflation remained low. Progress was underpinned by generally more robust fiscal and monetary policy and greatly aided by a remarkably benign external environment (high global liquidity, low international interest rates, high commodity prices, and intensified cross-border market integration). Still, compared with trends in other regions in the world, the most recent Latin American trend has not been especially stellar. While per capita income growth in Latin America during 2004–06 exceeded that of the advanced economies and Africa, it was substantially below that in other regions, especially emerging Asia but also central and eastern Europe. The post-2003 increase in growth was hardly sufficient to arrest the long-term trend in Latin America whereby its per capita income has diverged more and more from that in OECD countries (figure 2).

Moreover, the macroeconomic improvement in the most recent period has not dispelled the disenchantment that Latin Americans feel with market-

F I G U R E   2. Per Capita Income Relative to That in OECD Countries, 1975–2004[a]

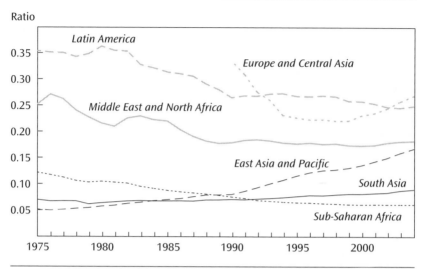

Source: WDI (2006).
a. Purchasing power parity, in current international dollars.

oriented reforms, their deep concerns about economic insecurity, and their frustration with the functioning of political systems. To be sure, technical analyses of the effects of structural reforms—trade and financial liberalization, opening of capital markets, privatization, and deregulation—suggest that Latin America would have been worse off without them. Per capita income and output would have been lower, volatility higher, and poverty deeper.[2] But the fact is that structural reforms (with the possible exception of financial sector reform) have not been politically viable and have stalled in the majority of Latin American countries since 1999 (figure 3). Recent public opinion polls do show a rising share—albeit from a relatively low level—of Latin America's population believing that the economic situation today is better than the past and is likely to

2. Lora and Panizza (2002) estimates that reforms increased annual growth rates by 1.3 percent on average in 1991–93, 1 percent in 1994–96, and 0.6 percent in 1997–99, generating a cumulative increase in the region's average per capita income of 11.4 percent. See also Escaith and Morley (2001) and Loayza, Fajnzylber, and Calderón (2005) for other estimates of the impact of reform on growth in Latin America.

F I G U R E   3. Structural Reforms Index, Average for Latin America[a]

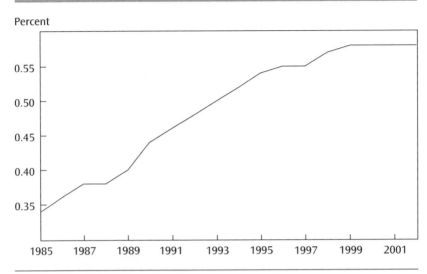

Percent

Sources: Lora (2004, 2001).
a. Extent of reforms as percent of total possible reforms.

improve further in the near future, a belief that is consistent with the recent increase in per capita income growth. However, they also show that Latin Americans are resentful of the reforms, especially privatization; tired of high unemployment and stagnant wages; and increasingly worried about violence, crime, and delinquency. Although a majority of those surveyed in 2006 endorsed democracy as the most preferable form of government, they tended to believe that their countries were ruled for the benefit of a few, self-serving, powerful groups, and they were dissatisfied with the actual functioning of their democracies.[3]

Those perceptions are not independent of Latin America's very slow progress in reducing poverty and its offensively high and persistent inequality in the distribution of income and assets. The share of the population living below the poverty line (as measured by ECLAC) fell only marginally from the early 1990s, to about 40 percent in 2005–06, while the number of poor people in 2006 was the same (around 205 million) as

3. Latinobarómetro (2006). Latinobarómetro is an annual public opinion survey of approximately 19,000 interviews in eighteen countries in Latin America.

F I G U R E   4. Latin American Population Living under the Poverty Line, 1980–2006[a]

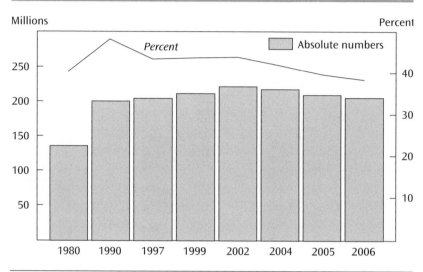

Sources: ECLAC (2006a).
a. Based on special tabulations of household surveys in eighteen countries in the region, plus Haiti.

in 1997 (figure 4).[4] At the same time, measured income inequality in Latin America remained among the highest in the world and in some countries has increased since the early 1990s (figure 5). And while certain measures of living conditions—infant mortality, completion of primary school, and access to clean water—have improved significantly, other key measures, such as urban violence and crime, have deteriorated alarmingly throughout most of the region.[5]

4. ECLAC (2006a). ECLAC's poverty line is defined as "the minimum income household members must have in order to meet their basic needs." That income is based on the cost of a basic food basket in each country that takes into account consumption habits, availability and relative prices of foodstuffs, and differences between metropolitan and other urban and rural areas, to which is added an estimate of the resources that households need to cover their basic non-nutritional needs. ECLAC (2006a) estimates that the monthly equivalent in dollars of the poverty lines in the region varies between US$45 (Bolivia) and US$157 (Mexico) in urban areas and between US$32 (Bolivia) and US$98 (Mexico) in rural areas.

5. On health and education indicators, see, for example, ECLAC (2006a, 2005) and PREAL (2001, 2006); on crime and urban violence, see Heinemann and Verner (2006) and Londoño and Guerrero (1999).

F I G U R E 5. Gini Coefficients of the Distribution of Household Per Capita Income, Various Regions and Years[a]

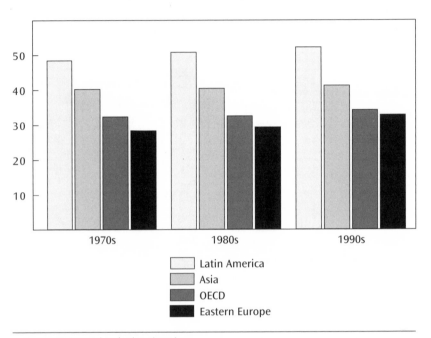

Source: De Ferranti and others (2004).
a. Africa is not included because not enough observations on income inequality in that region are available.

From the discussion above, two disturbing facts stand out. First is the contrast between the intensity of the reform effort in the 1990s and the modest results of that effort—some growth, little change in poverty, and stubbornly high inequality. Second is the contrast between the recent significant recovery of growth with low inflation and the lingering strong sense of frustration with market-based reforms as well as with the functioning of the political systems. These facts have sparked a heated debate among economists and policymakers on the shortcomings of the reform agenda—whether the problem has been too little or too much market reform or the wrong types or sequence of reforms.[6]

6. See, for example, Rodrik (2006, 2005); Zettelmeyer (2006); Loayza, Fajnzylber, and Calderón (2005); Kuczynski and Williamson (2003); Lora and Panizza (2002); Ocampo (2002, 2004); Rojas-Suarez and Johnson (2008, forthcoming); and Singh and others (2005).

In this book we take the view that the problem was not so much a shortage of reforms per se but that the various reform packages were missing an authentic and explicit concern with equity. We believe that the lingering social and political malaise in Latin America reflects in large part the sense that economic arrangements in the region have been unfair for far too long. On that score, the market reforms of the last fifteen years may have made things worse—or at least failed to make them better.

This central problem with the reform agenda since the 1990s—the lack of any explicit inclusion of equity concerns—undermined the potential benefits of reforms for social cohesion, undercut the enthusiasm for further reform, and may even have reduced some of the benefits of reforms for growth, although the last effect is difficult to demonstrate.[7] The reform packages of the 1990s did not systematically include features aimed directly at reducing inequity. Even if the reform agenda of the 1990s yielded faster overall growth and hence faster declines in poverty than would otherwise have occurred, it has not resulted in greater equality of opportunity, let alone in lower measured inequality. It is therefore not surprising that market reforms that focused on increasing efficiency and competitiveness failed, by themselves, to alter the perception that the region's economies work unfairly.

The growing anxiety stemming from perceptions of unfairness has been reinforced by the challenges that come with globalization.[8] Globalization's intensification of market competition has accelerated the Schumpeterian process of "creative destruction," whereby inefficient businesses are pushed out of the market by efficient ones.[9] That acceleration has raised economic uncertainty, especially for unskilled workers who feel at the mercy of global forces that they cannot control. The resulting sense of

---

7. For preliminary evidence that initial inequality may itself limit reform efforts (including but not necessarily reform of the labor market specifically), see Behrman, Birdsall, and Pettersson (2008, forthcoming).

8. See, for instance, De la Torre, Levy-Yeyati, and Schmukler (2002); Calvo (2005); De Ferranti and others (2000); and Rodrik (1997).

9. Economist Joseph Schumpeter proposed the idea that a market economy ensures growth by allowing new, better companies to topple the old through a process that he called "creative destruction," which is essential for sustaining long-term growth in market economies. Schumpeter believed that entrepreneurs are the ones who drive economies, generating growth and, through their successes and failures, setting business cycles in motion (Schumpeter 1975).

insecurity is of course much greater in countries where social safety nets are weak or truncated and where human capital (due to lack of educational and retraining opportunities) is inflexible, as those factors make the adjustment toward new employment unduly protracted and painful.

In short, we take the position that the reform agenda in the region has been incomplete—that it has left out what we call, in an allusion to a political expression invoked in the United States in the 1970s, the "silent majority." The economic reforms that did take place, with their emphasis on stability and competitiveness, were not meant to address a deeper underlying problem in Latin America: the poor distribution of opportunities and productive assets across households, regions, ethnic groups, and other divides. Measured income inequality in Latin America is simply a good proxy for the limited access of the poor to economic and social assets, of the low returns on the assets that they do have, and of their limited access to opportunities for advancement.[10] Given the low level of education of the silent majority (see chapter 9), and their poor access to land and credit (chapters 7 and 5), it is not surprising (at least in retrospect) that the majority of households did not benefit from rising wages for educated labor and could not exploit higher returns to business and other investment. Furthermore, the lack of explicit attention to equity considerations in economic reforms happened at the time when globalization was on the rise. Hence, growing economic insecurity was added to a longstanding perception of systemic unfairness, and that combination contributed significantly to Latin Americans' frustration with market reform.

As we write, in late 2007, the risk of a new round of populism and protectionism hangs over the region—an unsurprising result of historic injustices combined with, in most countries, rising anxiety about the future among the silent majority. That risk suggests that attacking inequality is a political as well as an economic necessity. Income inequality in Latin America is largely a function of the extremely high concentration of income in

---

10. Birdsall and Londoño (1997) shows that education and land inequality measured at the economy-wide level reduces the income growth of the poorest quintile twice as much as it reduces the income growth of the average household. The study also shows that Latin America is not different from other regions in terms of the effects of income distribution on growth; it is its much higher inequality in the distribution of land and education that makes it an outlier where growth is even lower than its income inequality alone can explain. See also Deininger and Olinto (2000).

the top decile. Indeed, measured inequality would be similar to that in the United States, except for the higher proportion of income captured by the richest 10 percent of households in Latin America.[11] The concentration of income at the top in Latin America reflects and reinforces a long history in which the economic elites were politically powerful—indeed, the economic and political elites often were one and the same, and they could abuse their political position to reinforce their economic privileges.[12]

What alternatives are there to the ultimately destructive course of populism and protectionism? What policies and practices can attack injustice while creating sustainable economic opportunities for all and helping unleash more fully shared growth? What concrete policy actions will give the region's silent majority the sense that they and their children have a chance for a better future?

In this book we suggest that Latin America should turn to a new focus—on equity, or fairness. We look beyond the Washington Consensus to an agenda explicitly designed to improve job opportunities and create assets for the region's silent majority—an agenda that attacks inequality in the distribution of productive assets. We propose a "toolkit" of twelve sets of policies, mostly economic in nature, aimed specifically at making economic life in Latin America more fair.

At the same time, we have selected policies that do not sacrifice growth. What is known about the links among poverty, inequality, and growth in developing countries suggests that opportunities abound for win-win solutions—that is, solutions that can lead to simultaneous advances in growth and equity. Because the room for win-win solutions is larger where financial markets and other markets are weak and regulatory arrangements to compensate for their inherent imperfections are inadequate, it is larger in Latin America than in developed countries.[13] In effect, where financial and labor markets do not work well, the poor and the unskilled are more likely to be elbowed out of access to credit, jobs, and other opportunities to be

---

11. IDB (1999, p. 16). This comparison is for the late 1990s and does not take into account the growing concentration of income in the top 1 percent in the United States since 2000.

12. Karl (2001) elaborates on the corrosive interaction of economic and political privilege in the region. See Engerman and Sokoloff (2002) for the historic origins of this interaction.

13. Birdsall (2007) emphasizes weak markets and poor government policy as key factors in making inequality a problem in developing countries. See Barro (2000) for evidence that inequality reduces growth more in poor than rich economies.

productive. The opportunities that they lose as individuals and households are lost to the economy as a whole, reducing overall growth. An example is the inability of small business owners with movable collateral to borrow where the legal and regulatory framework does not guarantee that creditors can seize that collateral in the event of default.

In developed countries, by contrast, more competitive markets and stronger institutions help ensure more equitable access, which reduces the room for win-win situations for growth and equity. But where capital and other markets do not work well and government policy and institutions do not either, market and policy failures combine with high inequality to undermine opportunities not only for the poor, but for growth itself. That implies that there is room to reduce inequality while enhancing efficiency and growth.[14] In other words, there need not be a trade-off between "economic" policies—for example, to maintain macroeconomic stability and enhance growth—and "social" policies to reduce poverty and inequality. Indeed, they can be mutually reinforcing.[15] Put another way, there need not be a trade-off between efficiency and equity.

In the remainder of this introduction we set out the facts with respect to growth, reforms, and changes in poverty and equity since the early 1990s. We suggest the relevance to job and wage insecurity of the increasing integration of Latin America into global trade and capital markets and the implications of growing integration for our equity agenda. We then introduce and summarize our agenda for 2007 and beyond in the form of a twelve-part equity policy toolkit.

1990–2006: Economic Reforms, Disappointing Results, Reform Fatigue

In the 1990s, Latin America championed open market reforms. Fiscal and monetary discipline cut the inflation rate to single digits almost everywhere,

---

14. Birdsall (2007). That is not to say that there can never be a trade-off between growth and inequality. But when inequality is as high as it is in Latin America, it is probably a source of inefficiency, so the likelihood of a trade-off is smaller. There is, in other words, plenty of room for achieving both, well inside what economists call the production frontier defining the trade-off between equity and efficiency. Birdsall (2001) defines "equity" as distinct from inequality.

15. For essays on this theme applicable to Latin America, see Birdsall, Graham, and Sabot (1998).

F I G U R E 6. **Progress with Structural Reforms in Latin America**[a]

Percent

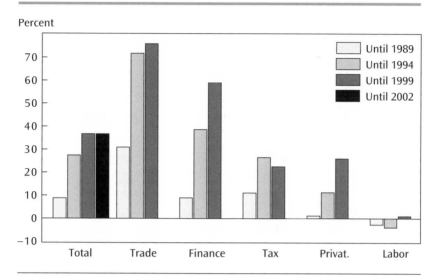

Sources: Lora (2004); Lora and Panizza (2002).
a. Extent of reforms as percent of total possible reforms.

and trade liberalization brought average tariffs down from more than 40 percent to nearly 10 percent. Financial liberalization was just as aggressive: direct credit controls were abandoned, interest rates deregulated, foreign direct investment (FDI) regimes opened, and foreign exchange and capital account controls dismantled. Banks, power plants, telecommunications systems, and, to a lesser extent, roads and water services were sold to the private sector (figure 6).

Implementation varied across countries, but the overall quality and extent of economic reforms in Latin America in the 1990s were far greater than at any time in memory. By reducing expenditures, writing off debt (in some cases using proceeds from privatization), and adopting steadier monetary and exchange rate policies, Latin American governments reduced inflation and volatility, at least in countries that escaped the financial crisis of the late 1990s.

But real GDP growth in the region was a modest 1.5 percent per capita per year for the decade—higher than in the crisis-laden "lost decade" of the 1980s but well short of per capita GDP growth in Asia (figure 1) and of Latin America's own growth in the 1960s and 1970s.[16] Since 2003, the region's economies have done better, expanding at about 3.5 percent per capita per year,[17] bolstered by robust global demand (especially from China) and strong commodity prices.[18] Macroeconomic stability and exchange rate flexibility contributed to the region's improved external sector performance and increased resilience to shocks.

But even with those gains, growth continues to lag that in other parts of the world—including, more recently, Africa and the Middle East, which once trailed Latin America. Most Latin American countries are growing more slowly than the developing world as a whole and, in some cases, even more slowly than the developed countries (figure 2).

Perhaps even more worrisome is the fact that labor productivity growth has been minimal.[19] Compared with investment in the rapidly growing economies of Asia, both public and private investment in science and technology to foster learning and innovation are low in Latin America.[20] And

16. Annual GDP growth in Latin America averaged 2.5 percent per capita in 1960–70 and 3.2 percent per capita in 1970–80 (ECLAC 2004b).

17. Real growth in Latin America is projected to be around 4.9 percent (3.5 percent per capita) in 2007 and 4.2 percent (2.9 percent per capita) in 2008 (IMF 2007a).

18. Latin American exports grew by 21 percent in 2006 (building on 19 percent growth in 2005 and an exceptional 23 percent increase in 2004), largely as a result of the robust growth in the United States and the strong demand for commodities from rapidly expanding Asian economies, particularly China and India. Countries like Argentina, Brazil, Chile, and Peru benefited significantly from China's strong demand for soy and copper. Net oil exporters such as Colombia, Ecuador, Mexico, and Venezuela also posted strong trade performances. In 2005, the overall price index for commodities exported by Latin America rose by 21 percent (15 percent excluding energy products such as crude oil, petroleum products, and natural gas). In 2004, average prices for commodities exported by the region increased by 29 percent (Cornejo Azzarri, Mesquita and Shearer 2006; ECLAC 2006c, 2006d; IMF 2006a).

19. Between 1990 and 2005, labor productivity growth averaged 0.4 percent in Latin America, while it was 3.3 in emerging Asian economies and 1.5 in the advanced economies over the same period (IMF 2007b). IDB (2004a) shows that between 1985 and 2000, nine Latin American countries experienced negative growth rates in productivity per worker (Panama, Venezuela, Colombia, Honduras, Ecuador, Bolivia, Paraguay, Peru, and Nicaragua) and only four (Chile, the Dominican Republic, El Salvador, and Uruguay) exhibited growth rates above 1 percent a year. The study finds no statistically significant difference in the rate of labor productivity growth in the region for 1985–90, 1990–95, and 1995–2000. Low labor productivity growth explains the low wage levels and painfully slow increases in wages in Latin America over the last decade (Ocampo 2004).

20. Malkin (2006) shows that Latin America invested US$11 billion on research and development (R&D) in 2002, US$1 billion less than South Korea's R&D investment in 2003. Ten years ago, China and Latin America shared similar levels of R&D investment (0.6 percent

despite clear improvements in fiscal positions, public debt levels remain high—averaging an estimated 52 percent of GDP in 2006—and far exceed levels during the mid-1990s.[21] Although there is some evidence of export diversification, most countries are still heavily dependent on primary commodity or "maquila" (apparel) exports.[22] With trade overall constituting a low percentage of GDP (figure 7) and debt remaining high, many economies in Latin America continue to be vulnerable to shifts in financial market sentiments and declines in commodity prices, even given their accumulation of high reserves (as of late 2007). Finally, Latin American countries (except Chile) rank poorly in most indexes measuring ability to compete in the global economy.[23]

Relatively slow growth and commodity dependence have added to the sense of vulnerability in the region, especially to competition from Asia. While China is an important and growing market for Latin American commodity exporters, it also is a significant competitor in the manufacturing sector.[24] China's accession to the World Trade Organization (WTO) in late 2001 and the removal in 2005 of OECD quotas on textile

---

of GDP). By 2005, China had more than doubled its ratio of R&D investment, to 1.4 percent of GDP, while Latin America saw overall R&D investment shrink by 3 percent in the same period.

21. IMF (2007b); reference is to weighted averages. Between 2002 and 2006, Latin America's debt-to-GDP ratio dropped 24 percentage points, reflecting the effects of strong primary surpluses, faster growth, and appreciating exchange rates as well as relatively benign global circumstances (IMF 2006a). More public debt is now domestic rather than external, but it continues to be short-maturity debt, implying that governments have traded a currency for a maturity mismatch and still face high rollover risk in the event of a financial or other crisis. See also IDB (2006).

22. Commodities constitute about 50 percent of Latin America's exports, and the share in the Andean region is even higher, about 84 percent (ECLAC 2007a). Most countries still specialize in goods that are not dynamic in world trade. The little diversification that has taken place recently in Latin America (for example, in Mexico) owes more to the decisions of foreign companies and preferential access to the U.S. market than to the traditional tools of export promotion and development. Central American countries have succeeded at curbing dependency on traditional commodity exports, but El Salvador and Honduras are now increasingly concentrated on exporting maquila manufactures (goods assembled from imported inputs for export). Export concentration has increased in Guatemala in recent years (ECLAC 2006e, 2004a; ECLAC-SIGCI 2007; World Bank 2005a; IMF 2007c).

23. See, for example, the World Bank's Doing Business indicators (World Bank 2006a; www.doingbusiness.org) and the World Economic Forum's Global Competitiveness Index (Lopez-Claros and others 2006).

24. For further discussion, see Perry and others (2007a); Blázquez-Lidoy, Rodríguez, and Santiso (2006); Schott (2006); Lora (2007); Mesquita Moreira (2007); and Hummels (2006).

F I G U R E   7. Trade as a Percentage of GDP, Various Regions, 1990–2004

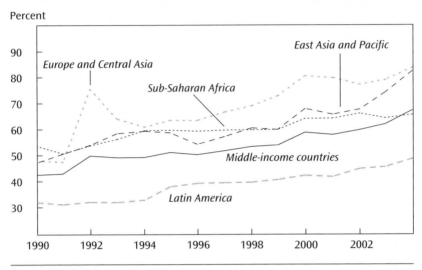

Source: WDI (2006).

and clothing imports pose a special challenge for producers in Central America. Mexico in particular has an export structure that is very similar to that of China. Once in the top position in the U.S. imports market after Canada, Mexico has seen its share of exports to the United States decline, and its economy is threatened all the more by the eventual erosion of its NAFTA preference, which will come with multilateral liberalization. Other countries in Central America that had taken small steps to get into manufacturing (and services) also are experiencing losses in market share, especially in the United States, to more competitive Chinese and Asian products. Between late 2001 and 2004, China's share of U.S. imports of textiles and apparel doubled from 9 to 18 percent while that of Mexico and the Caribbean dropped by a similar amount.[25] So far, analysts who

25. Chinese exports to the United States of textile and apparel products liberalized under phase 3 of the WTO's Agreement on Textile and Clothing (ATC) (for example, selected home furnishings of cotton, selected fabric and yarn products, and several types of commercially important apparel accessories) grew fourfold, and China's share in those categories jumped from 15 to 45 percent between 2001 and 2004. India and Pakistan also saw increases of 29 and 24 percent respectively in their market share over the same period. Mexico's exports of the same products dropped 11 percent, and CAFTA saw an overall decline of

predicted that the combination of proximity and preferences would preserve Latin America's market share have not been vindicated.[26]

In short, after more than a decade of open market reforms, Latin America still has not found its competitive legs. Although the region is ahead in terms of absolute income, the economic escalator is moving faster in other parts of the world. More than fifteen years after the embrace of market reforms throughout the region, only Chile (where market reforms began earlier) can claim strong and continuous, crisis-free growth.

What about poverty and inequality? At the beginning of the 1990s poverty rates declined from their peaks in the late 1980s, helped by reduced inflation. But progress slowed in the late 1990s in the context of low growth and financial crises and recovered in most countries only when economic growth increased in the last few years (2004–06). In 2005–06, close to 40 percent of the region's population still lived in poverty, about the same rate as in 1980, and in absolute numbers another 73 million people had been added to the poverty rolls.[27] Even where poverty fell, income inequality stayed high. Between 1990 and 2005, only Uruguay and Panama (and to a lesser extent Honduras) showed any marked improvement in already high levels of income inequality (figure 8).[28]

5.5 percent in exports in this category, although El Salvador, Honduras, and Nicaragua saw modest increases (Bhattacharya and Elliott 2005).

26. Bhattacharya and Elliott (2005). Several studies show that East Asian suppliers are ahead in adopting technologies that allow them to operate as full-package apparel suppliers (that is, they manage the process from procuring materials and assembling apparel to labeling, packaging, and shipping the product to stores) and to respond rapidly to orders. China has the workforce and the infrastructure to deliver high-quality apparel at competitive prices on a timely basis throughout the world (many Chinese firms are full-package suppliers). India (and perhaps Pakistan) also has an advantage in global textile and apparel markets because it has access to local inputs and a large pool of low-wage workers. Mexico and much of Latin America stand to lose market share because their wages are relatively high (compared with those of other apparel exporters, including China, where manufacturing wages are four times lower than in Latin America) and because Latin American producers have not made the move to providing full-package services (Blázquez-Lidoy, Rodríguez, and Santiso 2006).

27. We are referring to country-specific poverty lines (as measured by ECLAC; see note 4). In countries like Bolivia, Honduras, and Nicaragua—where poverty rates reach or exceed 60 percent—the proportion of the poor failed to drop much if at all between 1990 and 2004–05. Poverty actually increased slightly in Bolivia and also in Paraguay, Uruguay, and Argentina in the same period. In Venezuela, the proportion of poor people rose significantly before dropping again with the boom in commodity prices since 2002 (table 1).

28. On inequality in the 1990s, see also Székely (2001).

F I G U R E **8.** **Gini Coefficients of Income Distribution, Selected Latin American Countries**[a]

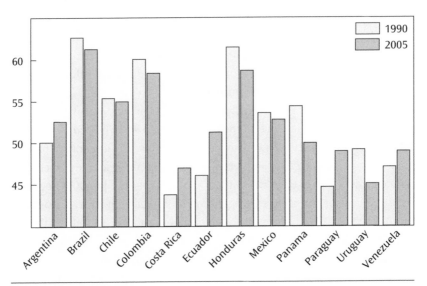

Source: ECLAC (2006a).

a. Data are for 1990 and 2005 or closest available year. For Ecuador, Panama, and Uruguay, data refer to urban areas. Data for Argentina refer to Gran Buenos Aires and for Paraguay, to the Asunción metropolitan area. Gini coefficients come from different household surveys and may not always be comparable.

Such results were all the more frustrating considering that since the 1980s Latin America has seen significant increases in the level of public spending on basic health and education (figure 9); devolution of revenue and authority for local services to local governments; and institutional innovations such as programs providing cash transfers to participants who keep their children in school or who use health services, which target the poorest households in Mexico, Brazil, and Chile (see chapter 3 in this volume).[29]

Not surprisingly, public opinion surveys in the early 2000s indicated that in country after country, citizens were discouraged. The majority of Latin Americans surveyed believed that their economies and democracies

29. On the recent trends and orientation of public social spending in Latin America see, for example, ECLAC (2005, 2001); see also Clements, Faircloth, and Verhoeven (2007). For an overview of the gradual change over time in the criteria to design and implement social policies and programs in the region, see Birdsall and Székely (2003); and Cohen and Franco (2006).

F I G U R E   9. Public Social Spending in Latin America

Percent of GDP

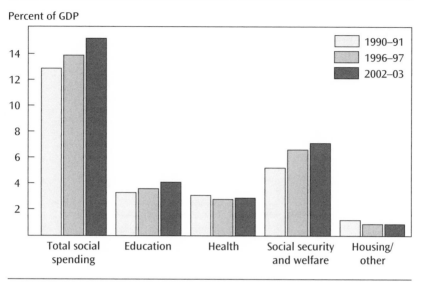

Source: ECLAC (2005).

were not functioning well (figures 10a and 10b), and that their quality of life was lower than that of previous generations (figure 10c). In the same surveys, citizens consistently expressed the sense that the region's societies were fundamentally unjust (figure 10d)—no doubt a reflection of the underlying inequity in opportunities for schooling, jobs, and participation in the political system.

There has been a recent increase, consistent with the current gain in growth, in the proportion of Latin Americans who believe that their economies are improving (figure 10a). However, opinion surveys highlight the political unpopularity of reforms across the region. In country after country, voters are increasingly unhappy with the market reforms of the 1990s and doubtful about their potential benefits (figure 10e).[30] That sentiment was especially strong among middle-income families. Opposition to privatization, for example, increased in the late 1990s among survey respondents with some secondary or technical education from more than

30. On the unpopularity of reforms in Latin America, see also Panizza and Yañez (2006); Lora and Olivera (2005); and Lora and Panizza (2002).

F I G U R E   1 0 a.   How would you describe your country's present economic situation?

Percent of respondents

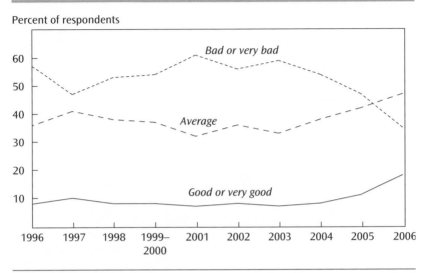

Source: Latinobarómetro (2006).

F I G U R E   1 0 b.   How satisfied are you with the way that democracy works in your country?

Percent of respondents

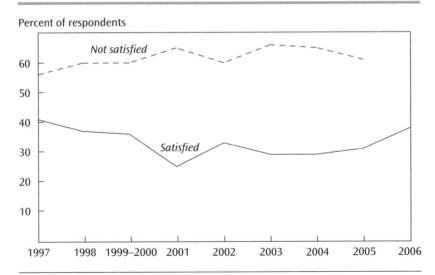

Source: Latinobarómetro (2006).

F I G U R E   1 0 c . **Would you say that your quality of life today is higher than, similar to, or lower than that of your parents' generation?**

Percent of respondents, 2001

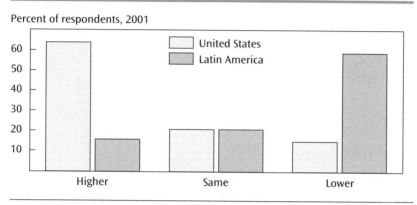

Source: Graham (2002), from U.S. General Social Survey (2001) and Latinobarómetro (2001).

F I G U R E   1 0 d . **Do you think that the income distribution in your country is very fair, fair, unfair, or very unfair?**[a]

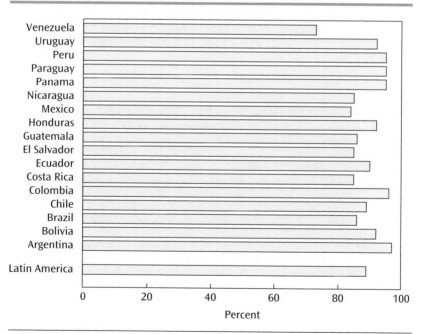

Source: Latinobarómetro (2001).
a. Percent responding unfair and very unfair, 2001.

F I G U R E   1 0 e. Support for Privatization and the Market Economy in Latin America, 1998–2003[a]

Percent

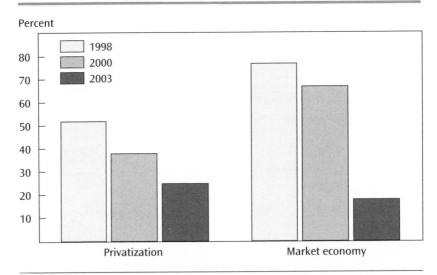

Privatization   Market economy

Source: Panizza and Yañez (2006) based on Latinobarómetro surveys.
a. Percent of respondents who think that the privatization process was beneficial for the country; percent of respondents who think that a market economy is good for the country. Note that Latinobarómetro surveys from 1998 and 2000 ask "Do you think that a market economy is good for the country?" For the year 2003 the question was "Are you satisfied with the functioning of the market economy?"

45 percent to more than 65 percent, while the increase for the overall population was from 40 percent to 50 percent (figure 11).[31]

In all, the adoption of the Washington Consensus turned out to be a costly political affair for reformers. A few incumbents were favored by voters for their success in taming inflation, but little electoral recognition was accorded those who advanced the rest of the macroeconomic and structural policies deemed necessary to accelerate growth and ensure stability.[32] It is

31. Lora and Panizza (2002). On the middle-income issue, see Birdsall and Menezes (2005) and Birdsall (2002). Birdsall, Graham, and Pettinato (2000) uses Latinobarómetro survey data on attitudes toward reform to assess the extent to which attitudes differed among poor, middle-income, and rich respondents. They report regression results indicating that middle-income respondents were more supportive of reforms early in the process and were least supportive later, indicating an increasingly negative overall attitude.

32. Lora and Olivera (2005) found that between 1985 and 2002 in seventeen Latin American countries the incumbent's party was rewarded in presidential elections for reductions in the rate of inflation and (although less) in legislative elections for increases in the rate of growth. But the electorate seems averse to pro-market policies, irrespective of their effects

F I G U R E   1 1. Negative Opinion of Privatization, by Educational Level[a]

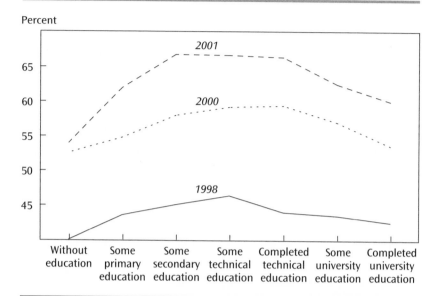

Percent

Source: Lora and Panizza (2002). Authors' calculations based on Latinobarómetro 1998, 2000, 2001.

a. Percent of respondents who believe that privatization has not been beneficial. Survey question: "State-run public services of water and electricity have been privatized. Taking into account price and quality, are you today much happier, happier, less happy, or much less happy with privatized services?" Here only "much less happy" and "less happy" responses are illustrated.

no coincidence that since 1999 the structural reform index for Latin America has flattened out (figure 3).[33] Although a widespread reversal of open market policies and a return to the irresponsible populism of earlier decades seems unlikely, the momentum for continued reform has dissipated.[34]

on growth or inflation. The authors' estimates imply that the typical reduction in the inflation rate—from, say, 20 percent to 8 percent during a president's term—boosts the vote for his or her party by 21 percent. If the same incumbent also introduces the average number of pro-market reforms, however, the party loses 23 percent of the vote on that account. (The evidence of adverse pay-offs in legislative elections is weak.)

33. Since 2000, in Argentina, Uruguay, Brazil, and Bolivia, voters have chosen presidents who emphasized the needs of the poor and working-class population (Juan Forero, "Populist Movements Wrest Much of Latin America from Old Parties," *New York Times,* April 20, 2006, p. A8; "The Battle for Latin America's Soul," *Economist,* May 18, 2006; "The Return of Populism," *Economist,* April 12, 2006).

34. Developments in 2006 in Bolivia—including a decree by President Evo Morales renationalizing oil and gas—suggest that a return to populism in Latin America is not out of the question. In 2007, President Hugo Chávez of Venezuela also announced plans to nationalize

Globalization, Jobs, and Middle-Income Households

Globalization has almost certainly contributed to the growing sense of economic insecurity among the silent majority of middle-income and poor households in Latin America. As with domestic market reforms, the greater integration of Latin America's economies into global financial markets has not worked as hoped or as advertised.[35] Along with financial globalization came more frequent financial crises (although not necessarily because of globalization per se), with large economic and political costs. The collapse of the Mexican peso in 1995 was followed by major financial crises in Brazil (1999), Ecuador (1999–2000), Argentina (2001–02), Uruguay (2002), and the Dominican Republic (2003), some of which involved a triple collapse (currency, banking, and debt) and a widespread breakdown of contracts.[36] Latin American economies have been especially vulnerable because of their heavy reliance on external savings, relatively high debt levels, and widespread currency and maturity mismatches on debtor balance sheets. The crises probably increased insecurity despite the benefits of the increased foreign direct investment and expansion of investment and export volumes brought by greater integration and open markets.

The silent majority has not escaped the effects of the crises. To be sure, global markets have brought economic insecurity to middle-income households everywhere.[37] But in Latin America insecurity is a far greater

---

energy and telecom companies (Simon Romero and Juan Forero, "Bolivia's Energy Takeover: Populism Rules in the Andes," *New York Times,* May 3, 2006, p. A8; "Now It's the People's Gas," *Economist,* May 4, 2006; "A Hard Bargain," *Economist,* November 2, 2006; "Tin Soldiers," *Economist,* February 15, 2007; Andy Webb-Vidal, "Chávez to Nationalise Telecoms, Power," *Financial Times,* January 8, 2007; Juan Forero, "Chávez Sets Plans for Nationalization," *Washington Post,* January 9, 2007, p. A10; Andy Webb-Vida, "Chávez Elaborates on Nationalisation Plans," *Financial Times,* February 02, 2007; Benedict Mander, "Venezuela Takes Over U.S. Oil Projects," *Financial Times,* June 26, 2007).

35. For middle-income countries, integration into the world's financial markets has not led to such expected benefits as a truly countercyclical monetary policy, consumption smoothing, deepening and diversification of domestic financial markets, noticeable reduction in the cost of capital, or significant availability of long-duration financial contracts denominated in the domestic currency (De la Torre, Levy-Yeyati, and Schmukler 2002).

36. De la Torre, Levy-Yeyati, and Schmukler (2002); De la Torre, Gozzi, and Schmukler (2007b).

37. See Birdsall, Graham, and Pettinato (2000).

TABLE 1. **Poverty Rates in Selected Countries, 1990–2005**[a]
Percent of population

	1990	1994	1997	1999	2002	2004	2005
Argentina	21.2	13.2	17.8	19.7	41.5	25.9	22.6
Bolivia	n.a.	n.a.	62.1	60.6	62.4	63.9	n.a.
Brazil	48	45.3	35.8	37.5	38.7	37.7	36.3
Chile	38.6	27.6	23.2	21.7	20.2	18.7	n.a.
Colombia[b]	56.1	52.5	50.9	54.9	51.1	51.1	46.8
Costa Rica	26.3	23.1	22.5	20.3	20.3	20.5	21.1
Dominican Republic	n.a.	n.a.	n.a.	46.9	44.9	54.4	47.5
Ecuador	62.1	57.9	56.2	63.5	49	47.5	45.2
El Salvador	n.a.	54.2	55.5	49.8	48.9	47.5	n.a.
Guatemala	69.4	n.a.	61.1	n.a.	60.2	n.a.	n.a.
Honduras	80.8	77.9	79.1	79.7	77.3	74.8	n.a.
Mexico	47.7	45.1	52.9	46.9	39.4	37	35.5
Nicaragua	n.a.	73.6	69.9	n.a.	69.3	n.a.	n.a.
Panama	39.9	30.8	29.7	25.8	25.3	22.4	24.4
Paraguay	n.a.	49.9	46.3	49	50.1	59.1	55
Peru[b]	n.a.	n.a.	47.6	48.6	54.8	54.7	51.1
Uruguay	17.9	9.7	9.5	9.4	15.4	20.9	18.8
Venezuela	39.8	48.7	48	49.4	48.6	45.4	37.1

Source: ECLAC (2006a).
a. Data are for 1990, 1994, 1997, 1999, 2002, 2004, 2005 or closest available year. For Ecuador, Panama, Paraguay, and Uruguay, data refer to urban areas. Data for Argentina are for metropolitan areas.
b. New measurement starting 2001, data are not strictly comparable with previous years.

worry for far more households, because "middle-income" households are far from "middle class."[38] In the United States, the median national income is about 73 percent of average national income.[39] In Brazil, it is only about 33 percent of average income, and in Honduras (between 1989 and 1996) it was lower than the World Bank poverty line of US$2.00 a day.[40]

Because so many middle-income households are close to the poverty line, short-term economic downturns like the one in Argentina in 2001 can create an entire class, the newly poor. Indeed, by 2002, as many as 45 percent of individuals in Argentina were counted as poor (almost double the share of just two years earlier) (table 1). Crises have tended to

38. See Birdsall and Menezes (2005).
39. DeNavas-Walt, Proctor, and Hill Lee (2006, table A-1); reference is to median and average national household income.
40. Birdsall (2002). In Chile, median income has been about half of average income.

increase poverty, with the incidence remaining higher even after a crisis has passed.[41]

In retrospect, the failure to focus on job creation in the 1990s may have undermined the success of the standard market reforms—trade liberalization, privatization, and opening of the capital markets—and hampered the region's ability to capitalize on the potential benefits of globalization.[42] Jobs and the labor market were not part of the reform agenda of the 1990s. Job growth was extremely weak in the 1990s, about 2.2 percent a year, and it failed to keep up with the rate of growth of the working-age population; moreover, it was concentrated for the most part in low-productivity activities.[43]

At the end of the 1990s, unemployment in most countries was as bad as or worse than it was at the beginning (figure 12). It remained high through the early 2000s and reached record levels in 2002–03.[44] Indicators of deterioration in job quality were even more widespread. Almost everywhere, salaried employment decreased as a percentage of total

41. See Lustig and Arias (2000). Cline (2002) estimates that at least 40 million people were pushed into poverty during the crises in Mexico (1995), Thailand and Indonesia (1997), Korea and Russia (1998), Brazil (1999), and Argentina and Turkey (2001). Poverty increased significantly more in countries in which crisis management was unsuccessful—for example, Indonesia, Russia, and Argentina.

42. Evidence in Heckman and Pagés (2004, 2000) suggests that labor market inflexibility (severance payments and other forms of employment protection) in Latin America has a significant negative impact on the level and distribution of employment and substantially affects the efficiency of labor markets. In particular, job security reduces the job prospects—and possibly wages—of younger and less experienced workers. Evidence in Besley and Burgess (2004) from another setting, India, suggests that job protection and other rigidities inhibited productivity, output growth, investment, and job growth in the registered manufacturing sector between 1958 and 1992. Labor inflexibility (or pro-worker regulations) was also shown to increase informal sector activity. The authors' empirical model compares the experience of two states and predicts that without its pro-employer reforms, the state of Andhra Pradesh would have registered manufacturing output that was 72 percent of its actual 1990 level and manufacturing employment that was 73 percent of its 1990 level. Had the state of West Bengal not passed any pro-worker amendments, it would have enjoyed registered manufacturing output that was 24 percent higher than its 1990 level and an employment rate that was 23 percent higher.

43. See IDB (2004a) for a comprehensive discussion of labor market issues.

44. Between 1990 and 1999, the average unemployment rate in Argentina rose from 7.5 percent to 14.3 percent; during the same period, unemployment in Colombia and Ecuador increased from 10.5 to 19.4 percent and from 6.1 to 15.1 percent respectively. In 2003, unemployment reached more than 16 percent in Argentina, Colombia, the Dominican Republic, Panama, Uruguay, and Venezuela and was near or above 10 percent in Bolivia, Brazil, Chile, Ecuador, Nicaragua, Paraguay, and Peru (ECLAC 2007a; ILO 2006).

F I G U R E   1 2. Urban Unemployment, 1990–2006

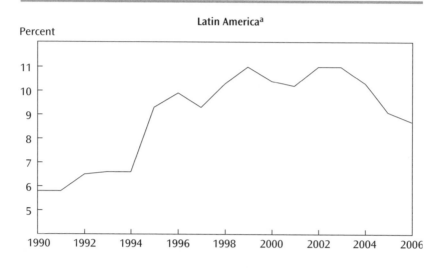

Latin America[a]

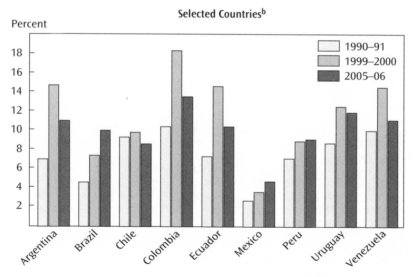

Selected Countries[b]

Source: ECLAC, Economic Development Division, Social Statistics and Indicators (BADEINSO).

a. Beginning in 1991, includes an adjustment in the data for Argentina, Brazil, and Mexico to account for changes in methodologies in 2002, 2003, and 2005, respectively.

b. Data for Chile and Venezuela refer to nationwide total. Data for Brazil are for six metropolitan areas and for Peru are for metropolitan Lima. New measurement starting 2003 and 2002 for Argentina and Brazil, respectively; data are not comparable with previous years. Mexico data from 1997 onward are not strictly comparable with previous years because of methodological changes and alterations in geographical coverage.

employment.[45] Most countries saw increases in the share of jobs considered low quality, such as temporary employment, involuntary part-time work, self-employment, and jobs in microenterprises and small firms.[46] Employment finally picked up beginning in 2004 as growth recovered, but the 2006 unemployment rate, at about 9 percent, was still higher than in 1990.

Meanwhile, average wages stagnated or declined almost everywhere (rising only slightly in 2005–06).[47] In most countries the majority of new jobs created between 1980 and 2005 were in the informal sector,[48] helping to keep average wages low. Yet the topic of wage levels was surprisingly absent from political discourse, as was that of jobs.

The impact of the overall reform package on productivity and investment growth was modest for many reasons, including the difficulty of avoiding exchange rate appreciation. But a key missing element was the politically charged issue of reducing "protections" in formal sector jobs, which ended up protecting only a fortunate minority. Unattended labor rigidities appear to have limited job creation not only directly but indirectly, by reducing firms' capacity to adapt to changes in the economic environment and by making adjustment to the financial and other shocks of the 1990s more difficult.[49]

45. ECLAC (2006a). While wage employment as a share of total employment rose between 2002 and 2005 (from 67.5 percent to 68.5 percent), the average figure is still lower than in 1990 (71 percent).

46. ECLAC (2006a); ILO (2006). Between 1990 and 2002, about seven of every ten newly employed workers in Latin America were in the informal sector and about six of every ten new wage and salaried jobs had no social security coverage. During the 1990s, self-employment grew by an average of 2.8 percent a year and domestic work by 3.9 percent a year. The recent upturn in employment and partly in wages in response to the period of growth in 2003–06 has not significantly improved the quality of new jobs in the region (ECLAC 2006a; ILO 2003).

47. ECLAC (2006a, 2006c); and Duryea, Jaramillo, and Pagés (2003).

48. ECLAC (2006a).

49. Bertola (1990) finds for a sample of industrial countries that employment protection reduces job destruction but also inhibits job creation. Caballero and others (2004) shows that job security regulation hinders the creative destruction process, with negative effects on the annual speed of adjustment to shocks and productivity growth. Loayza, Oviedo, and Servén (2005), in an analysis of a large sample of industrial and developing countries, suggests that a heavier regulatory burden—particularly in labor and product markets—reduces growth and induces informality.

It is not surprising that working-class, middle-income households felt particularly squeezed by the economic reforms, which, although they made industry more competitive, failed to create good jobs.[50] By undermining job creation in the formal sector, long-standing labor rigidities (see chapter 6) may have made the effects of other reforms not only less efficient but also less politically acceptable.

Part of the problem is that in societies that start with high levels of inequality and highly segmented labor markets, new market opportunities alone are not likely to reach those lacking good education and financial and other assets. Latin American countries that liberalized other markets but not their labor market saw increases in the size of the informal employment sector but not in wages or productivity, as the cost of capital but not the cost of labor in the formal sector fell.[51] Probably because easier and cheaper access to capital tends to raise the demand for skilled but not for unskilled labor, job opportunities and salaries of skilled labor in the formal sector increased disproportionately, widening the gap between the returns on higher education and those on secondary and primary education and between the wages for high-paying jobs and those for low-paying jobs.[52]

The job problem goes a long way toward explaining Latin American middle-income households' sense of insecurity and anxiety regarding the opening of economies and the other reforms of the past fifteen years. Arguably, the massive public protests that erupted in Argentina, Ecuador, and Bolivia in the last several years were fueled in part by discontent over high unemployment and economic instability.[53] The protests themselves

50. See Birdsall, Graham, and Pettinato (2000) on the middle-income squeeze in Latin America.

51. For example, in Mexico between 1996 and 1998, GDP per capita increased by 9.7 percent in real terms, but poverty hardly declined. In fact, the incomes of the poorest 30 percent of the population contracted during that period. The huge increase in average income was due entirely to income gains among the richest 30 percent, particularly the richest 10 percent of the population (Székely and Hilgert 2001; Attanasio and Székely 2001).

52. Behrman, Birdsall, and Székely (2003) concludes on the basis of an econometric analysis covering eighteen countries that structural reforms in the 1990s led to a widening of the gap between returns to more-educated workers and returns to less-educated workers in Latin America.

53. In Argentina, Ecuador, and Bolivia protests led to the ousting of incumbent presidents. However, it would be an exaggeration to blame their departure on the reforms.

involved other concerns, such as indigenous rights in the case of Bolivia and Ecuador. Still, their experience highlights the fact that open market economic reforms do not make for good politics anymore, if they ever did.

A Policy Toolkit for Promoting Equity and Growth

In this book we discuss what we call an "equity toolkit" for the region— a dozen tools to build more visibly just societies in which not only the elite but the silent majority have full access to economic, social, and political opportunities. We believe that our equity agenda is not only fully consistent with growth but that it may actually accelerate growth, by better tapping the potential of all the region's people. Some of the policies and programs in our toolkit already are familiar in the reform debate in the region (for example, those regarding education, fiscal policy, and pension reform). But we propose that the debate about even these familiar reform challenges be reshaped to incorporate issues of fairness more explicitly.

Our equity toolkit also is designed to help make market-oriented policies more politically sustainable. A new, politically visible agenda for improving fairness would help governments, civil society, and businesses address a key political economy challenge for the region today: how to give new impetus to reforms in an increasingly hostile political environment. It is difficult to believe that there will be popular support for more reforms if there is no sense that they will improve fairness.

We distinguish our equity toolkit from anything that might be called "populist." For example, our toolkit takes into account the demands and constraints of an open economy. Latin American economies need to remain open if they are to exploit the potential benefits of integration into the global economy. But without attention to fairness, the integration process will increase economic insecurity and produce too many losers and too few winners.

Behind our twelve tools is a simple theory of change. We believe that there is "policy space"—that there are politically realistic win-win options for equity that will not sacrifice and can even enhance growth. They need not sacrifice growth because, for the most part, they are not a matter of money but of the rules of the game and of political and civic leadership. Even when money is needed—say, for education—using these tools, though fiscally costly today, can be politically rewarding. And, of course, it will yield more than ample economic returns tomorrow.

Some are options that have been taken up in some countries of the region but not in others, and thus there are experiences to be shared. Some are options that are understood to be about "growth" but that have not been politically shaped or sold as also being about "fairness." Some, such as a more progressive tax structure, are politically (and even economically) controversial and create major policy challenges with many moving parts; those options demand political leadership of the first order, the engagement of civil society, and the support of the business community. Some are more like plumbing, a matter of know-how; they involve detailed technical and regulatory fixes, such as protecting minority shareholders' rights and promoting markets for factoring and leasing.

Some can and ought to be taken up by civil society—such as charging reasonable tuition for public university students from wealthy households. Some need the active involvement of the banking and business communities in developing and monitoring detailed changes—such as new prudential rules to minimize the tendency of temporary booms to lead to overexpansion of access to credit.

Finally, our focus is on domestic policy and practices. But responsibility also lies with the industrialized countries, whose actions entail high costs to workers and the poor in Latin America, especially with regard to trade. The demands of fairness justifiably apply to rich countries and to multilateral banks and other international donor organizations (as well as to international nongovernmental organizations), from which much of the rhetoric about poverty reduction—and more recently about equity—emanates.

We have organized our twelve equity tools into four key categories. We first emphasize mainstreaming poverty and equity considerations into economy-wide policies (tools 1–4). We focus next on workers (tools 5–7), since jobs and the labor market were neglected in the reform agenda of the last decade. We then discuss policies and practices that would better respond to consumers and citizens (tools 8–11); these are relevant to both the rich and the vast majority of non-rich households in the region. Finally, we address global opportunities and constraints (tool 12), focusing primarily on how the United States can help advance the ideas and the reality of fair growth in Latin America (box 1).

BOX 1. Equity Toolkit

Mainstreaming Poverty and Equity Considerations into Economy-wide Policies

1. Rule-based fiscal discipline. Lack of fiscal discipline—evident when governments consistently spend more than they collect and more than they can easily finance through sustainable borrowing—has high costs for the poor and the emerging middle class. Commitment to fiscal discipline must go beyond making idiosyncratic efforts to developing a healthy budget grounded in transparent rules and procedures.

2. Smoothing booms and busts. Economic booms are better for the rich; busts are worse for the poor. The fiscal and monetary policies and tough banking and other financial standards needed to manage volatility and minimize crisis cannot be improvised. They should be locked in when times are good.

3. Social safety nets that trigger automatically. A modern system provides an income floor for working and middle-class households as well as the poor. During slumps, spending should kick in automatically for emergency public works employment and for subsidies to encourage families to keep their children in school.

4. More taxes on the rich and better spending on the rest. Latin America relies heavily on regressive consumption taxes. Closing income tax loopholes and reducing evasion would increase revenues without adding to the tax burden of working-class and middle-income households.

Responding to Workers in a Global Economy

5. Giving small businesses a chance. Weak financial and judicial systems and onerous red tape block talented small entrepreneurs from expanding their businesses. Improving enforcement of credit contracts and shareholders' rights, ending the practice of offering insiders credit from state-owned banks, and increasing access to information and professional services would help create more small firms and more jobs.

6. Protecting job mobility and workers' rights. The poor bear the cost of a job contracting environment that has the wrong kind of worker protections and too many legal rules. Latin America needs more aggressive protection of workers' rights of association and collective bargaining, more independent and democratic unions, and more unemployment and other social insurance to replace inflexible rules that discourage job mobility and growth.

7. *Repairing rural markets.* Land titling and investment in rural infrastructure, research and development, and extension services can help boost the productivity and increase the competitiveness of rural markets in Latin America, finally giving the rural poor a fair chance.

Responding to Consumers and Citizens

8. *Tackling corruption head on.* Corruption undermines competition, reduces investment, and weakens government, hurting small businesses, consumers, taxpayers, and—especially—the poor. An independent judicial system, greater transparency, and an active civil society are essential elements in a serious anticorruption agenda.

9. *Schools for the poor, too.* Education systems in Latin America suffer from low levels of quality, efficiency, and equity. Critical reforms include more school autonomy and accountability to parents, reduced subsidies to better-off students for higher education, and more public spending on preschool programs.

10. *Dealing openly with discrimination.* A serious attack on poverty and inequality has to include a visible attack on discrimination. Political leadership can help break down the social and political barriers against members of Afro-descendent and indigenous groups—and, in some arenas, against women.

11. *Consumer-driven public services.* Shortcomings in infrastructure, public health, and regulatory services such as consumer protection have cost the poor and the near-poor dearly. Poor and other low-income consumers must now be at the heart of a new culture of service delivery.

Global Opportunities and Constraints

12. *How the United States can help: opening markets and more.* A practical agenda for how the U.S. can help diminish poverty and inequality in Latin America includes buttressing free trade agreements through aid programs that compensate and help the losers and pressing the financial community to encourage U.S.-based remittance senders and Latin-based receivers to open bank accounts to facilitate the process.

Choices and Caveats

We have five important caveats. First, we cannot pretend that there is any consensus on the content of our toolkit. We believe that the business elite is prepared to embrace an agenda that focuses on more widely shared opportunities, if only to reduce social tensions and stave off antigrowth populism. But we have no real basis for that intuition. In any event, although our focus on fairness as a fundamental goal is new, some of our tools are not. They already are fully endorsed by the business elite; indeed, some were included in the Washington Consensus.

Second, we do not directly address health, despite its crucial link to equity. There is nothing close to a technical consensus about the right approach to organizing and financing health systems, as there is with the issues that we do tackle. The health issue is also, from an institutional and policy point of view, so different in different countries and so complex that it would have been even more foolhardy to attack it in this short volume than it has been to tackle the twelve issues that we chose. However, the lessons of chapter 11 are relevant to public provision of health services.

Third, our toolkit focuses narrowly on economic and social policies, yet fairness concerns a much broader arena of public policy. Good governance goes well beyond our toolkit—to promoting democracy, extending civil liberties, and ensuring the rule of law, all actions that are central to equity. With one exception—corruption (see chapter 8)—we refer to these political and institutional topics only tangentially, when they have obvious links to economic and social policies.

Fourth, our toolkit is not a substitute for rigorous, case-by-case diagnosis of the binding constraints to growth and equity in a given country. It does not identify the main problems in a specific case, nor set out priorities, nor delineate the main components of a needed policy strategy, nor provide guidance on reform sequencing. That can flow only from diagnostic work on individual countries, for which our toolkit cannot substitute.[54] We just provide a set of "tools" that should come in handy once such a diagnosis has been performed.

Fifth, our toolkit approach does not pretend to completely understand the links between policy reforms and outcomes. If we have learned anything

54. On this approach to analysis, see Rodrik (2006).

over the past twenty years or so, it is that such links are elusive and that outcomes often do not correspond to initial expectations. While we believe that the appropriate use of the policies in the toolkit can help to improve equity without sacrificing growth, we do not claim to fully understand the transmission channels that link policy actions to outcomes.

That said, we do not want to be too modest. It is high time for leaders (in government, business, and civil society) in Latin America to embrace fairness as a fundamental goal. Latin America has undertaken one set of changes in order to develop more open and competitive market economies. The benefits of that first step now need to be complemented and reinforced by a second set of changes—changes aimed at fairness and at emphasizing jobs and access to key productive assets for the silent majority. Long-standing inequality in the region has fostered a deep sense of unfairness and injustice. We hope that our agenda rekindles hope that open markets and democratic institutions will, finally, make a difference.

A Dozen Equity Tools

ONE

Rule-Based Fiscal Discipline

I n the last fifteen years the countries of Latin America have made great progress in taming their budget deficits, helping to finally overcome the inflation that plagued the region before and during the 1980s. But in many countries deficit reduction still relies mostly on competent finance ministers, who in turn depend on the support of their heads of state, and on "emergency" revenue and tax measures that create their own inefficiencies and distortions. For example, Argentina, Brazil, Colombia, Ecuador, Peru, and Venezuela have all periodically boosted tax revenues by imposing a financial transactions tax, which at higher rates and over time has coincided with significant welfare losses and financial disintermediation.[1] Other countries have contained fiscal deficits by unduly compressing public investment and social spending—ultimately, an unsustainable option. In many countries, the costs of servicing debt remain high, requiring governments to run primary surpluses to contain further debt increases (table 1-1).

Missing in many countries are the institutional rules, political arrangements, and structural fixes—for example, reform of unduly generous and inequitable public pension systems—that would give investors confidence

---

1. Kirilenko and Perry (2004) estimates that, on average, financial transaction taxes have resulted in financial disintermediation of between 4 and 44 cents for every dollar in revenue, with well-above-average values of 46 cents in Argentina, 58 cents in Brazil, 64 cents in Colombia, 48 cents in Ecuador, 66 cents in Peru, and 49 cents in Venezuela. See also Baca-Campodónico, Mello, and Kirilenko (2006) and Kirilenko and Summers (2003).

TABLE 1-1. Public Debt and Primary Surpluses, 2003–06
Percent of GDP

	Public debt[a]								Primary surplus[b]			
	2003		2004		2005		2006					
Country	Gross	Net	Gross	Net	Gross	Net	Gross	Net	2003	2004	2005	2006
Argentina	145	125	132	111	89	n.a.	n.a.	n.a.	3.0	5.0	4.4	n.a.
Brazil	77	57	72	52	75	52	73	51	4.3	4.6	4.8	4.3
Chile	45	13	39	11	32	8	28	3	2.2	4.5	7.3	8.6
Colombia	53	45	50	39	46	34	45	32	1.5	3.2	4.0	3.1
Mexico	50	44	46	41	44	39	43	38	0.3	1.3	1.8	2.1
Peru	47	33	44	28	38	n.a.	32	n.a.	0.5	1.0	1.6	3.0
Uruguay	104	95	92	88	69	n.a.	64	n.a.	2.7	3.8	3.9	3.7

Sources: IMF, country reports; Panizza and others (2006); Banco Central do Brasil.
a. Includes domestic and external debt of the general government (central government, states or provinces, and municipalities).
b. Surplus net of interest on government debt.

that budget deficits will not get out of control in the future. Uncertainty persists about whether countries will sustain fiscal discipline when governments change from one administration to another or when political pressure grows during periods of low growth to spend too much and spend badly. Some countries suffer because excessively fragmented legislative bodies prevent the formation of stable coalitions or congressional majorities—or because decentralization undermines the government's capacity to keep overall public sector spending in check.[2]

Fiscal indiscipline—seen when governments consistently spend more than they collect and more than they can easily finance through sustainable borrowing—has had high costs for the poor in the region. In most of Latin America past fiscal laxity too often induced governments either to print money, fueling inflation, or to issue large amounts of debt, driving

2. For example, in the 1990s Colombia more than doubled the share of centrally collected revenues transferred to local governments without transferring spending responsibility and political accountability. See Acosta and Bird (2003) and Alesina, Carrasquilla, and Echavarría Soto (2002) for further discussion on Colombia. Ahmad and García-Escribano (2006) reviews the challenges of fiscal decentralization in Peru, including the need to clarify subnational-spending responsibilities and financing sources that increase local accountability. On the experience of Argentina, see Cuevas (2003).

real interest rates to onerous levels.[3] Inflation hurts poor people because their capacity to protect their earnings—through indexed savings, for example—is limited.[4] In contrast, fiscal discipline protects poor people's consumption and allows for lower interest rates than would otherwise prevail, unleashing new investment and job creation. Public savings also allow governments to use countercyclical policy to protect poor and working-class families during economic downturns.

Of course, inflation has fallen dramatically in the region over the last decade, thus reducing its regressive effect.[5] But creditworthy small firms and poor households still face high real interest rates. Since they have no alternative to the local market for their financing needs, this limits their expansion, and thus reduces overall investment and employment.[6] To bring down interest rates requires a host of institutional and structural fixes, but good fiscal policy is key (box 1-1). Good fiscal policy entails holding down deficits, including in good times, both to allow for countercyclical public spending in bad times (see chapter 2) and to reduce reliance on public borrowing, which in the past has led to unsustainable

3. Real interest rates were very high in Latin America in the 1990s, reaching more than 10 percent on average for the majority of countries, compared with 6 percent on average in Southeast Asia (Indonesia, Malaysia, Philippines, South Korea, and Thailand) and about 5.6 percent in the United States in 1990–2000 (WDI 2006). Since 2001, interest rates have fallen against a backdrop of fairly low inflation in most Latin American countries, but they remain well above those in other regions, especially in Brazil (IMF 2007c; Gelos 2006; ECLAC 2006c).

4. See Easterly and Fischer (2001) for evidence on the impact of inflation on the poor. Estimates in Behrman, Birdsall and Székely (2001), based on household data from seventeen Latin American countries over the last two decades, suggest that inflation and volatility in per capita GDP worsen poverty.

5. The average inflation rate in Latin America declined from close to 600 percent in 1990 to just under 10 percent in the last three years of the decade, with more than half of the region's countries recording single-digit rates. In 2000–06 average inflation remained at around 7.3 percent in the region (IMF 2007a). Carstens and Jácome (2005) finds that institutional reforms aimed at increasing the central banks' autonomy and accountability in the region, together with macroeconomic policies, played a key role in bringing down inflation to single digits.

6. Interest rates remain high because, given high ratios of public debt to revenues, creditors price in default risk and because of high public borrowing (in part to finance servicing of existing debt). Although in the OECD higher real interest rates have been shown to contribute to higher unemployment (Blanchard and Wolfers 1999), estimates of the relationship show no statistically robust effect in Latin America. The data are, however, much "noisier" on real interest rates (due to noncaptured inflation volatility itself), the credit markets are much more segmented, and employment and unemployment data are less reliable.

BOX 1-1. The Fiscal Policy of Presidents Cardoso and Lula in Brazil

Throughout his presidency, Brazil's Fernando Henrique Cardoso (1995–2002) was widely criticized by the left for making macroeconomic discipline a priority at the expense of much-needed investments in the social sector. His successor, Luiz Inacio Lula da Silva (2003–), has faced similar criticism for continuing the disciplined macroeconomic approach, including from members of his own cabinet and Workers' Party. But their critics are missing the point. Fiscal discipline and sound management of the government's debt constitute good social policy. In effect, the vulnerability of the government's fiscal stance and of public debt to economic and financial shocks goes a long way toward explaining the high level of the domestic real interest rate.[1] Hence, additional and durable improvements on the fiscal and public debt fronts are important in the quest for lower real interest rates, which encourage job creation. Real interest rates in Brazil were extremely high during the 1990s, averaging 21 percent for 1997–99. They have stabilized since then but remain very high by international standards, averaging about 13 percent in 2003–06. In order to lower interest rates to single digits, Brazil will have not only to sustain the fiscal gains achieved to date but also to push through with further fiscal reforms, including politically difficult reforms in pensions and taxes.

1. World Bank (2006b).

levels of public debt.[7] Some public debt (to finance small deficits) is reasonable, especially when economic growth ensures that the ratio of debt to GDP is not continuously rising beyond a safe range. In effect, there is a growing consensus that emerging market economies, with their history of inflation and volatility, should meet a tough standard of public debt to GDP—the IMF suggests no more than 30 percent—which is tougher than the standard for developed countries.[8] In Latin America, only Chile currently meets that standard.

7. Although we emphasize surpluses and deficits, additional indicators are used to assess a country's fiscal solvency in the medium and long term, including accounting and economic measures of government net worth (see Easterly, Irwin, and Servén 2007; Traa and Carare 2007). Fiscal deficits are obviously easier to manage and make compatible with long-term public debt sustainability where economic growth is vigorous.

8. IMF (2003a) estimates a benchmark debt-to-GDP ratio for emerging markets at 25 percent of GDP and for developing countries at 30 percent of GDP. Artana, López Murphy,

In short, a fiscal policy aimed at sustained "fairness" for the great majority of citizens today requires building an institutional culture of rule-based discipline and in many countries managing a string of primary surpluses that are demonstrably sustainable—that is, not based on unrealistic spending cuts and distortionary taxes inimical to efficiency and growth.[9] Until the markets are convinced that deficit spending is justified by the prospect of high growth and investment-intensive public spending, the hard reality is that most countries of Latin America will benefit their poor most by managing actual (not just primary) surpluses in good times to build confidence and in bad times to create space for deficit spending (see chapter 2).[10] In fact, despite a few exceptions in the last couple of years (most notably Chile), governments in the region have run overall fiscal deficits since 1993.[11]

Maintaining fiscal discipline from one administration to another requires a budget process that is fully institutionalized within a country's legal and regulatory systems and in its legislative procedures.[12] Examples of fiscal discipline measures include the following:

---

and Navajas (2003) suggests a Maastricht-type debt limit of 30 percent of GDP for the region once reasonable levels of indebtedness are reached, which is half the EU level. That reflects Latin America's narrow domestic capital markets, higher interest, and lower revenue shares relative to GDP. See also Reinhart, Rogoff, and Savastano (2003).

9. Dervis and Birdsall (2006) notes that governments now are stuck with high primary surpluses in order to finance debt service while minimizing total deficits. Calderón, Easterly, and Servén (2003a, 2003b) estimates that over half of the total fiscal adjustment in Argentina, Bolivia, Brazil, Chile, and Peru during the 1990s reflected infrastructure compression, which in turn may have lowered long-term GDP growth by more than 1 percent a year. A similar case of excessive budgetary rigidity is found in the example of Ecuador in Cueva (2007), which estimates that about 90 percent of central government expenditures are nondiscretionary. In most highly indebted countries, achieving a positive fiscal balance that is demonstrably sustainable will require structural fixes—pension reform and so forth—that are politically very difficult. For high-debt countries, Dervis and Birdsall (2006) recommends a large facility at the IMF or World Bank that would be used to lend at below-market rates to help them reduce the debt that creates the need for primary surpluses, without cutting back on key investments in development.

10. In the short run, given existing debt-service burdens, the primary surpluses needed just to get a zero fiscal surplus or deficit would be as high as 8 percent in Brazil and near 6 percent in Uruguay (estimates based on 2003–06 data from IMF country reports.) In the medium term, the real issue is the ratio of net debt to GDP and revenue base. Some nominal deficit would be consistent with avoiding increases in these ratios.

11. ECLAC (2006c, 2000).

12. An example of movement in this direction is Brazil's Fiscal Responsibility Law, which since its approval in 2000 has encouraged fiscal consolidation across all levels of government

- ◆ Prohibition of unfunded expenditures (defined over the business cycle, with saving taking place during good times and dis-saving during bad times)[13]
- ◆ Legal ceilings on total public sector indebtedness relative to GDP
- ◆ Standards and obligations for disclosure of the entire fiscal cycle—budget preparation, approval, and execution—to improve accountability of fiscal authorities and enable better monitoring by voters
- ◆ An independent source of published estimates of actual and projected government revenue and expenditures (as in the case of the U.S. Congressional Budget Office) to provide the public an alternative to the executive branch's estimates
- ◆ Fiscal contingency funds that set aside unexpected revenue due to high world prices of oil, copper, and other natural resources (see also chapter 2).

---

and increased fiscal transparency. In Colombia and Peru, following a generally poor start and repeated modifications, fiscal responsibility laws recently have helped to contain discretionary procyclical spending (Corbacho and Schwartz 2007, forthcoming; Mello 2006). For a comprehensive analysis of different instruments and approaches (including various types of fiscal rules, fiscal responsibility laws, and fiscal agencies) to improve the incentives for governments to maintain fiscal discipline, see IMF (2007, forthcoming).

13. In Brazil, recognizing the risk of a continuously rising tax burden—which in turn has been pushed up by ever-increasing current expenditures—the government introduced a new measure in the 2006 budget law to establish ceilings, as a share of GDP, for the federal government's revenue and expenditure estimates in the annual budget law. Unfortunately, the measure did not survive congressional scrutiny without an amendment that basically undermined its original intent, and the government decided not to include the same or a similar proposal in the budget for 2007 (World Bank 2007a).

TWO

Smoothing Booms and Busts

High financial and economic volatility—together with low growth and high inequality—is a Latin American trademark. The region's volatility, including the frequency of devastating financial crises, has been among the highest in the world.[1] It has reflected a wide range of external and homegrown factors: major swings in foreign capital flows (partly reflecting imperfections in the international financial architecture), sharp fluctuations in commodity prices (on which many economies are still unusually dependent), lack of credible domestic monetary policies, weaknesses in domestic financial sectors, and stop-go patterns of fiscal spending. Economic volatility in Latin America stands out regardless of the indicator chosen to measure it, whether it is the real exchange rate, the real interest rate, the budget deficit, banking system credit, or the growth rates of consumption, income, and employment. And while after the 1980s, as countries left hyperinflation behind, volatility did not increase in some dimensions (and even declined somewhat), it arguably rose along other dimensions, especially with respect to international capital flows.[2]

Hopes have been raised in recent years that volatility may be on a downward trend, given the region's stronger fiscal and external positions, improved financial regulation and supervision, and more flexible

1. See De la Torre, Levy-Yeyati, and Schmukler (2002); De Ferranti and others (2000); Hausmann and Gavin (1998); Singh (2006); and IDB (1995).
2. For instance, the variance in growth of real income and consumption did not increase in the 1990s above the level in the 1980s.

exchange rate regimes. However, the recent calm may be mainly a reflection of currently benign international financial conditions, such as abundant investable funds in major financial centers seeking yields throughout the world in the face of low interest rates in OECD countries, as well as buoyant export markets due to the strong demand in China for mining and agricultural products. These conditions cannot be expected to last indefinitely.

Volatility is bad for growth.[3] The uncertainty of returns on investment in human and physical capital undercuts total investment and biases the direction of investment toward shorter-term and riskier projects. Volatility is especially costly in Latin America because the region's underdeveloped financial markets fail to enable smaller firms to invest in technological adaptations and innovations and low-income households to invest in education, skill building, and health.

Equally worrying but less remarked, volatility in the form of financial crises involves inequitable wealth transfers that create major and enduring adverse distributional effects, including for those who do not directly participate in the financial system.[4] Volatility is particularly costly to poor and near-poor households. To be sure, the income of the rich fluctuates more, but a smaller fluctuation for a poor household can be much more costly. The poor benefit less during booms (when individuals with real and financial assets tend to gain most), and they are the first to lose jobs during busts.[5] For the poor, even short-term losses can have long-term implications. Evidence from Mexico and elsewhere suggests that many children who drop out of school to work in bad times never return.[6]

So, policies aimed at explicitly and systematically reducing volatility can exploit a vast terrain for win-win solutions to simultaneously advance the goals of growth, equity, and poverty reduction.

3. For more on Latin America's history of macroeconomic volatility and financial crisis and its impact on growth, see Singh (2006). On volatility and its relationship to growth, see Sahay and Goyal (2006); Hnatkovska and Loayza (2004); Ramey and Ramey (1995); and Easterly and others (1993).

4. See, for instance, Halac and Schmukler (2004). Dervis and Birdsall (2006) discusses the mechanisms by which high public debt in emerging markets generates inequality.

5. See Birdsall (2007, figure 7).

6. See Székely (1999); Lustig (2000); Duryea, Lam, and Levison (2007); Skoufias and Parker (2006); Blanco and Valdivia (2006); Guarcello, Mealli, and Rosati (2003); and Rucci (2004).

Policies to manage macrofinancial volatility and thus reduce the probability of crises cannot themselves be unpredictable or subject to constant improvisation. Instead, policies must be designed ex ante to lock in politically sustainable actions and responses. At the same time, rigid precommitments such as currency pegs can increase volatility over the longer horizon. Generally speaking, fiscal targeting and other institutional arrangements that put the emphasis on rules over discretion are a superior way to go. In particular, a framework should be established at the outset to constrain opportunities for political manipulation, thereby ensuring that a cushion of adequate savings is accumulated—not squandered—in good times and guaranteeing that mechanisms for compensatory spending (for example, on the social safety net discussed below) are triggered automatically in bad times.

In short, smoothing booms and busts requires fiscal, monetary, banking, and other policy tools that not only are well designed but also are underpinned by sound institutional fundamentals.[7]

Fiscal Tools

◆ *Rules to lock in additional fiscal effort during booms.* Such rules help avoid sharp fiscal contractions, thereby stabilizing spending on social programs in bad times, preventing spending binges when a country is enjoying a bonanza, and keeping public investment plans on track throughout the business cycle.[8] They also can help protect

---

7. A country could conceivably mitigate the consequences of volatility through market-supplied insurance, but it is at best thinly supplied in international capital markets. Hence, the emphasis unavoidably has to be placed on self-insurance (private and public savings accumulated in good times for use in bad) and self-protection (policy actions to reduce the likelihood that adverse shocks and sharp fluctuations will occur).

8. Governments in developed countries enjoy the benefits of countercyclical fiscal policy. During recessions they are still able to borrow at low cost in local and international financial markets; as a result, they can engage in deficit spending to stimulate their economy and provide a social safety net for their citizens. In Latin America, however, governments have been compelled to tighten fiscal policy (and even generate surpluses) in bad times—thereby exacerbating the economic downturn—because they tend to lose access to financial markets precisely when they need access most. Few countries, with the possible exception of Chile, command sufficient confidence in external markets to borrow in bad times. Building the capacity to undertake countercyclical fiscal policy therefore is a key priority for Latin American countries, and it begins with saving in good times.

access to financial markets in bad times. Specific standards for adopting a primary budget position—the fiscal position net of interest costs—that can be sustained over a long horizon need to be defined in each country (see chapter 1). In all cases, however, year-to-year fiscal policy targets should be defined, taking into account not just the country's long-run solvency but also its business cycle (cyclical deviations from actual and potential output). The "structural budget rule" used in Chile to determine year-to-year fiscal targets is a good example of how countercyclicality can be built into the budgetary process.[9]

◆ *Stabilization funds to smooth government spending during good times and bad.* Such contingency funds ideally operate under rules set by the national congress, stipulating that excess revenues earned during good times will be saved or used to pay down the public debt. If funds are saved, the government can draw down the funds in times of revenue shortfalls to help maintain critical spending. The Chilean copper stabilization fund is a good example.

Monetary Tools

◆ *A framework for countercyclical monetary policy that emphasizes building a credible record of low and stable inflation in the context of exchange rate flexibility.*[10] Monetary policy should enhance the role of the local currency as a store of value for savings, thereby providing a reliable currency of denomination for credit contracts. A reliable currency is essential to minimizing currency mismatches

---

9. The Chilean "structural budget balance" is a measure of the fiscal position adjusted for the output cycle (the difference between potential and actual GDP) and the "excess" or "shortfall" in copper-related revenues relative to trend. For a detailed discussion of the main issues and experience with the Chilean structural budget rule, see LeFort (2006); Rodríguez, Tokman, and Vega (2006); and Velasco and others (2007). For further discussion of structural balance, see Dos Reis, Manasse, and Panizza (2007) and Balassone and Kumar (2007, forthcoming).

10. The feasibility of introducing a monetary policy framework that allows a government to maintain low and stable inflation while maintaining a flexible exchange rate depends on sound fiscal and debt fundamentals, in particular controlling deficits and borrowing so that monetary authorities are not unduly constrained in raising interest rates by fear of increasing the government's debt burden.

and ensuring that currency depreciations do not have adverse balance sheet effects; it also makes exchange rate flexibility more feasible. Given Latin America's openness to capital flows, exchange rate flexibility is necessary to allow for the countercyclical monetary policy that has eluded Latin American countries for decades.[11]

Banking Tools

◆ *Prudential standards (for capital, provisions, liquidity) that follow best international practices yet are appropriately adapted to country circumstances.* Latin America must strive to converge toward the worldwide trend of enhancing the sensitivity to risk of bank regulation and supervision. Such efforts need to match the increasing sophistication of risk management systems among leading financial entities, take into account the implications of financial globalization, and reflect the growing complexity of financial products and markets. International accords and standards can help Latin American countries with that task. However, such standards must be adapted to better address specific features of the banking systems in individual countries—including higher volatility, illiquidity of securities markets, financial dollarization, and high exposure to government debt paper, among others.

◆ *Countercyclical loan-loss provisioning requirements to dampen the amplitude of the credit cycle and protect banks' solvency during downturns.* Banks would then have to build countercyclical provisions in times of high credit growth to use during the downswing of the credit cycle to absorb the losses from downward loan reclassifications and asset write-downs.[12]

◆ *Countercyclical liquidity or reserve requirements.* Such requirements would be higher in good times (with buoyant deposit growth) and

11. Monetary policy in Latin America has tended to be procyclical, with interest rates typically increasing sharply at the worse of times and thus magnifying the recessionary effects of adverse shocks. See, for instance, Calvo and Reinhart (2002) and Hausmann, Panizza, and Stein (2000).

12. The system of "statistical" provisions introduced in Spain is an interesting and useful example of countercyclical provisions.

lower in times of systemic liquidity crunches.[13] Such requirements do not exist in industrialized countries, but they can help in Latin America at least until creditor rights are much more consolidated in law and enforced in the region.

Other Policy Steps

◆ *Encouraging the entry of first-rate foreign banks, which in countries like Mexico, Chile, Peru, and Colombia have enhanced the stability and resiliency of the domestic banking system.* Foreign banks bring sounder banking practices and access, through the parent bank, to external capital and liquidity. They typically operate under the stricter regulatory and supervisory procedures of their home country, setting a high standard in the local market.

◆ *Promoting the development of local currency–denominated debt markets and reducing the exposure of government debt to rollover, interest, and exchange rate risks.* Mexico has made substantial progress on this front. Reducing the exposure of governments to risks associated with their debt entails generating a debt profile that takes into account risks, not just costs. CPI-indexed instruments can complement local debt market development in a way that is consistent with reducing currency mismatches.[14] To lengthen the term of private sector debt while limiting instability in capital inflows, Chilean-style reserve requirements discouraging excessive short-term indebtedness may be considered.[15]

---

13. These requirements should be complemented by management of adequate international reserves and, if possible, by arrangements for automatic access to international lines of credit in the event of a liquidity squeeze. The idea of Argentina's international repo facility, which was negotiated in the second half of the 1990s, was to lock in automatic access to hard-currency liquidity in good times for use in bad times. However, the repo contract gave Argentina the option of using government bonds, valued at market prices, as collateral to obtain liquidity from international banks. The price of those bonds declined steeply as fears of default rose and financial conditions in Argentina deteriorated in 2000 and 2001, precisely when the bonds were needed most.

14. See Goldstein and Turner (2004) on controlling currency mismatches. See also De la Torre and Schmukler (2004).

15. See Williamson (2005, 2000) for a brief discussion of Chile's uncompensated reserve requirement.

Multilateral financial institutions, such as the World Bank and the Inter-American Development Bank, can buttress such efforts by issuing or guaranteeing growth-linked bonds[16] and by exploiting their own balance sheet (obligations and income in a country's currency) to lend in borrowing countries' local currency, while hedging such positions in international markets—for example, by issuing bonds denominated in individual local currencies or in a suitable basket thereof.[17]

◆ *Continuing efforts to diversify trade and increase foreign direct investment, including by negotiating multilateral, regional, and bilateral agreements.* In the face of the entry of exports from the Asian giants (China and India) into the world markets, it is even more critical for Latin America to build broader markets for nontraditional export products, reducing its excessive dependence on a few commodity exports whose prices are subject to large fluctuations. Openness to foreign direct investment makes sense in this context because it is more stable and permanent than other forms of capital inflows, such as portfolio investment and short-term debt.

◆ *Diversifying catastrophic risk.* Many countries in the region are disproportionately exposed to natural disasters (earthquakes in Central America, hurricanes in the Caribbean). These disasters are particularly damaging for the poor, whose homes and livelihoods they destroy. Global financial markets offer little help in managing catastrophic risk in developing countries. But there is room for domestic authorities to cooperate regionally and internationally, with multilateral financial institutions and private firms, to create special catastrophe insurance programs. Such programs would tap the international capital markets to insure the domestic economy and victims of natural disasters against at least part of their losses.

16. See Borenzstein and Mauro (2004); Council of Economic Advisers (2004); and Chamon and Mauro (2006).

17. Eichengreen, Hausmann, and Panizza (2005) and Levy-Yeyati (2004) offer interesting proposals in this regard. In 2001 the World Bank began offering some of its emerging market borrowers financial products denominated in their domestic currencies, but at modest volumes. In 2005 the Inter-American Development Bank approved on a pilot basis a local currency option for disbursement of a US$300 million loan to Mexico. See also CGD (2006, 2005).

THREE

Social Safety Nets That Trigger Automatically

Ideally, a publicly financed social safety net serves two purposes. First, it protects the many people vulnerable to income losses, especially during economic downturns—including not only the 32 percent of all households that are poor in Latin America (as measured by ECLAC) but also another 20 to 30 percent of middle-income households. Safety net programs establish a floor below which households are not allowed to fall. Some programs, such as food stamps, protect households hit by sudden disability, unexpected job loss, death of a major breadwinner, and so on. In addition, an arsenal of these and other measures—emergency public works jobs, special school subsidies—should be available in times of increased unemployment and real wage declines. Second, an adequate public safety net provides cash and in-kind transfers to chronically poor households to minimize the most dangerous risks associated with deep poverty—such as child malnutrition and missed schooling. (Social safety nets can be distinguished from social insurance programs. Social safety nets transfer income in one way or another to the needy. They target the chronically poor as well as other households that are put at risk of poverty by economic shocks. In contrast, social insurance programs—contributory pensions, unemployment insurance, and so forth—are largely related to earnings and need not include any transfers, although some may contain an element of cross-subsidization, as when pension programs find ways to provide cash transfers to those who have not made adequate contributions).[1]

An Income Floor

Only a few countries have developed systematic programs to provide temporary or "emergency" income support for working-class and middle-income as well as poor households hit by sudden job loss due to exogenous shocks or a major economic downturn.[2] Such programs must be carefully designed to avoid encouraging abuse and dependency. A few initiatives undertaken in the 1990s, such as Argentina's Trabajar and Chile's Chile Joven, seem to have worked relatively well, but they were mostly ad hoc emergency programs that were not fully institutionalized, and they have been discontinued.[3] (In 2002, Argentina launched Jefes y Jefas de Hogar, replacing Trabajar, which served as the government's main safety net response to the economic crisis of 2001–02. Despite targeting flaws, it seems to have helped mitigate the impact of the crisis somewhat, especially among the extremely poor.[4] Although Chile Joven no longer exists, Chile has developed smaller, more focused programs—like

1. The World Bank makes the following distinction: "Social insurance programs help households manage risk, but before the fact. Safety nets take up the load where households cannot participate in social insurance schemes or when the benefits from those are exhausted." "Safety Nets and Transfers" (http://go.worldbank.org/RJP1CF2CM0 [June 2007]; Grosh, Blomquist, and Amde 2002, p. 5). This chapter is concerned with the latter. We discuss pensions in chapter 4 and unemployment insurance in chapter 6.

2. For a review of programs introduced in Argentina, Chile, Colombia, and Peru since the 1990s, including a summary of the results of their impact evaluations, see Bouillon and Tejerina (2006). In practice, some of the workfare programs have become tools in the general effort to combat poverty and high unemployment, operating even after a recession or crisis has passed, as in Argentina, Chile, and Uruguay in recent years. Some have lasted longer than intended because of a lack of appropriate guidelines for bringing them to a close once the crisis is over (ECLAC 2006b).

3. See Paredes (2005); Santiago Consultores Asociados (1999); and Bravo and Contreras (2000) on Chile Joven, a training program for unemployed youth. See Jalan and Ravallion (2003); Ravallion (2000); and Coady, Grosh, and Hoddinott (2004) on Argentina's Trabajar, a labor-intensive public works program.

4. At its peak in 2003, Jefes y Jefas reached nearly 2 million beneficiaries, who were required to work or participate in training activities for at least twenty hours a week in exchange for a cash transfer. Coverage has since declined by about 20 percent. Galasso and

Programa Especial de Jóvenes—that finance job training for out-of-school, unemployed youth, targeting areas with the highest incidence of poverty or youth unemployment).[5] Across countries, specifically counter-cyclical programs are even rarer than initiatives such as these.

To meet the challenge of spending on countercyclical or emergency programs, governments normally need to spend more during recessions or periods of low growth, when they are collecting less. That is why in chapter 1 we emphasize the need for fiscal surpluses or low deficits and in chapter 2 we highlight the advisability of saving in good times (see also box 3-1 for the role of the IMF).[6] Emergency programs should be permanently available, but spending on them must be short-lived and disciplined. Given their debt burdens and fiscal pressures, many countries in the region will need to rely for some years on external support to finance counter-cyclical social safety net programs, but that support should not be seen as being available indefinitely.

We highlight three guidelines for emergency programs:

♦ Automatic kick-ins. Programs need to be established before a downturn occurs, and a commitment must be made to maintain steady levels of adequate spending during fiscal tightening. A minimum spending level should always be maintained for primary education and health programs. Countercyclical spending should kick in automatically to provide for emergency public works employment and subsidies to families to keep their children in school.

♦ Sunset clauses. Countercyclical programs need to have clear "sunset" or exit clauses to preserve the fiscal integrity of the budget and reduce program vulnerability to political pressures.

Ravallion (2004) shows that about 40 percent of Jefes' participants in its first year came from the poorest 20 percent of the population and 90 percent fell below the official poverty line—which is better than average for social programs in the country but not as well-targeted as its predecessor, the smaller-scale Trabajar. Many of Jefes' beneficiaries were new entrants into the labor force (mostly women) as opposed to workers who had lost their jobs as a result of the crisis. All in all, for 2002, the program helped reduce aggregate unemployment by about 2.5 percent and prevented an extra 2 percent of the population from falling into extreme poverty.

5. For further details on Chile's Programa Especial de Jóvenes (short for Programa de Formación en Oficios para Jóvenes de Escasos Recursos), see Universidad de Chile (2006) and Quapper and Valenzuela (2005).

6. Birdsall (2002) and Birdsall and Menezes (2005) elaborate on these points. See also Braun and di Gresia (2003) and Hicks and Wodon (2001).

BOX 3-1. The Role of the IMF

Governments' social spending and programs critical to the most vulnerable groups come under increased pressure during economic shocks or budgetary retrenchments. Spending on personnel salaries is politically invulnerable so spending on complementary but critical inputs (books, medicine, and so forth) is often cut drastically. For example, during the 1999–2000 crisis, hospitals in Ecuador adjusted by cutting spending on vaccines. In 2003, the IMF board approved a recommendation (based on a report from the fund's Independent Evaluation Office) to encourage fund staff during Article IV consultations to invite national authorities to suggest whether they would want to see programs protected in the event of a negative shock and if so, which ones.[1]

Systematic and thoughtful implementation of this nonintrusive approach would help countries protect fiscal adjustment from untoward political pressure. It would also help the IMF itself, rescuing it from the widespread perception, which is ultimately harmful to its effectiveness, that its support for fiscal discipline mindlessly and callously pushes spending reductions that hurt the poor.[2]

---

1. IMF (2003b).
2. Nancy Birdsall, letter to Horst Kohler, managing director of the International Monetary Fund, January 8, 2004 (Washington: Center for Global Development). For more on the role of the IMF, see CGD (2007).

◆ Targeting mechanisms. For emergency employment programs, self-selection works best; accordingly, the wage offered must be slightly below the market wage so that the jobs created are of interest only (or mainly) to the population targeted. Chile's emergency public works program, which employed millions during the country's recession in the 1980s, is a good example.[7]

Chronic Poverty

Latin America has a long history of uncoordinated programs to help the chronically poor, often driven by populist clientelism and marred by

7. See Subbarao (2003, 1997).

weak, arbitrary, and politically unsustainable funding.[8] But in the 1990s Brazil, Mexico, and other countries introduced a new generation of well-regulated, targeted programs that are reaching a large proportion of poor households, often while spending less than 1 percent of GDP (box 3-2).[9] Such programs often have taken the form of "conditional cash transfers"—for example, transfer to mothers who keep their children in school. These institutional innovations represent effective public investment, including in human capital formation, at the same time that they protect the poorest families from destitution in the worst economic times.

If a program is to protect the very poor against the worst risks of deep poverty, it must have the following four characteristics:

♦ Commonsense targeting of poor individuals and households. Adequate targeting requires a reliable system of information gathering on household living standards and a heavy dose of common sense, which dictates some geographical targeting of poor neighborhoods and poor regions, as in conditional cash-transfer programs in Honduras and Nicaragua.[10] Systems of information gathering—Chile and Mexico

8. Lindert, Skoufias, and Shapiro (2006) examines the evolution of public transfers in the context of the broader welfare state in Latin America. Their findings, based on fifty-six interventions in eight countries, suggest that public social transfers have been largely regressive in the region—primarily because the bulk of funds goes toward social insurance (pensions, unemployment), which are highly regressive (see chapter 4). Social assistance transfers are more progressive in absolute terms, with the average program transferring 38 percent more to the bottom quintile than would be the case with a random allocation. Still, 35 percent of programs are regressive. Conditional cash transfers are the best targeted. In Mexico's Oportunidades, the poorest quintile receives nearly nine times more benefits than the richest. Targeting efficiency is also impressive in Brazil's Bolsa Família, where 73 percent of transfers reach the poorest quintile of the population. Other types of cash transfers, however, show mixed results. Mexico's farmer-support program, PROCAMPO, is regressive, with 43 percent of benefits going to the richest quintile and 12 percent to the poorest. School-based meal programs tend to favor the poor, but other meal programs show mixed results. Finally, scholarships are found to be quite regressive, with 37 percent of benefits going to the richest quintile and only 8 percent for the poorest quintile.

9. Another good example of an innovative cash transfer program is Chile's Solidario, started in 2002, which provides cash transfers to extremely poor families, many of which are indigenous. See Galasso (2006) and Palma and Urzúa (2005).

10. Most conditional cash transfer programs in the region rely on a combination of geographical targeting and household assessment mechanisms to determine eligibility. When selecting communities to participate, programs like Colombia's Familias en Acción and Nicaragua's Red de Protección Social also look at each community's capacity to respond to increased demand in health and education services (Rawlings and Rubio 2005; Rawlings 2005). Coady, Grosh, and Hoddinott (2004) suggests that combining multiple targeting

BOX 3-2. Two Successful Safety Net Programs

Mexico's Progresa, started in 1997, was designed to provide school subsidies, nutritional supplements, and cash food payments to poor families in rural areas of the country. Based on community feedback, household information, and geographical targeting of poor regions, Progresa showed what poverty reduction programs can do to promote growth-inducing investments in the country's future. In the first three years, the program reached close to 3 million rural families, about 30 percent of the estimated poor in the country, making a substantial difference in such indicators as school enrollment.[1] Renamed Oportunidades, the program began a gradual roll-out to urban areas in 2002, expanding its coverage to 4.2 million households (close to one-fifth of the country's population) the following year at a cost of MXN$22.3 billion (US$2.1 billion), or 0.32 percent of GDP. By 2007, the program reached about 5 million families (24 percent of the population) with a budget of MXN$39 billion (US$3.5 billion), or 0.39 percent of GDP.

Oportunidades now includes high school students, who also participate in a savings plan called Jóvenes con Oportunidades. The program offers a bonus that grows each year and turns into a savings fund if the student completes high school before turning twenty-two years of age. Students can use the bonus to help fund higher education or buy health insurance; they also can put it up as collateral for microcredit or use it to make a down payment on a house. Since 2003, Jóvenes con Oportunidades has opened more than 270,000 savings accounts on behalf of Oportunidades beneficiaries. Its impact has not yet been formally evaluated.

Between 1995 and 1998, Bolsa Escola guaranteed a minimum-wage income to poor families in Brazil's Federal District as long as their children (ages seven to fourteen) attended school regularly. In 1996 the program covered more than 44,000 children (12 percent of public school enrollment that year) at a cost of less than 1 percent of the district's total budget, and it made a substantial difference in such indicators as school drop-out and repetition rates as well as the employment rate of children ages ten to fourteen. The program was later adopted in other cities and states.

---

1. See De Janvry and Sadoulet (2006) for a discussion on how to make conditional cash transfer programs more efficient by targeting and calibrating grants.

(continued)

BOX 3-2. Two Successful Safety Net Programs (*continued*)

In 2003, the Brazilian government combined what was by then a federal Bolsa Escola program (Bolsa Escola Federal) with three other federal conditional cash transfer programs to create Bolsa Família, promoting education, health, and nutrition. With a budget of R$5.9 billion (US$2 billion), or 0.30 percent of GDP, Bolsa Família reached 7 million families by the end of 2004, transferring on average about US$25 per family per month through an electronic card (*cartão de benefício social*) issued and distributed by local branches of a government bank. As of 2007, the program reached 11.1 million families (100 percent of the estimated poor based on a program-specific poverty line of R$120 a month, about US$2 a day) and had an annual budget of R$8.8 billion (US$4.1 billion), or 0.35 percent of GDP.

An important feature of both programs is that cash transfers go mainly to women, who usually are the caregivers in the family. Many research studies have shown women are more likely than men to spend the money on their children.

Sources: On Mexico's Progresa-Oportunidades, see México-SEDESOL (2007); Behrman, Parker, and Todd (2007); Cruz, de la Torre, and Velázquez (2006); Gertler, Martinez, Rubio-Codina (2006); Levy (2006a); Skoufias (2000, 2005); Schultz (2004); Gertler (2004); and Skoufias and Parker (2001). On Brazil's Bolsa Escola/Bolsa Família, see Lindert and others (2007); Vaitsman and Paes-Sousa (2007); Brasil-MDS (2007); Brasil-MP (2007); De Janvry, Finan, and Sadoulet (2006); Soares and others (2006); Draibe (2006); De Janvry and others (2005); Cardoso and Souza (2004); Bourguignon, Ferreira, and Leite (2003); and Caccia Bava and others (1998). De Janvry and Sadoulet (2005) outlines key lessons from both the Brazilian and Mexican programs. De Janvry and others (2006) finds that the conditional transfers in Mexico have helped protect school enrollment from the impacts of economic shocks. Overviews of other experiences in Latin America can be found in Morley and Coady (2003); Rawlings (2005); Rawlings and Rubio (2005); Villatoro (2005b); Handa and Davis (2006); and De la Brière and Rawlings (2006).

mechanisms tends to yield more accurate results. The authors rank eighty-five antipoverty programs in thirty-six developing countries on the basis of their targeting performance. Argentina's Trabajar appears at the top of the list as the best-targeted intervention, with 80 percent of the benefits on average going to the poorest quintile of the population.

have made good progress—can function only if they allow analysts in- and outside government full access to the data and provide for full public dissemination.[11]

♦ Politically transparent rules that govern how money is spent. Programs have to be immune to clientelism, political manipulation, and corruption in procurement. It makes sense to include nongovernment officials in program governance or to find other ways to insulate program leadership from political changes.

♦ Community involvement. Active participation of the community should be an integral part of the program, and opportunities for communities to form partnerships with nongovernmental organizations should be provided.[12]

♦ Evaluation. The costs associated with rigorous evaluation can represent as little as 1 percent of total program costs.[13] The experience of Mexico, which has sponsored independent evaluation of its cash transfer program (box 3-2), shows that the returns to evaluation are high, in terms of both increasing the effectiveness of spending through design adjustments and making the political case for sustaining good programs.[14]

11. Chile and Mexico examples are from Castañeda and others (2005).

12. Some of the existing programs, like Oportunidades in Mexico, include community mechanisms for validating beneficiaries (Villatoro 2005a). Community participation in Argentina's Jefes y Jefas program helped reduce political and social conflict (Kessler and Roggi 2005). For further discussion of community-based targeting in social safety net programs, see Conning and Kevane (2002) and Pritchett (2005).

13. IDB (2003a).

14. See the recent report by a CGD working group on why good impact evaluation is too rare (Savedoff, Levine, and Birdsall 2006). For further details on Mexico's experience, see Behrman and Skoufias (2006) and Cohen, Franco, and Villatoro (2006). For the experiences of Latin American countries with the monitoring and evaluation of government programs in general, see May and others (2006) and Zaltsman (2006).

FOUR

More Taxes on the Rich and Better Spending on the Rest

I n the 1990s some Latin American governments succeeded in broadening their tax base and improving revenue collection. The emphasis was on improving the efficiency of the tax system to increase revenues, without much regard for the incidence of the tax burden on different income groups. Only Chile made the incidence of government spending measurably more progressive on the expenditure side.[1] Progress thus was limited in making the fiscal system overall—taxes and expenditures—more progressive.

The Tax Side

Most economists endorse the view that tax systems should not bear the burden of income redistribution—that the focus should be on efficiency, with any redistribution handled primarily through expenditures. But although government expenditure is and will continue to be the better instrument to deal with redistribution, it is time in Latin America to consider equity in taxation too, for at least three reasons.

First, most tax systems in Latin America are not good at generating revenue, and their ineffectiveness is a major constraint on using the expenditure side of the budget to reduce the region's high income inequality. Tax revenues average about 18 percent of GDP, well below what might be

1. ECLAC (2005).

58

expected given average per capita income.[2] (Brazil is an exception; there taxes are actually too high, at more than 35 percent of GDP.)[3] Changes in tax policy and more efficient tax collection could increase revenues while reducing the regressivity in actual tax collections. Raising more revenue would allow for increased spending. That would reduce inequality simply because in Latin America the proportion of government spending transferred to the bottom half of the population is larger than that population's share of national income. For example, although only 10 percent of government spending goes to the poorest 20 percent of families, that poorest 20 percent accounts for only 4 percent of national income. So, increasing the absolute amount of government spending would improve the overall distribution of real income, even without any change in the distribution of spending.

Second, most tax systems in the region are unusually regressive compared with those in OECD nations. They tax an equal or greater portion of the income of poor and middle-income households than of rich households; estimates from one study of Argentina suggest that of the high Gini coefficient of 55.9, as much as 7 points reflects the increase in inequality due to the regressive effect of taxes.[4] Tax systems are regressive for at least

2. Latin America's tax ratio is from ECLAC-ILPES database, based on 2005 values, except for Brazil, Colombia, and Ecuador (2004), Bolivia (2003), and Uruguay (2002). Data for Argentina, Bolivia, Brazil, Chile, Colombia, Costa Rica, Ecuador, and Uruguay refer to general government (central government, states or provinces, and municipalities); data for the rest are for central government. "For the development level of the countries, average tax burdens ought to be 24 percent of GDP. The primary deficiency in tax collection is for taxes on income and property, which on average amount to only 4.5 percent of GDP; in keeping with the development level of the countries, those taxes ought to generate 8 percent" (IDB 1999, p. 183).

3. Brazil's revenue ratio, though high by international standards, is the result of an overly complex and distortive tax system that depends heavily on cascading federal, state, and municipal indirect taxes with heavy burdens on labor and production. See Pessino and Fenochietto (2007, forthcoming) and OECD (2005a) for further discussion.

4. Pessino and Fenochietto (2007, forthcoming) estimates that in Argentina, the Gini coefficient calculated on the distribution of income before taxes is 48.7; after (personal) income, VAT, and payroll taxes it increases to 55.9. The impact of VAT alone raises the Gini coefficient to 53.5 (personal income taxes alone raise the Gini to 49.9). In 1996 the after-tax Gini coefficient for Chile was 49.6 and the before-tax Gini was 48.8 (Engel, Galetovic, and Raddatz 1999). In Central America, the regressivity of tax systems is reflected in higher after-tax Gini coefficients for El Salvador, Honduras, and especially Nicaragua, where the before-tax Gini coefficient was 50.1 and the after-tax Gini was 69.2 in 2000 (Agosin and others 2005).

three reasons: revenues are derived largely from neutral or regressive taxes (value-added tax, other consumption taxes, and single-rate payroll taxes); effective taxation of high-income people is low; and enforcement of corporate and personal income tax regulations is weak.

The value-added tax and other taxes on consumption account for about 60 percent of total revenues in the region; the figure is about 30 percent in Europe.[5] Despite various exemptions on such basic necessities as food and medicine, the value-added, excise, trade, and other consumption-based taxes tend to be regressive.[6] They collect a higher percentage from the incomes of the poor than from those of the rich, in large part because the poor spend a larger share of their income than the rich.

Payroll taxes—which are set at a rate of more than 15 percent in most countries—also are regressive.[7] Although in principle they finance specific health and pay-as-you-go pension benefits and therefore can be thought of as "contributions," the relationship between the value of the contributions and the benefits has been weak.[8] The de-linking of contributions and benefits is due in some cases to overgenerous pension benefits (which exceed the contributions plus a reasonable imputation of a rate of return)

5. Tanzi and Zee (2000). Martner and Aldunate (2006) estimates that indirect taxes accounted for about 56 percent of total tax revenues in Latin America and 31 percent of tax revenues in Europe in 2003–04.

6. Pessino and Fenochietto (2007, forthcoming) shows that while various exemptions on food, durable goods, and education reduce the tax burden imposed on the poor, they reduce the burden on the rich even more and make tax systems more susceptible to evasion and cheating. In Argentina, the two richest quintiles receive 76 percent of the exemptions on education and 59 percent of all other exemptions on different goods and services. Those exemptions reduce the tax burden on the poorest quintiles by 25 percent, with the exemptions on food like bread, milk, and meat helping the most. But the cost is several times what they receive: each US$1 of exemptions in education (which goes mostly to the rich) costs US$17. In the case of milk, each US$1 costs US$5.

7. Economists have generally concluded that in the long run, the burden of payroll taxes falls on workers, not consumers. Brazil collects close to 8 percent of GDP in payroll taxes while Argentina collects about 5 percent of GDP. Payroll taxes are capped in some countries, so the average tax rate declines as income increases. In Argentina, prior to elimination of the cap in 2005, the burden of the full tax (without deducting presumed benefits) represented around 28 percent of the wage of the poorest quintile, 33 percent of the wage of the middle quintile, and 21 percent of the wage of the richest quintile. In Chile, payroll taxation fell significantly as a result of the privatization of pension fund administration (Pessino and Fenochietto 2007, forthcoming).

8. See Levy (2006b) for evidence of a wide wedge between the costs and the value of social security contributions in Mexico.

and in other cases to severe deterioration in the quality of health services and erosion in the real value of pensions as a result of inflation.

Finally, personal income tax rates are progressive on paper because they apply only to high-income taxpayers—as few as 3 percent to 5 percent of all households in some countries. But with few taxpayers affected and the high rates of evasion discussed below, the personal income tax cannot compensate for the inherent regressivity of other taxes. Though statutory marginal rates rise as income rises in most countries, with top rates around 40 percent or higher, effective tax rates are much lower. In Argentina, Chile, and Guatemala in the mid-1990s, for example, effective tax rates for the richest 10 percent of households were a mere 8 percent of income.[9] In contrast, average effective tax rates on top income earners in the United States are closer to 40 percent, including federal and state taxes.[10] Overall revenue collection can only be poor when households that control more than 50 percent of income contribute so little in taxes.

Why is it that in most countries of the region personal income and other nonconsumption taxes fail to compensate much if at all for efficient but regressive value-added taxes and payroll "contributions"? In many countries, most households with above-average income are exempt from personal income tax because of relatively high minimum personal exemption levels.[11] Minimum taxable levels and multiple exemptions and other loopholes combine with underfunded and ineffective tax administration, lax enforcement, and widespread evasion (box 4-1) to minimize the taxes paid by high-income households. Exemptions of income from capital allow many high-income households to reduce their tax burden dramatically. And in some countries it is all too easy to shelter personal income in shadow "corporations" with high expenses.

There is no need to raise personal income tax rates. They already are high and, on paper, highly progressive. However, there is room to reduce overall regressivity and enhance fairness in the region's tax systems by reducing

9. IDB (1999).

10. Schmitt (2005).

11. Minimum personal exemption levels have increased from a regional average starting at 60 percent of per capita GDP in the mid 1980s to 2.3 times per capita GDP in the 2000s. The minimums are as high as eight times the average income in Nicaragua and four times the average income in Colombia (Bird 2003; IDEA 2007; Stotsky and WoldeMariam 2002).

BOX 4-1. Tax Evasion in Argentina, Brazil, and Chile

Tax evasion rates are very high throughout Latin America and affect all major taxes.[1] The level of personal income tax evasion is estimated at almost 50 percent in Argentina, 55 percent in Brazil, and 56 percent in Chile, while corporate income tax evasion is estimated at about 46, 42, and 35 percent respectively.[2]

TABLE 4-1. Tax Evasion Rates in Argentina, Brazil, and Chile, 2000[a]
Percent

Tax	Argentina	Brazil	Chile
Value-added tax (VAT)	39	. . .	20
Payroll tax	43	55	17
Personal income tax	49	55	57
Corporate income tax	46	42	35
Informal economy as percent of GNP	40	39	. . .

a. Payroll tax figures are for 1999 (1998 for Brazil). Personal and corporate income taxes for Brazil are for 1998. VAT figures for Chile and Argentina are for 1997. Estimates of tax evasion vary widely. For example, the official estimate for VAT evasion in Argentina in 2004 was 25 percent; an independent study's estimates of evasion of VAT and payroll taxes in the country in 2004 were around 29 percent and 52 to 56 percent respectively (Cont and Susmel 2006; Cont 2006).

Estimates suggest that a 30 percent reduction in evasion of VAT, personal and corporate income taxes, and payroll and wealth taxes would generate a 17 percent increase in tax collection in Argentina, 14 percent in Brazil, and 12 percent in Chile.

1. The discussion in this box is based on Pessino and Fenochietto (2007, forthcoming).
2. An average-wage employee in Argentina who is a non-evader pays on average more than 50 percent of his or her income in taxes (including payroll taxes) while an informal worker who complies only with VAT and some property taxes pays only 12 percent. So, of a total tax burden of 24 percent, non-evaders pay 50 percent while full evaders pay around 12 percent.

evasion and eliminating loopholes that tend to favor high-income households. In principle, increasing the actual tax burden on high-income earners could create negative work or other incentive problems, but we believe that any effect would be small. Revenue increases might also be small, but the tax systems would be perceived, finally, as reasonably fair. Similarly, even the fear that taxing income from capital would lead to capital flight

Increasing compliance is no easy task. Implementing a system to improve the collection and cross-indexing of information on potential taxpayers (identifying individual social and fiscal attributes), such as that based on the Social Security number in the United States, would help detect and reduce evasion. Increasing the perceived probability of auditing by implementing an information-crossing system would also have a positive impact on compliance. In the 1980s, Chile became the first country in the region to institute a tax identification number to facilitate the identification of individuals and their transactions and assets. Chile is more advanced than Argentina and Brazil in crossing personal, tax, and social data, which may explain its better tax collection level and expenditure management.

But more progress is needed. In Argentina, the SINTyS project—Sistema de Identificación Nacional Tributario y Social (National Tax and Social Identification System)—was initiated in the office of the chief of the Cabinet of Ministers. Since its start, the project has collected data of relevance in tax administration. But so far there has not been collaboration between the office responsible for tax administration and the SINTyS project office in building a shared database of key information to cross with information on income or wealth taxes. An exception occurred in late 2001, when the tax administration crossed information on deposits or funds sent abroad (which came to light when depositors went to court to demand the return of deposits that had been confiscated by the administration of then President Fernando de la Rua in the wake of the economic crisis) and used it to detect evasion, catching several noncompliant taxpayers.

States, municipalities, and other subnational government units also need to fight evasion. A first step is to create an incentive for them to do so in the many countries where these units receive fixed transfers from the central government, often independent of their own revenue efforts.

may well be exaggerated. Other factors—unstable prices, poor contract enforcement—are equally probable sources of capital flight. Indeed, compared with the United States, where effective average tax rates already are as high as 40 percent for higher-income households, Latin America is not close to bumping up against the traditional economists' concern that enforced high tax rates will discourage work, innovation, and investment.

BOX 4-2. Politics of Tax Reform

The recent literature on taxation in Latin America suggests that making tax systems more progressive is a major political challenge. In a 2004 World Bank report, *Inequality in Latin America: Breaking with History?* the bottom line was not much of a bottom line: although "there is almost certainly some potential to make tax systems somewhat more progressive . . . the extent to which this is possible will depend on issues of overall political and social consensus as much as on the details of tax instruments." In a 2003 background paper for that report, "Taxation in Latin America: Reflections on Sustainability and the Balance between Equity and Efficiency," Richard Bird, a distinguished authority on tax issues worldwide, wrote: "Some specific suggestions are made in [this] paper with respect to how both the efficiency and the equity outcomes of Latin American tax systems might be improved. My general conclusion, however, is . . . somewhat pessimistic. . . . a more democratic and sustainable outcome cannot, as it were, be induced by better fiscal institutions. On the contrary, a more encompassing and legitimate state is itself the key ingredient needed for a more balanced and sustainable tax system."[1]

But might "overall political and social consensus" and a "more encompassing and legitimate state" be in part the product of a more and visibly fair tax regime? Is politics the problem or the solution? Politics was never said to be an impossible barrier to reform of macroeconomic or trade policy or to privatization of state-owned enterprises. There is surely political room to build a constituency favoring, for example, reduced evasion, some property taxes, and—in the interests of job creation—reduced reliance on payroll taxes. The key change may need to come from political leaders who decide to champion tax systems built on the principles of fairness and transparency.

---

1. De Ferranti and others (2004, p. 255). See also Bird (2003, p.2).

Compared with increasing the value-added tax, increasing tax collection from the few high-income earners (say, the top 10 percent) might not raise much revenue in the short run. But that should not be an excuse for inaction. Now that an initial round of tax reforms is in place (establishing and consolidating the value-added tax), the democratic governments of the region should put a premium on making tax systems more visibly fair (box 4-2). Tax systems that are fair—and perceived to be fair by the majority of the population—make transparent the connection between tax payments and citizenship. An increase in reliance on personal and wealth taxes would help inform citizens at all income levels of the taxes that they pay, raising awareness among Latin Americans about their responsibilities as well as their rights as citizens—bearing in mind that the value-added tax, for all its merits, is an invisible tax (box 4-3). If citizens, particularly the working poor, understood how much they are paying their governments, they might be more easily mobilized to press for public services and for accountability from their elected officials.

More visibly fair tax systems might also make higher ratios of taxes to GDP more politically acceptable (as would, of course, more efficient public spending and less corruption.)[12] And higher tax-to-GDP ratios would allow for increased spending, benefiting the bottom half, by income, of the population.

The key steps to making tax systems both more effective and fair are to

◆ Reduce high rates of evasion of all types of taxes (see box 4-1), eliminate loopholes, and lower the thresholds below which income is exempted.[13] Where top marginal tax rates are punitive for those who actually pay (one example is Brazil), a package of reduced top rates and stiffened enforcement makes sense.

◆ Improve tax administration. Doing so is critical to better enforcement.[14] Tax administrations in most countries are weak, inefficient,

12. Public opinion polls show that on average only 23 percent of Latin Americans surveyed in 2003 believed that tax collection was "impartial" and only 15 percent trusted that tax revenues would be well spent by the government. In 2005 about 21 percent of respondents trusted that their tax money would be put to good use (Latinobarómetro 2003, 2005).

13. Pessino and Fenochietto (2007, forthcoming) estimates that eliminating all personal income tax exemptions and privileges would increase collections by 47 percent in Argentina, 62 percent in Brazil, and 40 percent in Chile. They argue against eliminating income tax exemptions indiscriminately, since many promote savings or investment and their elimination could increase capital flight. They recommend eliminating exemptions on indirect taxes that are granted as political privileges, such as exemptions for promotion of particular industries or regions or for communications media, although doing so would not markedly increase revenues. Exemptions on capital, medical, and educational expenses in Argentina and Brazil are most likely benefiting middle- and high-income households and might be worth eliminating, but their effects are more ambiguous and need further research. In Colombia, the fiscal cost of exemptions is calculated at 9.2 percent of GDP; in Guatemala and Mexico, it is calculated at 7.3 and 6.3 percent of GDP respectively (IDEA 2007).

14. Tax administrations in Latin America have not relied much on scientific analysis (theoretical or empirical) of tax noncompliance in designing measures to reduce evasion. In most

BOX 4-3. Citizens as Taxpayers

Linking citizens' rights and the payment of taxes is crucial to legitimizing tax reform in Latin America. Because the value-added tax and other consumption-based taxes are folded into the price of goods, consumers may not know that they pay taxes on their purchases. That is also true in other regions, but in Latin America an unusually high proportion of all revenue comes from such taxes. Independent research and policy institutes could help by publishing analyses of how much tax different income groups actually pay.[1]

The same problem applies to payroll and income taxes. Many workers need not file individual tax returns, given the minimum income rules. As a result, Latin Americans are rarely conscious of the taxes deducted every month from their paychecks and often are unaware of their pretax income; of what percentage of their wages goes for contributions to pension, health, and other social insurance programs; and of what percentage goes to general taxes.

A system based on tax rebates for those with incomes below a given threshold would be more transparent than the current system.[2] Implementing it would be expensive and demand a very good, efficient tax bureaucracy, something that is scarce in the region. But its merits would more than outweigh its costs.

FIGURE 4-1. Personal Income Tax Revenue in Latin America and in OECD Countries, 2004[a]

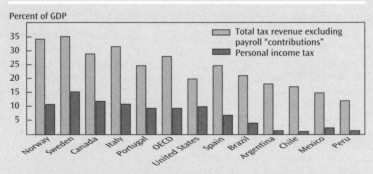

Percent of GDP

Total tax revenue excluding payroll "contributions"
Personal income tax

Sources: ECLAC-ILPES database for Brazil, Chile, and Peru; OECD (2005a) for OECD countries including Mexico; Pessino and Fenochietto (2007, forthcoming) for Argentina.

a. Payroll contributions encompass pensions and unemployment, health, and other such insurance, depending on the country. Figures are for general government, except those for Peru, which are for central government. All data are for 2004 or closest available year.

1. Martinez-Vazquez (2001) suggests that in Mexico, lack of information on the actual distribution of tax burdens has contributed to the lack of voluntary compliance with tax laws because of the general perception that many do not contribute their fair share of taxes.
2. This point is convincingly elaborated in De la Torre (2002).

understaffed, and underfunded.[15] Reforms are needed to increase their ability to effectively audit tax returns, detect errors and evasion, and enforce collection, especially among the wealthy, who tend to wield significant political influence. Such changes require increasing their technical expertise and providing them with political backing.[16] They should also be allowed to recover evaded taxes through administrative channels before resorting to the justice system. The U.S. Internal Revenue Service already does that.[17] Peru's success in tax administration in the 1990s and the experience of Ecuador's internal revenue service indicate that more revenue can be raised without

---

countries there is no systematic effort to measure tax evasion levels on a consistent annual or biannual basis. Chile is the exception, where the tax administration relies on an annual in-house study of VAT evasion to design tax policy goals (Baer 2006). Many countries, among them Argentina and Brazil, designed so-called simplified regimes based on the popular belief that tax complexity is one of the key reasons for tax evasion. While tax complexity may be a factor, the extent of its relationship with tax evasion in Latin America has never been rigorously studied (Pessino and Fenochietto, 2007 forthcoming). Moreover, there have been very few empirical investigations of any of the reasons for tax evasion in the region. Fenochietto (1999) is among the earliest, most comprehensive tax evasion surveys in the region.

15. In Chile, Brazil, and Argentina, tax administrations cite lack of resources, personnel, and training as obstacles to performing efficiently. Pessino and Fenochietto (2007, forthcoming) shows that among the three, Chile's tax administration is the most productive. While Argentina's tax administration has 1,000 employees per percentage point of GDP collected and processes 277 tax reports per employee, Chile's has 146 employees per percentage point collected and processes 899 reports per employee. In Brazil, the government has resorted to higher taxes or new distortive ones to improve collection instead of focusing on tax administration performance. In many countries, performance is measured by increases in tax collection, leading to incorrect evaluations because an increase in revenue can depend on other factors, like GDP growth, tax legislation, and changes in the tax base.

16. The degree of political independence of tax administrations varies across countries. Chile's tax administration is an autonomous decentralized public agency whose director is appointed by the president. Efforts to decentralize tax administration, to allow directors to be nominated by the president and approved by the Senate, and to establish tenure of six years for the director failed in Argentina in the 1990s. In Brazil, the 1988 constitution abolished tenure for the tax administration's director and staff as part of efforts to reduce job security among public officials. But in this case, the lack of job stability makes the tax administrator easily replaceable and very susceptible to political interference. In Chile, the director has more stability than in other countries. Between 1974 and 1999, Chile's tax administration had just five directors while Argentina had eleven. Note, however, that stability of tenure might not be a good idea in all countries and under all circumstances.

17. For further discussion on this point, see Baer (2006). Tax administrations in many Latin American countries suffer from the inefficiency and slowness of the justice system in penalizing evaders. Even when evasion is detected, an inefficient (and corrupt) judiciary makes it extremely difficult to recover large outstanding debts.

major changes in tax regimes.[18] Chile also has shown that it is possible to achieve high productivity in tax administration.

♦ Reduce reliance on high, single-rate payroll taxes. Lowering payroll taxes would increase collection from both payroll and value-added taxes (through reduced evasion) and, along with other policy changes, would reduce the high cost of labor (see chapter 6), in turn reducing the level of informal employment. But to make room for lowering payroll taxes, governments must tackle head on the difficult problem of benefits. In many countries, it would make sense to drop payroll "contributions" for pension and health benefits and finance minimum entitlements from general, progressive taxation.

♦ Implement progressive taxes and make tax payments more visible to taxpayers. In addition to better enforcement of the personal income tax, there are at least three other possibilities. One is to tax property (implying investment in municipal tax administration). A second is to tax gross assets; the tax could be treated as a minimum corporate tax, deductible on corporate income tax. Mexico has implemented a reasonably effective minimum corporate tax. A third, more controversial possibility is to establish procedures for taxing income from assets held abroad. That would require bilateral agreements with countries such as the United States to share access to information on assets of nonresidents.

The Expenditure Side: Pensions and More

Substantial improvement in redistribution can be achieved through sensible government spending. In the interests of equity, more spending on health, education, and public infrastructure such as roads makes sense. Greater spending could benefit not only the poor (as in Mexico's Oportunidades or in Brazil's Bolsa Família; see chapter 3, box 3-2) but also the many other

18. Personnel and technology were at the center of Ecuador's tax administration reform, initiated in 1998, which established its internal revenue service (Servicio de Rentas Internas). Of the 1,700 employees of the old tax administration system, all but five accepted buyout offers and resigned in the wake of the reforms. The newly formed agency was granted institutional autonomy, which limits political interference and enhances its authority. Previously, fiscal agents were unable to win a single tax collection case in court. As a result of reforms, tax collections nearly doubled in three years, from US$1.4 billion (7.3 percent of GDP) in 1998 to US$2.3 billion (13 percent of GDP) in 2001 (Drosdoff 2002). Fuentes (2006) discusses recent tax administration reform efforts in Central America.

households whose per capita income is well below the average—in most countries as much as 70 percent of all households.

It is a question not just of more spending but of more efficient spending. Our discussion of other policy areas (education and consumer-driven public services) focuses on radical new approaches to make public spending both more efficient and more fair. One simple way is to spend more on preschool-age children in poor households (see box 4-4). Here we concentrate on a single big-ticket item—pay-as-you-go pensions. Through such pensions, public spending benefits disproportionately households with above-average income.[19]

In Latin America the biggest problem plaguing pension systems in terms of their effect on equity is their low coverage—low not just in absolute terms but also in terms of what would be expected given per capita income.[20] Across countries, formal coverage does tend to rise with per capita income. But even in Colombia, where per capita income is higher than the Latin America average, less than 25 percent of the economically active population is covered. In Argentina, the figure is nearly 40 percent; in Chile, about 60 percent. In the region overall, pensions are far from universal, and they usually exclude workers in the informal sector and in agriculture.[21] Effective coverage, furthermore, is much lower because many workers, especially women, fail to qualify for pensions because they never manage to document sufficiently long and continuous employment in formal sector jobs.[22]

19. In Latin America, the richest quintile of the population receives on average about 61 percent of net pension benefits (full benefit amount received minus total contributions), while the poorest quintile only receives 3 percent (Lindert, Skoufias, and Shapiro 2006).

20. Gill, Packard, and Yermo (2005); Lucchetti and Rofman (2006). We do not comment here on other valid objectives of pension programs, such as being fiscally sustainable and promoting savings.

21. In nearly half the countries in Latin America, less than 30 percent of the economically active population is covered by a pension system. Between the mid-1990s and early 2000s, the proportion of the labor force with pension coverage fell in nine countries (Argentina, Bolivia, Brazil, Colombia, Chile, Costa Rica, Paraguay, Uruguay, and Venezuela). Across countries, coverage is much higher in wealthier quintiles and urban areas than in poorer quintiles and rural areas. A simple average shows that in seventeen countries fewer than four of every ten persons age sixty-five or older directly receive some type of pension income (Lucchetti and Rofman 2006).

22. For example, in Colombia, where less than 25 percent of the labor force is covered by the pension system, only half of those covered will meet the minimum contribution period required to qualify for a monthly pension; instead, they will receive their accumulated contributions in a lump sum payment at retirement.

BOX 4-4. Investing in Children in Unequal Societies

In unequal societies that have a high level of poverty, investments in disadvantaged children almost automatically reconcile equity and efficiency goals. Early childhood interventions aimed at improving nutrition, health, and cognitive development are crucial to helping children from poor families overcome the disadvantages that too often prevent them from building the most important of all assets—human capital. Efficient government investment in disadvantaged children brings higher rates of return than investment in low-skilled adults.[1] In rural Colombia, the Community Childcare and Nutrition Program, through which poor children received food and childcare from one of the mothers in the community, had a significant effect on the nutritional status of young children (three to five years of age)

---

1. Heckman and Masterov (2007) and Carneiro and Heckman (2003) make a strong productivity case for investing in early childhood interventions based on evidence from the United States. Garces, Thomas, and Currie (2000) shows the long-term effects of Head Start, a U.S. early childhood development program. Studies of early childhood development programs in developing countries suggest robust benefits for all children, with cost-benefit analyses showing returns of US$2 to US$5 for every US$1 invested. In general, children who participate in an early childhood program show improved health and school achievement—for example, higher enrollment rates in later schooling, less repetition of grades, and less dropping out—when compared with nonparticipants in similar circumstances (World Bank 2005c; Attanasio and Vera-Hernández 2004; Behrman and others 2006; Grantham-McGregor and others 1991; Engle and others 2007; Curi and Menezes-Filho 2006; Morán 2003). Schady 2006 reviews the literature on the impact of early childhood interventions in the United States and discusses evidence from Latin America.

Low effective coverage today means a high and growing incidence of people who will fall into poverty during their old age. Moreover, the pay-as-you-go pension systems that are actuarially underfunded—that is, where the expected present value of contributions is less than the expected present value of pension benefits promised under the system—introduce intergenerational inequity, because workers who are currently contributing to the system will have to pay more in taxes or receive lower pension benefits (or both) than those who are currently retired. Because of low coverage and actuarial deficits, pensions systems in most of the region are exacerbating rather than mitigating income inequality.[23]

23. Despite formal membership contributions, virtually all public social security regimes in Latin America run significant deficits, which are financed by general tax revenues (for example, about 56 percent of federal social security benefits in Argentina and 89 percent in Peru) (Lindert, Skoufias, and Shapiro 2006).

who had been enrolled since birth, resulting in a relative increase of almost four centimeters in height. Children ages thirteen to seventeen who had benefited from the program were more likely to be in school later. In rural Guatemala, nutritional supplements for preschool children increased their probability of attending school and led to higher completed schooling and higher adult cognitive achievement test scores.[2]

Democracy, decentralization, and the increasing role of civil society are all increasing effective political demand for public investments in children in the region. To make growing political support more sustainable, advocates of these programs can

- Push for earmarked taxes to fund child programs. Earmarking, never ideal, may be necessary given the region's political realities.
- Build on the initiatives of small community groups, civil society, and local governments.
- Promote a political constituency of consumers by using direct subsidies to poor and working-class families for investment in children. They would then demand good-quality, sustained programs.
- Build a supplier constituency by hiring and training mothers to start and manage their own small daycare services, while providing public subsidies to help poor neighbors pay for such services.

---

2. Attanasio and Vera-Hernández (2004); Behrman and others (2006).

Unfortunately, the Chilean-style pension reforms introduced in several Latin American countries during the 1990s seem to have done nothing to expand effective coverage.[24] And rather than augmenting coverage by providing a broad-based pension floor for the elderly, the pay-as-you-go pension systems that remain in the region tend to increase inequality by

---

24. Chilean-style reforms have been introduced in several countries since 1992, including Argentina, Bolivia, Colombia, El Salvador, Mexico, Peru, and Uruguay. In essence, these reforms consist of a shift away from government-administered, pay-as-you-go, defined-benefit pension systems toward systems that rely mainly on the so-called "second pillar"—that is, mandatory, privately administered, defined-contribution pension funds (Gill, Packard, and Yermo 2005; Kay and Matijascic 2006). That this type of reform has failed to widen coverage is illustrated in Chile itself, where coverage has failed to expand beyond 60 percent of the labor force, the same as in the old pay-as-you-go system (Larraín Ríos 2005). For in-depth analysis of pension reform experiences in Mexico, Costa Rica, Brazil, Peru, Uruguay and Argentina, see Kay and Sinha (2007).

offering benefits only or mainly to formal sector workers. The problem of providing coverage to the very poor may require a solution that goes beyond expanding the formal pension system. There will always be many people outside the system who will be deeply poor when they are old. Because coverage of the formal pension scheme will never be sufficient, some type of noncontributory income support program in old age may be the only answer.[25]

Perhaps the most egregious forms of regressivity in pension systems in the region are found in certain separate pay-as-you-go pension schemes for certain classes of public sector employees—for example, those in the education system, the judiciary, the police, the military, and public enterprises. Because such systems offer overgenerous pension benefits—that is, pensions that vastly exceed what is warranted by accumulated contributions—to a privileged few, they are a huge and hugely regressive drain on public finances.[26] In part, the excessive benefits reflect past public sector wage negotiations that were often resolved by agreements to limit current wage increases in return for future pension and other benefits. But those future benefits were never funded; the result has been high and often exploding public sector unfunded liabilities. To protect their benefits, politically powerful groups have resisted incorporation into the general pension system, so taxpayers bear the burden.[27] In Brazil, the annual

25. In developed countries, social protection systems often include noncontributory old age income support programs to protect the very poor. In Latin America, with the exception perhaps of Brazil, very little effort has been made in that area. Brazil's rural pension system extends pension coverage to the rural poor through noncontributory mechanisms, financed in part by taxes levied on the sale of agriculture products (ECLAC 2006b).

26. Excessive generosity takes the form of a retirement pension that vastly exceeds what is warranted by accumulated contributions. In practice, this is the result of one or more factors: low contribution rates, low retirement age, pensions that are based on the recipient's last salary, and so forth.

27. In Chile, the social security programs for the Armed Forces were left out of the reforms and their administration was maintained under the National Defense Social Security Fund (Caja de Previsión de la Defensa Nacional) and the General Department of Social Security for the Police Force (Dirección de Previsión de Carabineros de Chile). The pension scheme runs at a deficit, and benefits are nearly totally (93–95 percent in 1997) financed by the central revenue budget. Peru has a highly regressive pension system for a select group of civil servants, the Cédula Viva, managed by the federal government, which provides significantly more generous benefits than the country's national pension regime, which is open to all workers. In 2004, the public subsidy to the Cédula Viva equaled 99 percent of its cost. That same year pension reforms closed the Cédula Viva to new entrants and empowered the legislature to reduce current benefits and make it more difficult to raise future benefits (Lindert, Skoufias, and Shapiro 2006).

deficit on the civil service pension system, which covers only 13 percent of pensioners, constitutes around 3.8 percent of GDP.[28] In a country struggling to sustain a primary fiscal surplus target of more than 4 percent of GDP, that is a huge fiscal burden—and one that, short of reform, will grow as the population ages.[29] Future taxpayers, including poorer workers, will end up subsidizing more privileged workers.

Privileged pension programs for civil servants and the military are essentially a political economy issue. The high costs are well known. Yet the governments that have attempted reforms have so far been limited, after huge and costly political fights, to minor fixes. There is the usual collective action problem: losers are easy to identify (losses are big and concentrated among a politically vocal few) while winners are not (gains are small for each individual and spread out over many beneficiaries). To mobilize those who stand to gain requires making the imbalances clear to everyone—and in some cases embarrassing the losers with public information on the size of their benefits. (Protests erupted in Argentina in 2001–02 when the pension benefits of civil servants were revealed in the press.) When legal contracts bind current taxpayers, at the least the pension rules for the future should be fixed.

With equity as the objective, improved pension policy calls for

◆ Expanding coverage to reach more of the poor, while maintaining the financial viability of pension systems and avoiding fiscal damage.

---

28. World Bank (2005b). The figure refers to the deficit of the combined pension schemes for public sector workers at the federal, state, and municipal levels of governments in 2004. Pensioners in the public sector scheme received R$1,973 on average in 2003, nearly five times more than their counterparts in the private sector (for federal public servants, the average value of pensions can be up to twenty-five times greater than the average pension for private sector workers). Cash-strapped states and municipalities are obliged under the Federal Responsibility Law to constrain spending on salaries and pensions to below 60 percent of revenues. Expenditures on civil servant pensions often can constitute up to 50 percent of the total payroll of active/inactive employees and 30 percent of the total payroll, imposing an onerous fiscal burden that squeezes out development spending (World Bank 2005b; Ferreira Savoia 2007). Glomm and others (2005) and Glomm, Jung, and Tran (2006) examine the negative impact of Brazil's generous pension scheme and rising pension expenditure on consumption, public investment, and GDP growth.

29. The population in Brazil sixty years of age and older is expected to grow at an annual average rate of 3 percent in the next twenty years, while total population is growing at less than 1.4 percent annually. Although reforms that Brazil pushed through in 2003–04 are a step in the right direction, they save only about 0.2 to 0.3 percent of GDP (World Bank 2005b, 2007a; Ferreira Savoia 2007).

In economies with large numbers of informal and self-employed workers, that might require regulatory adjustments to allow groups of self-employed workers to invest together in the country's private defined-contribution systems.

◆ Including minimum benefits for low-income retirees enrolled in the formal pension system, if necessary financed from general revenues. Chile has set up a collective, or solidarity, scheme funded by employers and the state that pays benefits (partial insurance) to workers with insufficient funds in their individual accounts.

◆ Considering generic, non-contributory old age income support programs to protect the very poor, financed from general tax revenues.

◆ Promoting informed public discussion of the immediate and long-term costs of civil service, military, and state enterprise pay-as-you-go pension programs. That is the first step toward creating the political will and developing legislation to reduce the future tax burden of these programs.

FIVE

Giving Small Businesses a Chance

D oing business in Latin America is very difficult for small and medium-size enterprises (SMEs), in every dimension. In business surveys, Latin American SMEs report higher obstacles related to legal matters, financing, and corruption than do larger enterprises in their own countries and SMEs in developed countries.[1] Moreover, analysis of surveys indicates that equivalent obstacles hurt SMEs much more than other enterprises.[2] The silver lining of that finding is, of course, that any improvement in the business environment will bring a disproportionate benefit to SMEs. And there is indeed much room to improve. The available comparative indicators of the quality of business environments paint a grimmer picture for Latin SMEs than their peers in, say, developing Asia and eastern Europe (figure 5-1). Typically, a Latin American SME faces unduly slow and cumbersome bureaucratic procedures (which invite corruption), poorly designed tax regimes, onerous labor legislation, tight financing constraints, and costly transportation and communications infrastructure.[3]

1. As illustrated in the World Bank Enterprise Surveys (www.enterprisesurveys.org), Investment Climate Assessments (World Bank 2005d, 2005e), and World Business Environment Survey 2000 (Batra, Kaufmann, and Stone 2003).
2. Beck, Demirgüç-Kunt, and Maksimovic (2005) finds that the extent to which financial, legal, and corruption problems affect firm growth depends on firm size, with smaller firms being most affected by these factors.
3. In high-income OECD countries, it takes on average six steps over twenty-five days at a cost of around 8 percent of per capita income to open a new business. By contrast, Latin

F I G U R E   5-1.   Ease of Doing Business Index[a]

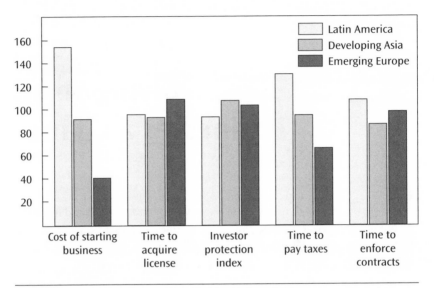

Source: IMF (2006b) based on World Bank's Doing Business Database.
a. Average across countries = 100.

American entrepreneurs on average go through eleven procedures over seventy days at a cost of 60 percent of per capita income to start a business, second only to their peers in sub-Saharan Africa. In Latin America, procedures to close a business take twice as long (3.6 compared with 1.6 years), bankruptcy proceedings cost twice as much (15.8 percent compared with 6.8 percent of the estate), and the recovery rate (how many cents on the dollar claimants such as creditors, tax authorities, and employees can recover from an insolvent firm) is about a third of that of high-income OECD countries (26 percent compared with 72 percent of debt, respectively) (World Bank 2006a). Senior management executives in Latin America report spending more than 10 percent of their time in a typical week dealing with government tax, customs, and labor regulations; dealing with government officials; completing official paperwork; and so forth. That figure is the highest of any region and compares with just under 3 percent in OECD countries (World Bank Enterprise Surveys). In Brazil, active SMEs surveyed in 2004 cited high levels of taxes and compulsory government payments as the main obstacle to doing business. The owners of failed SMEs also reported a high tax burden as a key reason for their failures (SEBRAE 2004). In Mexico, high energy prices affect the competitiveness of businesses across sectors and sizes. But the quality of electricity service is especially poor for SMEs, which often experience variations in frequency and voltage and service interruptions. Large firms have fewer quality problems because they generally are served by more reliable, high-tension wires (World Bank 2006d). On the effects of corruption, see chapter 8 of this volume; for more on infrastructure costs, see chapter 11.

Large enterprises in the region are, of course, not fully immune to those obstacles. But they have access to greater and more varied resources that help them to absorb the associated costs, they exert political influence to get special treatment, or they move operations to, and obtain financing from, foreign jurisdictions that offer a better business environment. Small businesses and microenterprises do not have those options. To minimize the costs of regulation and taxes, they often opt to remain informal as a way to stay in business, further reducing their ability to borrow, acquire new technologies, and expand in the long run.[4]

Reflecting the interaction between informality and smallness, the corporate sector in Latin American countries tends to be characterized by the so-called "missing middle." At one extreme, a few large enterprises account for a large share of a country's GDP and, at the other, many small firms and microenterprises account for a small fraction of GDP but a large share of employment and household income.[5] The missing middle reflects the difficulties that small enterprises face in breaking the size barrier to become medium-size firms.

Improving the business environment to level the playing field for SMEs is easier said than done. For example, significant reforms in the 1990s that

4. Informal, small firms operate without being registered, regulated, or taxed (Palmade and Anayiotos 2005). In Peru, nearly three-quarters of all microenterprises and small businesses operate outside of the formal economy; informality is much higher among microenterprises (75 percent) than among small firms (37 percent) (Perú–MTPE 2006). In Chile, there were 1.4 million microenterprises and small businesses in 2004, of which approximately half were informal. Chile's informal microenterprises were shown to have significantly lower sales than their counterparts in the formal economy as well as 25 percent less capital (Chile Emprende 2005). A recent assessment of informality in twelve Latin American countries suggests that burdensome procedures often deter micro- and small entrepreneurs who attempt to formalize their businesses, raising costs and forcing them to remain informal (see, for example, ILD 2006a-2006d). See also the discussion in Perry and others (2007b).

5. Angelelli, Moudry and Llisterri (2006) reports that large firms constitute less than 0.5 percent of total firms in Latin America and employ close to one-fourth of the private sector labor force. At the other extreme, microenterprises and small businesses together account for 97 percent of all businesses and 63 percent of total private sector employment. In five of seven countries with data available, microenterprises and SMEs together contribute to less than 50 percent of GDP. In Brazil, formal microenterprises and small businesses account for 98 percent of all firms, nearly 70 percent of total private sector jobs, and about 20 percent of GDP (SEBRAE 2006). In Peru, microbusinesses and small firms (both formal and informal, excluding self-employed individuals) account for 98 percent of total firms, employ 60 percent of the labor force, and contribute 42 percent to GDP (Perú–MTPE 2006, 2005).

produced more stable financial systems did not boost financing of SMEs to the extent expected.[6] At one extreme, large, reputable corporations can raise financing from local or international banks or securities markets.[7] At the other extreme, microenterprises have seen their access improve in recent years. In the middle are SMEs, for which financing, even for working capital, seems to have stagnated. In order to expand, SMEs must rely on retained earnings or borrow short term at high interest rates through credit cards or current account overdrafts.[8]

The need for renewed policy efforts to give small businesses a better chance is more urgent than ever given the growing competitive challenges of economic globalization.[9] Most of our equity tools (for example, for building infrastructure, smoothing booms and busts, and improving education) would benefit SMEs indirectly. We focus in this chapter on two areas in which policies could have direct effects: broadening access to financing and reducing other costs of doing business.

Broadening Access to Financing

For at least two decades, the singular focus of policy for improving the access of the poor to finance has been on "microcredit"—that is, on the

6. De la Torre, Gozzi, and Schmukler (2007a) and De la Torre and Schmukler (2004) discuss at length the nature of this gap with respect to the state of development of Latin American securities markets.

7. Segmentation of access to financial services can deepen with financial globalization (De la Torre and Schmukler 2004); for example, IDB (2005) provides evidence that foreign bank penetration (relative to GDP) tends to lower financing constraints, but mostly for larger firms, and that consolidation of the banking sector increases financing constraints for small firms. See also Clarke, Cull, and Martínez Pería (2001); Clarke and others (2005); and Beck, Demirgüç-Kunt, and Maksimovic (2003).

8. A 2000 survey in Argentina found that about half of industrial small and medium-size businesses were resorting to overdrafts, paying at that time an average interest rate of 2.7 percent per month (38 percent annually) in real terms (World Bank 2004a; Bebczuk 2004). Overall, credit to the nonfinancial private sector (as a share of GDP) remains low (about 9 percent in 2005)—and long-term credit, which is available at reasonable rates only to top-tier companies, remains scarce (World Bank 2006e; Bebczuk 2007). Small firms fare somewhat better in Chile, where less than a third report facing serious financing constraints and where bank credit finances about 25 percent of their investments. In Mexico, on the other hand, financing obstacles are a major problem for nearly two-thirds of small firms, and banks provide only 5 percent of their financing (World Bank Enterprise Surveys).

9. See note 7 for an example in the case of "financial" globalization.

creation of institutions, often by nongovernment groups, designed to make small loans to poor people, often women, and to very small "microenterprises" (a term that in Latin America is generally understood to refer to enterprises with ten or fewer employees.)[10] Progress in providing access to finance for microenterprises has been impressive in at least some countries, but financing for SMEs is still a major challenge.

Microfinance

Over the last two decades there has been considerable progress in Latin America on expanding access to financing for microenterprises, even in countries where the institutional framework is relatively weak—for example, Bolivia and Nicaragua.[11] The strong growth of the microfinance industry has been propelled by innovative lending techniques (for example, the use of credit scoring and e-banking) and the rising presence of credit bureaus, which have enabled microfinance institutions to reach the needed scale and bring costs down substantially.[12] As a result, microfinance has become a self-sustaining and highly profitable business in many countries.

10. There is no set definition of microenterprises or of small and medium-size enterprises. The definition used by enterprise surveys and statistical offices tends to be based on number of employees. Under that definition, microenterprises typically are considered to have ten or fewer employees, small enterprises to have between ten and fifty employees, and medium-size enterprises to have between fifty and 200 employees. For enterprise definitions in eighteen Latin American countries, see Angelelli, Moudry, and Llisterri (2006). For definitions in more than 100 countries, including in Latin America, see Marta Kozak, "Micro, Small, and Medium Enterprises: A Collection of Published Data," International Finance Corporation, January 26, 2007 (http://rru.worldbank.org/Documents/other/MSMEdatabase/msme_database.htm [March 2007]). Banks, in contrast, make their distinctions based on gross sales. For example, banks in Argentina and Chile would consider enterprises to be bigger than "micro" only if their annual sales total at least US$30,000.

11. Latin America has seen more rapid advances in the development of microfinance than any other region in the world. Today there are hundreds of institutions that specialize in microfinance, plus a growing number of commercial banks that seriously target this sector (Berger 2006). By 2005, microfinance institutions in Latin America served approximately 6 million clients (up from 1.8 million in 2001) and managed more than US$5.4 billion in loans (up from US$1.1 billion in 2001). Coverage of microfinance is significant in Chile, Ecuador, and Peru. Microlenders also have performed well in many of the poorest countries, such as Nicaragua, Bolivia, and Guatemala, where they reach 58 percent, 32 percent, and 22 percent of microenterprises respectively (Navajas and Tejerina 2006).

12. See, for example, Hardy, Holden, and Prokopenko (2003) for a description of how the availability of debtor information systems combined with scoring technologies has allowed Banco del Trabajo in Peru to become a commercially viable microfinance institution.

But microfinance penetration is still minimal in some places.[13] In Colombia, interest rate ceilings are a key obstacle. Elsewhere, monetary and banking authorities need to innovate, establishing a regulatory framework and prudential norms specific to and appropriate for microfinance institutions (including regarding capital, loan-loss provisions, and credit risk analysis and management). Special efforts on the policy and regulatory side are critical to support the interest of microfinance institutions in enabling the poor to save as well as borrow.[14] The authorities also should actively promote the modernization of debtor information systems (credit bureaus), with special emphasis on broadening their coverage to include debtors of both financial and nonfinancial institutions, improving the quality of information, and making the information accessible to bank and nonbank creditors (box 5-1). Examples of good practices in the region should be adopted more widely.

SMEs

As is the case for microenterprises, success for small and medium-size businesses requires that the best, most competitive among them be able to grow—from small to medium size and from medium size to large. Growth, in turn, requires that they have better access to credit at a reasonable cost.

But access to credit for SMEs continues to be a largely unsolved problem in Latin America, even in the countries that have made significant

---

Credit scoring is an automated statistical technique used to screen loan applicants. It involves analyzing a large sample of past borrowers to identify the characteristics that predict the likelihood of default. Scoring systems usually generate a single quantitative measure (the credit score) to evaluate the credit application (De la Torre, Gozzi, and Schmukler 2007b). Schreiner (2003) and Salazar and others (2003) present an overview of how scoring works and its application to microfinance.

13. Microfinance has been far slower to develop in larger countries such as Brazil, Mexico, Colombia, Argentina, and Venezuela, where the majority of the region's poor live and where more than half of all microentrepreneurs are based. In Mexico and Colombia, microfinance institutions reach 12 percent and 7 percent of microenterprises respectively. In Brazil and also in Venezuela, microfinance penetration is less than 2 percent; in Argentina, it is less than one-third of 1 percent (Navajas and Tejerina 2006). See also the analysis in Christen and Miller (2006).

14. Roodman and Qureshi (2006) points out why microfinance institutions have tended to expand in lending services more than in providing the financial service of savings and other deposits.

BOX 5-1. Microfinance Expansion

In Latin America—more than in Africa and Asia—microfinance has become self-sustaining and profitable. Several microfinance institutions (MFIs) take deposits as well as make loans, and many are able to borrow from banks or have guarantees from banks that enable them to lend. What has worked for MFIs in Latin America? We highlight the following three key contributors:

First, *scoring technologies* have played a crucial role in reducing costs, even where the contractual environment is deficient. Hardy, Holden, and Prokopenko (2002) describes how the availability of debtor information systems (credit bureaus) combined with scoring technologies has allowed Banco del Trabajo in Peru to become a commercially viable microfinance institution. Schreiner (2003) presents an overview of how scoring methods work and their application to microfinance. Encouraging the adoption of new technologies has allowed microlenders to reach the needed scale and to standardize their products.

Second, the establishment and continuous modernization of *credit bureaus* through legal and regulatory changes as well as through the catalytic role of public policy have also been critical. The credit information systems in Brazil, Chile, Argentina, and Peru fare the best.[1] Credit bureaus that disseminate information on debtors (positive as well as negative) allow new entrants to build a credit record and its associated "reputation collateral" and help drive down the costs of debtor screening and monitoring.[2] In order to facilitate transparency and arm's-length lending, the regulatory framework must encourage symmetry in making information available to lenders. Because credit bureaus benefit from economies of scale, public policy should facilitate cooperation among creditors (in order to avoid excessive fragmentation of the industry) while maximizing creditors' access to debtor information and adequately protecting privacy rights.

Third, successful MFIs have adopted adequate *risk management policies*. MFIs and banks are high-volume, low-margin businesses that manage high credit risk. So, as in the case of Calpiá Bank in El Salvador, they display significantly higher capital-to-asset ratios and have much more aggressive provisioning policies than typical commercial banks.

---

1. Most Latin American countries have well-established, good-quality public and private credit registries in which most banks participate. Factors like the absence of laws restricting information sharing within the financial sector, increased foreign investment in credit registries, and the long-time use of this tool in the retail sector help explain advances in the sector since the 1990s. Brazil's SERASA is the largest Latin American credit registry, with annual sales close to US$150 million. (The country's extensive chamber of commerce network operates a credit registry and bad-check list on a state-by-state basis.) Argentina and Chile also have strong private credit registries. As in other developing regions, the consumer side of credit registries appears to be more developed than the small business side.

2. Evidence in Djankov, McLiesh, and Shleifer (2007) suggests that credit registries have a positive impact on firms' access to bank finance, especially in poorer countries. See also IDB (2005) and Love and Mylenko (2003).

progress toward developing more resilient financial systems.[15] Part of the problem is that SME lending relies on local legal, information, and judicial systems, which are inadequate in most Latin American countries. Other forms of credit contracts, such as consumer loans and even microloans, have expanded more quickly, presumably because they rely less on the quality of financial statements and on local institutions for contract enforcement and because scoring techniques and credit bureaus appear to suffice for managing lender risks. As firms grow and become less homogeneous, however, scoring methods become less applicable and the relevance of financial statements, collateral laws, bankruptcy regimes, and judicial processes rises.[16] Because entering the SME lending business implies high fixed costs, banks move only reluctantly into this sector—and then only when other lines of business have been fully exploited. Moreover, in the absence of visible improvements in the contractual environment, even the modernization of credit bureaus, which helps microfinance, may have less impact on SME lending, because banks that invest in finding and building relationships with SMEs will avoid sharing with other banks the information that they gain about individual firms.[17]

For decades Latin American governments have tried to redress the poor access of SMEs to credit by creating public banks that made loans to this sector at below-market interest rates. But those banks have often been plagued with problems of governance and political interference. The resulting poor loan origination and collection practices, exacerbated by political pressure to grant debt forgiveness, in many cases led to recurrent claims on government budgets.[18] The banks' subsidized interest

15. Even in successful corporate bond markets like Chile's, access to financing is highly segmented. Between 2000 and 2003, 100 percent of all the corporate bond issues in the local stock market went to larger firms. In Argentina and Mexico in 2004, the top ten companies accounted for more than 70 percent of trading in domestic stock markets; in Brazil, Chile, and Peru, the ten largest firms accounted for roughly 50 percent of total stock market value traded that year (De la Torre, Gozzi, and Schmuckler 2007b). See Beck and De la Torre (2007) and De la Torre, Gozzi, and Schmukler (2007b) for a discussion of conceptual issues in access to finance.

16. See Beck and Levine (2005) for evidence on the impact of contractual and legal environments on financial depth.

17. IDB (2005) suggests that in Latin America (especially in medium-size markets) banks may be unwilling to disclose information on small business clients, at least not immediately, even if that would reduce their risk.

18. For example, in 2001 the Brazilian government absorbed the nonperforming loan portfolios of two public banks (Banco do Brasil and Caixa Econômica Federal) at a net cost

rates, furthermore, all too often favored rich and politically connected borrowers. By distorting price signals and incentives, subsidized credit programs probably slowed the creation of new small businesses and accentuated their disadvantages vis-à-vis large firms.[19]

In addition to ongoing improvements in debtor information systems and the diffusion of scoring techniques for evaluating smaller firms (see box 5-2 for the indirect effects of continued strengthening of the overall financial system),[20] key policies to encourage development of the SME finance sector include

◆ improving the institutional infrastructure that backs credit contracts: securing the legal rights of creditors, in terms of both executing guarantees and implementing timely corporate bankruptcy proceedings; securing the judicial and nonjudicial processes for contract enforcement; and strengthening titling and property registries.[21]

---

of about 6 percent of GDP. And in Mexico the government had to recapitalize Banrural (now Financiera Rural), a development bank providing financing to the rural sector, with more than US$1 billion in 1999, even after having significantly downsized its operations in previous years. See De la Torre, Gozzi, and Schmukler (2006). For further discussion of the role and record of public banks in Latin America, see IDB (2005) and Levy-Yeyati, Micco, and Panizza (2007, forthcoming).

19. Many state-owned banks have since become private, and often taxpayers are stuck with financing their losses, as governments assumed their debts. And little has arisen—either in banking or in debt or equity markets—to take their place.

20. Developing small business credit-scoring technologies would help in evaluating risk more efficiently and act as an effective account management tool. Evidence that doing so might be feasible in Latin America is provided in Miller and Rojas (2005). In the United States, FICO (Fair Isaac Corporation, the best-known credit score model in the United States) provides some 350 lenders with a highly developed set of credit-scoring models based on information on both small businesses and their owners. FICO contributes to approximately 900,000 lending decisions a year, considerably reducing loan processing time and costs. See also Berger and Frame (2007) on small business credit-scoring models in the United States.

21. Loan contracts are not enforced effectively in Latin America. Laws and judges tend to have an unduly pro-debtor bias in disputes, making it excessively costly for creditors to recover collateral in cases of default. In most of the region, titling and property registries are weak and poorly managed, which makes it difficult for creditors to establish the priority and seniority of their claims (IDB 2005; IFC 2006; World Bank 2006c). Countries that have implemented titling reforms perform better than those that have not; but there is still a long way to go if the region is to achieve international standards (see ILD 2006a-2006e). Djankov, McLiesh, and Shleifer (2007) finds that both better creditor rights and the presence of credit registries are associated with a higher ratio of private credit to GDP, controlling for total GDP, per capita income growth, and contemporaneous inflation. The study shows that private credit rises following either improvements in creditor rights (especially in the case of

B O X 5 - 2 . As Securities Markets Grow

Broadening SME access to financing requires more than a single-minded focus on a particular type of credit product or financial entity. Policies to promote access must take into account the overall functioning of the financial system. For example, while it is unrealistic to expect institutional investors (for example, pension funds) and securities markets to become the main source of *direct* financing to SMEs, the development of securities markets—especially debt markets—and the institutional investor base is nonetheless crucial to generate the *indirect* effects needed to improve the overall availability of financing for SMEs. In effect, as securities markets grow, they will attract the larger and blue-chip corporate clients away from banks, thereby forcing banks to move down market and seek new business by lending more to SMEs.[1] To be sure, expectations have to be tamed to the extent that the development of centralized securities markets depends significantly on liquidity, economies of scale, and network externalities, which can be very difficult to achieve in small emerging markets.

1. De la Torre and Schmukler (2004) outlines challenges in the development of securities markets for small emerging economies.

♦ facilitating the use of movable collateral (for example, accounts receivable, future wage earnings, livestock, machinery, and inventories); changing the legislation and civil codes on pledges and guarantees; modernizing the registries for movable assets; and streamlining the mechanisms for repossession of collateral.[22]

---

developed countries) or the introduction of credit registries (in the case of developing countries). Evidence in Haber (2006) suggests that in Mexico, weak contract rights and property rights are key explanatory variables for the low levels o f credit offered by Mexican banks.

22. In most countries, the requisites demanded by financial institutions for granting credit and accepting collateral remain very complex and costly. The process of establishing collateral and obtaining credit can take sixteen months and cost about US$3,500 in Guatemala; in Colombia it takes more than three years and costs around US$1,800 (ILD 2006b, 2006e). Peru has recently implemented a centralized collateral registry, which began operating in May 2006, as part of an effort to broaden access to credit. In Mexico, reforms in 2000 provided for the creation of a federal public registry of commerce on movable property, but collateral registries continue to be run by the states, with each state deciding how to operate the registries and how much to charge in taxes and duties, with no links among them. The process of converting registries to electronic access has been very slow; in some states security agreements still are manually transcribed on paper. Mexico has a law providing for out-of-court enforcement, but creditors cannot enforce a nonjudicial order if the debtor opposes it. Moreover, the debtor is likely to successfully challenge as unconstitutional any out-of-court enforcement action,

◆ enhancing minority shareholder rights as well as improving accounting and disclosure practices. Both are of special relevance if firms are
to break the size threshold by issuing equity and debt securities in
local and international markets.[23]

◆ instituting a set of policies designed to encourage diversification of
financial intermediaries and products: removing legal, regulatory,
tax, and other obstacles to the development of factoring and leasing,
which are key sources of working capital and investment financing
for small and medium-size businesses;[24] promoting competition in
credit markets by, for instance, allowing the entrance of non–deposit-
taking credit institutions—such as the Sociedades Financieras de
Objeto Limitado (Sofoles) in Mexico; and facilitating, through suitable
regulations, the establishment of bridges between credit institutions
and institutional investors (mutual funds, pension funds, and insurance companies).[25] Governments might also consider encouraging
reciprocal credit guarantee agreements to increase the availability of
credit to small businesses. In such agreements, lenders share loan
decisions and monitoring with agents who are in a better position to

---

regardless of the terms of the original contract. In the end, both parties often end up in court
anyway (World Bank 2006c; IMF 2007d). Brazil faces some of the same challenges as Mexico in facilitating the use of collateral (see IFC 2006).

23. Market participants in most of the medium-size and larger Latin American countries
typically consider bond or equity issues of less than US$50 million unlikely to whet the
appetite of large institutional investors, in part because smaller issues would not generate
sufficient secondary market liquidity to enable orderly exit. This sort of size threshold for
new issues is also needed to spread out the transaction costs of issuing, as discussed in Zervos (2004). However, $50 million is a hefty sum in relative terms for many Latin American
countries. It is, for instance, a multiple of the capital of most of the corporations within Latin
American countries and, hence, is a threshold that leaves only a handful of firms eligible to
participate through securities issuance in the local, centralized stock exchanges.

24. For a discussion of factoring markets and the possible role of government policy, see
De la Torre, Gozzi, and Schmuckler (2006) and Klapper (2006). Argentina is promoting
markets for invoice factoring through changes in the country's legal and regulatory framework. Some of the legal steps necessary include allowing and protecting the transfer of
invoices from small businesses to financial agents, establishing clear procedures to enforce
the buyer's payment of invoices, and strengthening the creditor rights of factoring agents vis-
à-vis the borrowing firm (IDB 2005; Bakker and others 2004).

25. In this connection, the Latin American Shadow Financial Regulatory Committee (2004)
recommends that countries fix their regulatory framework to allow for the emergence of mutual
fund–style institutions (for example, by defining responsibilities vis-à-vis shareholders, capital requirements, and so forth) whose assets are a diversified portfolio of loans to SMEs and whose
liabilities are shares owned by institutional investors that can be traded in the secondary market.

observe borrowers' effort or who have privileged information on or leverage over borrowers.[26]

◆ focusing on new reform strategies for development banks. Most important are reforms aimed at separating subsidies from financing. Subsidies in the form of below-market interest rates fuel misallocation of resources and mismanagement of risks and stifle the development of private markets. Promoting market-based and sustainable broadening of access for underserved sectors requires new and innovative instruments, such as technical assistance, matching grants, and special programs to modernize financial market infrastructure. In Mexico, the promotion by Nacional Financiera (NAFIN) of an Internet-based market for SME receivables discounting is a good example of a development bank playing a market-friendly role.[27]

The policies suggested above concentrate largely on improvements to the contractual and informational environment that can unblock credit to SMEs. These policies, while important, are of course not sufficient. In particular, they cannot by themselves give rise to high-quality entrepreneurship, profitable projects, and investment optimism in the SME sector. These latter ingredients are even more important, in the sense that they alone could unleash adequate financing to SMEs even where weaknesses remain in the contractual environment.

Reducing Other Costs of Doing Business

Latin American SMEs, compared with their peers in advanced economies, have limited access to information and technology. Incomplete information

26. See Llisterri (2006); Llisterri and others (2006); and Malhotra and others (2006) for further discussion.

27. In Mexico, NAFIN, a development bank, created an Internet-based system to provide factoring services to SMEs, ameliorating information problems, reducing transaction costs, and fostering competition among financial institutions. The system works by creating chains between buyers (large creditworthy firms) and their suppliers. Large buyers post the receivables into the system, preventing fraud. All financial institutions can bid to factor a specific transaction; the electronic platform allows wider participation, especially of smaller regional banks. Since the start of the program in 2001, NAFIN-supported market infrastructure has brokered more than 1.2 million factoring transactions (98 percent by SMEs). For more details on this case, see De la Torre, Gozzi, and Schmukler (2006). The study by De la Torre, Gozzi, and Schmukler (2007b) discusses the potential for market-friendly government interventions and examines a number of case studies, including that of NAFIN.

and uncertainty, together with practical difficulties caused by weak property rights in appropriating the gains from innovative effort, make these enterprises reluctant to invest in learning and innovation. Most countries have a long history of government programs that offer management and technical support for small and medium-size enterprises. But frequently such public programs have been of poor quality, being excessively supply-driven and failing to focus on the new and changing needs of small businesses.[28] A number of countries have expanded private sector participation in the design, implementation, and evaluation of SME support programs, with some positive results (see box 5-3). In Brazil and Chile, for example, small businesses are increasingly required to share the costs of the services that they receive. These are steps in the right direction.

Here are two additional specific steps:

♦ First, a major "spring cleaning" of government red tape—regulatory, tax, and bureaucratic intrusions—that affects small enterprises. Much of the bureaucratic nuisance that hinders SME development stems from regulations that have lost relevance but continue to be embodied—often unconsciously—in the inertia of administrative habits.[29] A high-level independent taskforce, with members from outside the government, can lend credibility and prestige to such a spring cleaning.

---

28. World Bank (2004a) highlights the excessive number of uncoordinated and overlapping support programs for small businesses in Argentina. With a few exceptions, programs showed low coverage and poor outcomes. Whether federal, provincial, or municipal, most suffer from insufficient strategic vision and coherence. There is also a lack of adequate monitoring and assessment mechanisms, making evaluation of cost effectiveness and impact very difficult. In Mexico, the number of firms participating in the largest public SME support program (which provides training services on a cost-sharing basis) fell sharply from about 94,000 firms in 2001 to 7,000 in 2005 because of the program's budget cuts and low efficiency (overhead figures were close to 60 percent). Among participating firms, the impact of the program on firm productivity was minimal (World Bank 2006d). See also Lopez-Acevedo and Tan (2005) for further discussion and evaluation of Mexico's SME programs.

29. Colombia has made significant progress in reducing red tape by means of interinstitutional coordination, simplification of existing procedures, and technological strengthening of government agencies. By mid-2006, hundreds of bureaucratic procedures had been simplified and dozens eliminated. Almost all formalities for starting a business in Colombia can now be completed in one day at one of the Centros de Atención Empresarial, which are established and managed by the Confederation of Chambers of Commerce and local governments. The process previously took from fifty-five to sixty days and involved seventeen separate procedures. Costs of starting a company have fallen by up to 75 percent for microenterprises and small businesses (Castro Forero 2007). See also Sislen and others (2007) for progress in reducing red tape in Lima, Peru.

BOX 5-3. Competitiveness and Innovation for Small and Medium-Size Enterprises

Argentina's Rafaela-Esperanza Enterprise Development Center (Centro de Desarrollo Empresarial) is part of a new generation of government-sponsored business development services—with the government program as intermediary. Rather than provide services directly to businesses, the public agency arranges for businesses to use consultants selected through competitive bidding. Small businesses pay some of the cost—not necessarily the full cost, but enough to ensure that they are committed to using the advice that they buy. The program combines reliance on private consultants with the recognition that small businesses need some subsidy if they are to get the best technical advice.

To improve the export performance of small and medium-size enterprises, Argentina's Business Restructuring Program for Exports (Programa de Reconversión Empresarial para las Exportaciones) departed radically from the traditional (failed) export promotion programs. Using a US$27 million grant from the government, it required individual firms to pay half the cost of consultants and other services of approved projects. The projects were chosen and the program managed by a private operator, selected by international tender. Between 1996 and 1999, the program attracted close to 1,000 clients; the number of approved projects exceeded expectations, despite economic uncertainties in Argentina's main export market, Brazil.[1]

---

1. In total, the program attracted 967 clients (the goal was 900) and approved 1,089 projects. Close to 30 percent of the participating firms increased their export markets, and 32 percent increased the number of exported products. It has since ended, due to a combination of neglect and interference from the public agency that provided partial financing.

Paraguay's Voucher Training Program for Microbusinesses (Sistema de Bonos de Capacitación) was initiated to remedy past failures in financing microenterprise training. Program beneficiaries (who ran microenterprises of just a few employees) received publicly funded vouchers. They used them to help purchase training and other services from prequalified private suppliers, who then redeemed the vouchers for cash when a trainee completed the course. Vouchers were valued at approximately U.S. $20 each, which covered up to 60 percent, on average, of the total cost of each course. Courses offered by private providers were evaluated by the participants and the results were made publicly available, allowing interested microentrepreneurs to make an informed choice of providers. The program helped create a market for private training: by increasing microentrepreneur's buying power, it encouraged training institutions to compete to attract clients. Between 1995 and 1997, more than 14,000 vouchers were distributed through the program, and many microentrepreneurs continued to pay for the courses in full after termination of the voucher program. The number and diversity of service providers rose markedly. Managed by an independent contractor, the program avoided problems common to this type of initiative when managed by governments, such as failure to reach the beneficiaries most in need, inappropriate services, and abuses of the support offered. Ecuador and Bolivia have implemented initiatives that build on Paraguay's voucher experience.

Sources: Ventura (2003, 2001); Goldmark (2006); Angelelli and Solís (2002); Oldsman (2000); and Addis Botelho and Goldmark (2000).

◆ Second, government promotion of clusters and productive chains, especially where comparative advantages are obvious and perhaps also where government smart signaling (for example, through strategic investment in infrastructure and human capital) can "crowd in" private investment and enthusiasm. That would help small businesses identify and gain access to new opportunities.[30] Policy tools to promote clusters and chains could include a judicious use of matching grants, which can improve small enterprise access to the markets for technical and professional services and, at the same time, foster the development of such markets.[31] While this requires a degree of pro-market activism on the part of the government, it is a far cry from the old-style industrial policy of "picking winners."[32]

30. Empirical evidence shows that in both developed and developing countries, when small firms are located in clusters they often are able to overcome some of the major constraints that they face, including lack of specialized skills and difficulty in accessing technology, inputs, market information, credit, and external services. Linking into clusters and value chains also offers an opportunity to access larger and foreign markets (Pietrobelli and Rabellotti 2006; Pietrobelli, Rabellotti, and Giuliani 2006). On the successful cluster of salmon farming and processing businesses in southern Chile, see Maggi Campos (2006). Gomes (2006) examines the case of small fruit exporters in three parts of Brazil who have managed to meet the rising demand of global markets through different strategies and levels of association with the public sector.

31. In general subsidies should go to the firm demanding the service, with participating private firms sharing substantially in the costs of contracting for consulting, technical, and professional services. Service contracting should be demand-driven to ensure the supplier firm's commitment to quality. Even the overall administration of the program can be subcontracted to a specialized private firm. Subsidies also can be used to encourage SMEs to cofinance training of workers.

32. See Recart (2005) on the success of Fundación Chile in fostering innovative business development in key Chilean clusters.

SIX

Protecting Job Mobility and Workers' Rights

Gainful, productive employment is crucial to enhancing equity and income growth and to reducing poverty.[1] But its importance goes well beyond that, making employment a legitimate policy concern in its own right, not just a means to other ends. Productive employment is not only about income. It is also about human dignity and a place in society.

In Latin America jobs and the labor market were not part of the reform agenda of the 1990s, and little progress has been made in this area compared with others (see figure 6 in our Introduction). Surprisingly, neither jobs nor wages were part of the political discourse in the 1990s. Yet recent surveys of attitudes indicate that lack of jobs and low wages are the main concerns in the region—ahead of crime and other social problems (figure 6-1).[2] That is not surprising. Unemployment rose in the 1990s (figure 12 in the Introduction), and only 50 percent of workers are employed in the formal sector (table 6-1).

Labor markets in the region, though highly regulated (figure 6-2), fail to protect the great majority of workers.[3] Regulation focuses on job security

---

1. Krugman (1994) singles out productivity, employment, and income distribution as the three things that matter most in economics.
2. See also Latinobarómetro (2003, 2004, 2005).
3. The exceptions are Chile and, by some measures, Uruguay. Mandatory transfers to workers are low in Uruguay, but the total cost of labor regulations is still relatively high—well above that in Chile and most developed countries, mostly because of high payroll taxes (social security contributions) (Botero and others 2003; Heckman and Pagés 2004).

F I G U R E   6-1. **What do you consider to be your country's most important problem?**

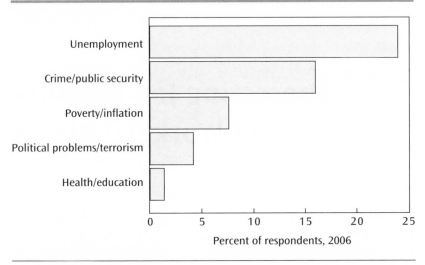

Percent of respondents, 2006

Source: Latinobarómetro (2006).

(for example, mandating certain forms of severance pay), not on rights of association or collective bargaining that would allow workers to negotiate directly with employers. Inflexible labor rules and practices discourage worker mobility and undermine the creation of productive employment in the formal sector.[4] Jobs and wage income are insecure—especially for the large majority of young, female, and unskilled workers. Training financed by employers benefits only the small percentage of workers who are more educated and skilled.[5] There is little or no public support during spells of

4. Labor rigidities became even more binding with the loss of real wage flexibility in the 1990s, as the policy crutch that inflation had (ironically) provided disappeared.

5. Surveys by the IDB and World Bank in 1999–2000 show that three of four Latin American firms provide training for workers, a percentage not that different from those in the United States and Canada. As in the United States and Canada, in Latin America more educated and skilled workers receive more training for longer periods. The difference is that the percentage of educated workers in the labor force is much higher in the United States and Canada, so a bigger share of the labor force ends up trained than in Latin America. Also, in Latin America a much smaller share of the workforce is employed in the kind of firms that provide training (IDB 2001; Duryea and Pagés 2002; World Bank 2006e).

TABLE 6-1. Structure of Urban Employment in Latin America, 1995–2005

Percent

	1995	2000	2004	2005
Informal sector	50.1	48.6	49.2	48.5
Self employed[a]	26.2	25.4	25.7	25.1
Domestic service	6.5	6.3	6.4	6.3
Microfirm[b]	17.4	17.0	17.2	17.0
Formal Sector	49.9	51.4	50.8	51.5
Public sector	13.2	12.8	12.8	12.8
Private firms[c]	34.7	36.4	35.8	36.5
Self employed	2.0	2.2	2.2	2.3

Source: ILO (2006).
a. Includes self-employed workers and workers with no pay.
b. Includes employers and salaried workers.
c. Includes businesses with 6 or more employees.

FIGURE 6-2. Index of Labor Market Rigidity[a]

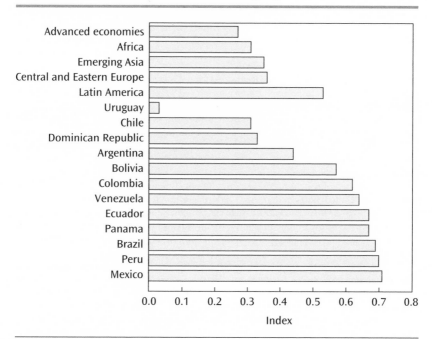

Source: Botero and others (2003).
a. 0 = low level of labor market rigidities; 1 = high level of labor market rigidities.

unemployment because few countries have society-wide unemployment insurance schemes.[6] Overall, fewer workers today are covered by full-benefit contracts (around 40 percent) than at the beginning of the 1990s.[7] Open unemployment remains high (figure 12 in our Introduction). A large informal sector in which labor productivity is low and workers lack minimal protection and benefits persists everywhere.[8] Labor laws and regulations are often ignored by employers and employees alike because they are obsolete and incompatible with the dynamics of today's markets. And the plethora of rules is such that even sensible regulations—say, on occupational safety—cannot possibly be enforced by ill-staffed labor ministries.

Ironically, severance payments—the insurance mechanism of choice in Latin America—are a costly regulation for workers. Applying only to

6. Five countries in Latin America have functioning unemployment insurance programs: Argentina, Brazil, Chile, Ecuador, and Uruguay. Where they exist, such programs do not work very well. Coverage is limited to workers with regulated, tax-paying contracts. More than 30 percent of government spending on unemployment insurance in the region goes to the richest quintile of the population; less than 10 percent is directed toward the poorest quintile (Perry and others 2006; Goñi, Lopez, and Servén 2006). The level and duration of benefits are low compared with those in more developed countries, and unemployment insurance systems generally lack any connection with training programs or national employment services (IDB 2004a).

7. ECLAC (2006b). In Mexico (1990–2001) and Argentina (1993–2001), more than 60 percent and 80 percent respectively of the unemployed who found jobs did not receive social security benefits in their new jobs (IDB 2004a).

8. The informal sector tends to act as a cushion (given the absence of unemployment insurance) that expands with the loss of formal sector jobs. Uncertainty and weaknesses in labor contracting have been associated not only with a large informal sector but also with the increased irrelevance of labor market regulations in the formal sector. Even when unenforced, unrealistic regulations are perceived as a threat that can cause firms to go informal. Informal sector employment now constitutes half of all nonagricultural employment in the region. In the United States in the early 2000s, the informal sector accounted for about 8.8 percent of the labor force (ILO 2006; Angelelli, Moudry, and Llisterri 2006). Informality is particularly widespread among the poor. IDB (2004a) estimates that 60 percent of working members of the poorest 40 percent of families in Latin America work in the informal sector. In Colombia, available estimates put overall informality at about 61 percent of the labor force, but that estimate rises to 91 percent of the poor (Departamento Nacional de Planeación, cited in Lindert, Skoufias, and Shapiro 2006). Recent studies suggest that the region's informal sector is very heterogeneous, with an upward tier of largely voluntarily informal workers (including most self-employed and some informal salaried workers) and a smaller lower tier for which the sector functions as a safety net. See Maloney (2004) and Perry and others (2007b). But even if voluntary, informal employment (including work in very small firms or self-employment) usually reflects low average productivity and wages (Perry and others 2006; IDB 2004a; Saavedra 2003).

those covered by full-benefit contracts in the formal sector, they are unrealistically generous, leading employers to find ways to avoid paying them. The result is less job security because employers often fire employees before severance payments are vested or become too onerous. There is little incentive for job creation; rather than accept the regulatory burden and risks of hiring new permanent workers, employers invest more in labor-saving capital equipment.[9]

In the 1990s, many countries (for example, Argentina, Peru, Colombia, and Brazil) introduced temporary and fixed-term employment contracts with no benefits or incentives for training as part of half-hearted, partial reforms to address labor rigidities. These are classic second-best measures: they probably are an improvement but they have perverse effects that have not yet been measured, such as reducing incentives for employer-financed training and increasing wage gaps between protected and temporary workers in the long run.[10]

Labor market reform has no doubt been politically difficult. The idea of deregulation and greater "flexibility" is highly inconsistent with the pre-1980s social contract based on industrial sector job protection, and in most countries an alternative safety net of unemployment and health benefits for unemployed workers and their families barely exists. But governments can no longer ignore the "jobs" problem. Lagging labor reform may already have cost countries a great deal by undermining the equity effects of other structural reforms in the region, as discussed in the Introduction.

---

9. Heckman and Pagés (2004, 2000) find that severance pay in Latin America has negative and high negative effects on employment, mainly for younger and less experienced workers. In Argentina, Pessino (2001) estimates that in 1999–2000 severance payments and advance notice layoff costs represented between 6 percent and 7.5 percent of firm payroll costs (excluding additional litigious expenses that may come up when layoffs occur).

10. IDB (2004a). Overall, temporary contracts accounted for most of the recent rise in formal wage employment in the region—only 4 percent of the jobs created between 2002 and 2005 came with a permanent contract (ECLAC 2006a). In Mexico, 62 percent of the increase in formal employment (covered by the Mexican Social Security Institute) in 2005–06 was accounted for by temporary contracts (which increased by 26.2 percent); only 38 percent corresponded to permanent contracts (which were up by 2.8 percent). In Colombia, the rise in seasonal employment (6.7 percent between January and September of 2006) accounted for all of the increase in manufacturing employment (2.1 percent); the level of permanent employment in the country fell by 1.5 percent in the same period (ECLAC 2006c).

Latin America's rigid labor laws and regulations are obsolete and incompatible with the dynamics of today's markets. In a global economy, creative destruction is the norm. Creative destruction—the process in the market economies whereby new, better companies are allowed to topple old, less competitive ones—creates new opportunities, promotes efficiency, and generates prosperity. But it also triggers an enormous degree of job instability and dislocation. Many new jobs are created, but many also are destroyed. The cost of being competitive in a global economy is, in short, some job insecurity and dislocation.

Those who lose their jobs are not always those who can easily find a job that has equivalent wages and benefits. That fact naturally creates an incentive for uncompetitive businesses to ally with workers demanding more job security and protection from the creative destruction process.[11] The way to avoid such a reaction is to make job changes easier for workers and to soften the blow of dislocation with a reasonable package of temporary unemployment payments and access to training and additional education for displaced workers. Developed countries instituted unemployment insurance when they were much poorer than they are today and not much richer than some countries in Latin America now. Unemployment insurance may not be the top priority in the poorer countries of Central America or in Bolivia and Paraguay. But there is a wider range of policy options that include facilitating the portability of pension and other benefits; protecting collective bargaining; and providing minimal tax-financed income security to workers without jobs. For example, governments could establish emergency programs like Argentina's Trabajar (see chapter 3) and subsidize firms to upgrade workers' skills through on-site apprenticeships for unemployed youth (box 6-1).[12]

The real challenge for governments is to go beyond "deregulation" and "flexibilization" to adopt a proactive stance that focuses on creating new

11. Rajan and Zingales (2004) argues that the group of opponents formed by workers tends to surface during economic downturns. Those who have lost out in the process of creative destruction unleashed by markets see no legitimacy in a system in which they have been proved losers. They want relief; since the markets offer them none, they try the political route.

12. Evidence suggests that unless workers' skills are upgraded, integration into international markets would increase wage disparities in the region, probably because capital tends to substitute for unskilled labor but to complement skilled labor.

BOX 6-1. Linking Work and Education:
The Role of Firms and Governments

Policies and practices crucial to encouraging the constant renewal and growth of the human capital of the labor force include the following:

◆ Governments: Offer tax incentives to encourage firms to give scholarships for short-term classroom training and on-site apprenticeships, particularly for unemployed youth. Scholarship stipends should be set low enough to avoid discouraging recipients from searching for jobs.

◆ Firms: Create jobs that allow young people (sixteen years of age and older) to work and attend school at the same time. That would offset the pressure to leave school in bad times to compensate for a decline in household income and in good times to take advantage of a booming labor market. It would also be an effective way for firms to recruit highly qualified youth for potential full-time employment. Legal or regulatory changes might be necessary to allow special contracts for young people who attend school—featuring flexible hours, below minimum wages, and greater ease of firing or quitting. To avoid cheating, school attendance should be required in youth training or apprenticeship programs.

jobs rather than protecting old ones and encourages individuals to prepare for job mobility throughout life rather than seek job permanence. A proactive stance also involves simplifying the legislative and regulatory framework in order to enable better enforcement and redefining the role of the labor ministry.[13] The function of the ministry would shift from making unrealistic attempts to enforce regulatory minutiae toward disseminating information (for example, on economy-wide productivity changes to help guide wage negotiations), setting broad standards (say, for occupational safety), and protecting a fair contracting environment for individuals and for unions.

13. Most Latin American countries have ratified most of the basic labor standards embodied in International Labor Organization conventions: free association, the right to collective bargaining, minimum working age, the prohibition of forced labor, and the prohibition of discrimination.

Specific policies to strengthen workers' rights include

◆ Protecting workers' rights of association and encouraging collective bargaining (covering wages as well as work conditions) at the firm level, within sector- or economy-wide guidelines.[14] Providing flexible guidelines for negotiation and conflict resolution. Raising penalties for illegal anti-union practices and easing regulations that discourage the creation of unions within firms. At the same time, establishing regulations that emphasize transparency and accountability in labor unions, including public sector unions, to ensure that unions are democratic and corruption free.[15] Supporting training programs for union leaders on emerging demands of their members—such as issues pertaining to women in the workplace—and education programs for union members on their rights and obligations.

◆ Ensuring that the law does not prohibit flexible hiring arrangements. Laws should allow employment contracts for hourly, part-time, and seasonal employment. These contracts should have adequate social protections, proportional to that in the law for open-ended contracts, to prevent large-scale substitution of workers with new contracts for workers with full-benefit contracts.

To increase labor mobility while reducing uncertainty for workers, governments should aim to empower workers to adapt to economic change, succeed in multiple career paths, and choose periods of self-employment.[16] Policy approaches include

◆ Certification of skills based on national standards. In Mexico, a system for certifying skills provides a bridge for workers between training and

---

14. Public sector unions in the region (for teachers, health workers, public enterprise workers) are strong in most countries, although often their leadership is more politically ambitious than is consistent with their members' interests. We refer here primarily to unions representing private sector workers.

15. Often the product of old, highly centralized systems for delivering public services, public sector unions (for teachers, health workers, public enterprise workers) have become an obstacle to privatization and political decentralization. While they often lack democratic structures, their militancy and political power bring their members job stability and other benefits, sometimes at the cost of other socially desirable public spending.

16. In addition to the ideas listed here, see emergency employment programs in chapter 3 of this volume.

jobs and from jobs back to formal education. It also requires a stronger partnership between the public and private sectors to better disseminate updated information on job vacancies and to develop effective job-search assistance programs.

◆ Pension, health care, and other benefits that are portable across and between jobs (see box 6-2 on Chile's program).[17] Developing the financial system to enhance workers' capacity to manage savings throughout their life would contribute much to achieving that goal.

◆ In the more advanced economies in the region, a system of unemployment insurance (in lieu of high severance payments) that covers all workers in regulated contracts. The system can be built on a partially self-financed program of mandatory employee and employer contributions to individual accounts, which can be rolled over into retirement funds, as in Chile.[18] Both individual accounts and collective insurance can be combined within the system to widen coverage and limit adverse effects on work effort.[19]

◆ Creation of health insurance, unemployment insurance, and pension systems for informal sector workers.[20] Spain has had success in implementing programs in these areas for the self-employed.[21]

17. In Chile, Bolivia, Costa Rica, El Salvador, and Peru, structural reforms have allowed governments to consolidate disparate systems, making pension portability possible (Mesa-Lago 2005).

18. For further discussion on Chile's unemployment insurance model, including its applicability in other developing countries, see Acevedo, Eskenazi, and Pagés (2006) and Sehnbruch (2006).

19. The Chilean unemployment insurance scheme includes a common fund built with a portion of employers' contributions and direct contributions from the state that pays for partial insurance benefits for workers with insufficient funds in their individual accounts.

20. While the goal of reform should be to bring as many people into the regulated segment of the economy as possible, in the short and medium term many workers and firms may remain out of the formal economy. It is important to address how to reach this large segment of the labor force.

21. For more information on Spain's program see ILO (1999).

B O X 6 - 2 . Portability in Chile

Chile has pioneered a funded, portable system of individual worker accounts that can be used for retirement, work injury insurance and disability, and survivors' pensions.[1] A separate component, a subsidy funded by the state out of general revenues, ensures a minimum retirement benefit level to workers with insufficient funds in their individual accounts.[2] The system has been a success financially, generating accumulated assets equal to about 64 percent of Chile's GDP as of early 2005 and fostering the development of financial markets, with spillover effects on foreign investment, productivity, and growth. The partially self-financed system is also more equitable and progressive than the old pay-as-you-go system, which in Chile applied different rates to different groups, depending on their political clout.

But coverage under the new system—at around 60 percent of the labor force—has not increased compared with that under the old system and so remains a serious challenge. Partly to blame are high job-turnover rates and high levels of informal employment and self-employment, which provide a disincentive to save in a plan that is not liquid. (Self-employed workers, who constitute at least 25 percent of the labor force, are not required to contribute and rarely do.) High and regressive management fees on workers' private accounts also are a problem.[3]

---

1. Other worker-initiated withdrawals are permitted only if the remaining balance in the worker's account is large enough to produce a pension that is at least 150 percent of the minimum pension guarantee and 70 percent of the worker's average wage over the past ten years. So far, very few workers have met that requirement.

2. The subsidy is paid to workers who have contributed for at least twenty years to a pension fund and whose savings have been exhausted. As of mid-2007, a new solidarity pillar was being debated in the Chilean congress as part of a comprehensive reform package submitted by the Presidential Advisory Council for Pension Reform that aims at, among other things, expanding coverage and increasing support to those with lower capacity to contribute.

3. Fees are calculated on gross wages instead of a percentage of the assets managed, as in developed countries. Insufficient competition also is a concern. There are about six private pension fund administrators in Chile, and they dominate the financial system.

Sources: Larraín Ríos (2005); Berstein, Larraín, and Pino (2006); James, Martinez, and Iglesias (2006); Arenas de Mesa (2005); Arenas de Mesa and others (2007); Marcel (2006).

SEVEN

Repairing Rural Markets

Because today only about 8 percent of GDP in Latin America comes from agriculture, rural markets may seem less relevant than in the past.[1] But nearly 20 percent of the region's labor force still relies on agriculture—in Guatemala, Nicaragua, and Honduras, the share is close to 40 percent—and nearly 40 percent of the region's poor, some 65 million people, live in rural areas.[2]

Inefficient rural markets in Latin America limit productivity growth in agriculture and fail to provide the great majority of rural families with enough income to cross the poverty line. Facing low incomes and increasingly limited prospects, many rural workers migrate to cities, where they join the informal, low-productivity workforce. Low incomes in the rural sector put downward pressure on the wages of unskilled workers in urban areas. Until agriculture is more productive, urban and rural poverty will persist.

A dynamic agricultural sector—characterized by high productivity and income growth—played the key role in the rapid, more equitable growth seen in South Korea, Taiwan, Thailand, Malaysia, and Indonesia during

---

1. WDI (2006).

2. WDI (2006) and De Ferranti and others (2005). Agriculture absorbs more than one-third of the labor force in Paraguay and about 20 percent of the workforce in Mexico, Brazil, and Colombia (WDI 2006). In Bolivia, Guatemala, Honduras, Nicaragua, Paraguay, and Peru, nearly 70 percent or more of the rural population lives in poverty (ECLAC 2006a).

the latter half of the twentieth century.[3] The agricultural sector was a source of capital and labor for the manufacturing sector. Resources were pulled into manufacturing by rising wages and returns, rather than squeezed out of agriculture by high taxes and stagnant or declining relative incomes, as in Latin America.[4]

Progress and Problems

There have been some signs of progress in the region in recent years. Chile has seen the continuation of the previous decade's upward trend in agricultural productivity and exports, which has had positive effects on other sectors and overall economic growth. Brazil also has experienced increased productivity in its large agro-industrial sector, driven for the most part by a surge in exports of soy, coffee, and sugar.[5] Increasing integration in international markets has expanded market access for more competitive sectors in various countries. Guatemala, for example, has seen rapid growth in nontraditional agricultural exports over the last decade; in the Cooperative Cuatro Pinos, smallholders have been successful in exporting fruits and vegetables.[6] Agricultural producers across the region

3. World Bank (1993).

4. Secure property rights and a relatively equal distribution of land, high investment in rural infrastructure and education, and limited direct and indirect taxation of agriculture meant that rural incomes and productivity rose more rapidly in East Asia than in other regions (World Bank 1993).

5. Since the mid-1980s, Chile has had a highly efficient agricultural sector, the result of a long history of reform, adequate macroeconomic management, and continued investment in knowledge and innovation in agriculture. Even after other countries implemented market reforms in the 1990s, Chile's agricultural productivity was outstanding compared with that of the rest of the region (Acquaye and others 2004). More recently, several countries— including Argentina, Brazil, Peru, and Uruguay in addition to Chile—have seen growth in agricultural production, reflecting the recent commodity boom and increasing demand and higher prices for regional exports. Argentina, Brazil, and Uruguay have expanded their farm exports on the strength of higher prices for soy and its by-products. Some economies were able to benefit from robust demand from high-performing Asian countries, notably China, for meat, cereals, coffee, minerals (copper, iron, tin, nickel, and lead) and agricultural raw materials (ECLAC 2006c, 2004a, 2004b).

6. De Janvry and Sadoulet (2004); Riveros and Santacoloma (2004); Lundy (2006). Other noteworthy examples include Costa Rica's decorative plants and tropical fruit exports; successful exporting to the United States of fruits and vegetables by irrigation farmers in northern Mexico; production of tropical fruits and vegetables for international

also have benefited from the increase in supermarkets and rising demand for value-added food products in domestic markets.[7] The return of macroeconomic stability has helped. In most countries, exchange rate regimes are no longer a tax on the agriculture sector.

But huge numbers of people in large areas throughout the region are still engaged in low-productivity agriculture, some despite relatively easy access to markets and good agro-ecologies. In Nicaragua, half of the extremely poor population lives in rural areas that are within four hours of the capital, Managua. In Guatemala, subsistence agriculture still dominates.[8] Global markets and the rise of supermarkets have so far left small, less productive farmers in the region further behind.[9]

---

markets in northeast Brazil; and recent expansion of palm oil exports from Colombia (De Ferranti and others 2004; Damiani 2007; Gomes 2006).

7. Domestic supermarkets have emerged as key players in Latin America's agrifood economy. Their share in national food retail sales jumped from 10 to 20 percent in 1990 to more than 50 percent by the early 2000s. Domestic supermarket demand for fruits and vegetables in the region reached US$24 billion in 2000 while total exports of these products were worth US$10.5 billion in the same year. Fruits and vegetables, dairy products, and value-added foods sought after by supermarkets and consumers in rich countries pay better than basic staples. They also tend not to have such important economies of scale in production, so the potential exists to increase farm income on a limited amount of land (Reardon and Berdegué 2002, 2006; Berdegué and others 2005).

8. De Janvry and Sadoulet (2004) and Alwang and others (2004).

9. In Colombia and Brazil, the regional impacts of trade liberalization have revealed a strong north-south differentiation, with the less competitive north generating far fewer gains than the more productive south (Hewings 2004). Even larger and more sophisticated farmers hoping to export their products must meet stringent international quality and sanitary standards. (See Henson 2007 for an overview of the significant capacities required of agricultural producers to gain access and succeed in high-value nontraditional agrifood export markets). In domestic markets, small producers have been largely excluded from the supermarket boom. Supermarkets' practices regarding quality and safety standards, cost, volume, consistency, and payment have a big impact on farmers, and small producers often are unable to compete due to lack of financing, management skills, and access to relevant technologies. Recent studies show that where medium and large producers are available to meet the year-round demand of processors and supermarkets (as in the case of tomatoes in Mexico), small producers are simply excluded. In other situations, a select group of small farmers, the commercial elite (who, according to evidence, tend to be more educated, to have more access to transport and roads, and to have greater prior holdings of irrigation and other physical assets such as wells and greenhouses), are the only small farmers participating in the modern retail supply channels. Asset-poor small farmers are left out. The few exceptions in the region tend to involve some type of donor or NGO support or subsidy. See Reardon and Berdegué (2002, 2006, 2007); Reardon (2006); and Hazell and others (2006).

Several factors contribute to pervasive low-productivity agriculture. One, of course, is the unequal distribution of land itself.[10] Government programs to redistribute land (with compensation to prior owners) have not worked well—even in Brazil and Colombia, where programs that benefited from extensive technical support financed by the World Bank and the Inter-American Development Bank have foundered in recent years.[11] An alternative approach is to support development of land markets, including rental and leasing markets, which in turn requires a big push to establish clear property rights.

Insecure property rights are a major constraint in most countries, and they affect the poor disproportionately. Land titling and registering programs have advanced slowly. In most of the region, less than 50 percent of farmers who cultivate small and medium-size holdings have legal title to the land, either because no title exists or because there is no official record of it. In the early 1990s, surveys showed that 63 percent of farmers in Chile, Colombia, Honduras, and Paraguay lacked legal title to their land.[12] The lack of an explicit title—and the insecurity of tenure more generally—reduces incentives for productivity-enhancing investments,

10. Latin America has the highest land inequality of any region. Gini coefficients of land distribution are on the order of 0.8, where 1.0 is perfect inequality and zero is perfect equality (De Ferranti and others 2004).

11. Recent initially promising market-oriented land redistribution efforts in Brazil and Colombia are faltering. See Birdsall and de la Torre with Menezes (2001) for a brief analysis of these efforts. Recent studies put part of the blame on the lack of sufficient public resources to make a serious dent in land redistribution through adequate and widespread compensation. Political considerations have often driven governments to target high-productivity areas for redistribution instead of high-potential areas, resulting in costly land acquisitions and little room for a sustained impact on productivity. (In practice, land reform programs in the region often were implemented to address political grievances, with poverty reduction and efficiency considerations taking a back seat.) See World Bank (2005e). Program failures have been also linked to lack of training, complementary inputs, and limited access of beneficiaries to credit (see De Ferranti and others 2004, 2005; Deininger 2003; and Deininger, Castagnini, and González 2004).

12. Tejo (2003); López and Valdés (2001); and De Ferranti and others (2005). ILD (2006e) finds that in Colombia, more than 75 percent of rural properties are outside the formal legal system of titles, registration, and other legal instruments that render property negotiable in the market; in Mexico, the corresponding figure is 70 percent (ILD 2006c). (This includes land without valid title or registry, with legal irregularities, or with restrictions on its transfer.)

limits use of land as collateral, and increases the potential for conflict. It is also a severe obstacle to realizing the efficiency and equity benefits associated with land rental activities, which is especially damaging in a region where land ownership and access is so unequal. In most countries, land rental markets are atrophied and socially segmented due to uncertain property rights and weak enforcement.[13]

Everywhere in the region, agricultural productivity is also limited by suboptimal investments in infrastructure and other public goods in rural areas.[14] In Peru only 5 percent of rural households have access to water, electricity, telephone service, and roads; around 74 percent have access to only one of those goods or to none.[15] Government expenditure in the rural sector has been highly regressive in most of the region and severely biased in favor of big subsidies to specific producer groups.[16] The lack of rural roads is a serious barrier to commerce and trade.[17] Access to credit in rural communities also is limited, especially for small farmers and producers,

---

13. Where property rights are weak and land tenure insecure, as in most of Latin America, landowners are reluctant to rent out for fear that tenants will establish a claim to the land. So rentals are few, informal, short term, and often restricted to closely related people to facilitate enforcement (Deininger 2003). In Nicaragua, insecure tenure has been shown to reduce participation on the supply side of rental markets (Deininger and Chamorro 2002). In the Dominican Republic, insecure property rights reduce land rental market transactions and cause market segmentation (Macours, De Janvry, and Sadoulet 2004).

14. Many countries expanded rural infrastructure services in the 1990s, but rural areas remain greatly underserved, especially compared with urban areas (see chapter 11).

15. Escobal and Torero (2005). The authors find that rural households in Peru with access to more than one service do much better economically than those with access to only one, with multiple services significantly increasing agricultural productivity and diversification beyond agriculture. On Peru's deteriorating, inadequate rural infrastructure see also Peltier-Thiberge (2006).

16. The share of private subsidies in public rural expenditure in Latin America has declined over the past fifteen years, but in 2001, a number of countries—including Costa Rica, Dominican Republic, Honduras, Panama, Paraguay, Peru, Venezuela, Ecuador, and Uruguay—still spent about 45 percent of their rural budgets on nonsocial subsidies (López 2005). In Colombia in 2005, out of the Ministry of Agriculture's investment budget of US$108 million, US$67.5 million (or 62.5 percent) went to private subsidies, mostly to large producers, about US$ 8.5 million (or 7.8 percent) went to programs to support small farmers, and US$8 million (or 7.5 percent) went to technology and technical assistance programs (Caballero and others 2007).

17. In Peru and Ecuador, only 8 percent of rural and local roads are in good condition. In Colombia, one-third of the rural population does not have ready access to the country's road network (Fay and Morrison 2007).

and credit and other market failures mean poor farmers and rural workers often are unable to exploit new technologies and market opportunities.[18]

Many of the region's poor, finally, live in difficult regions, where low productivity in agriculture reflects geographic isolation, severe lack of access to markets, and very low-productivity biophysical environments. Examples include high-altitude areas in Central America's Altiplano. These are areas where migration may well be the best route out of poverty but where historically the opportunity to migrate has been limited—by language, culture, and low income itself.

What to Do?

What can be done to repair rural markets and boost the potential for agricultural productivity growth in the region? Although local conditions differ, we suggest three priorities below.

Titling

Titling can be the next step to get land markets—rental as well as sales—working in rural areas.[19] Throughout most of the region, macroeconomic liberalization and the elimination of special privileges for large producers have helped to lower land prices considerably, reducing incentives for speculative land acquisition and bringing prices more in line with agricultural profits. In Brazil, following the elimination of tax exemptions on unused land and the end of hyperinflation, land prices dropped by as much as 70 percent in the early 1990s, making it easier to acquire land for productive purposes. In Colombia, overall land prices are now more in line with expected returns.[20] The key step now is titling to secure clear

18. Recent econometric analyses cited in De Ferranti and others (2005) show that in both Brazil and Mexico geographic location affects individuals' ability to gain access to credit regardless of personal, familial, and professional characteristics. Past government interventions in rural credit markets—including through regulatory reforms and interest rate subsidies by public banks—have not met with success. Most programs have struggled with limited outreach, low recovery rates, high costs, and little identifiable impact at the farm level.

19. De Soto (2000) argues persuasively about the benefits of property titling in promoting economic development and reducing poverty.

20. See Reydon and Cornélio (2006) and Reydon and Plata (2002) on the evolution of land prices in Brazil; see Lavadenz and Deininger (2003) on the case of Colombia. During

property rights. Titling increases incentives to invest in land and expands the scope for more efficient land use and greater access of the poor to land through rental transactions. In Nicaragua, Honduras, and parts of Brazil, the receipt of registered title greatly increased the propensity to invest in land, and titling was shown to have a significant positive effect on farm income in Paraguay and Honduras.[21] In Colombia, strengthened rental and sales markets have been more effective than government-sponsored land reforms in providing land access to poor but productive farmers.[22] Of course, with secure property rights must come credit and legal assistance and other competition-enhancing actions to help small farmers exploit land markets.[23]

---

periods of macroeconomic instability, investors may use land as a hedge against inflation; therefore an inflation premium is incorporated into the real land price. Because of lower inflation, using land as a hedge has become less attractive in Latin America. But the expected results of land liberalization in terms of greater market activity have only partly materialized, in large part because of low confidence in property rights.

21. In Nicaragua, Deininger and Chamorro (2002) finds that receipt of a registered title increased land values by almost 30 percent and greatly boosted the propensity to invest. Deininger (2005, 2003) reports that in the developing world increased tenure security has been associated with as much as a 50 percent increase in land investment returns and has raised land values by between 30 and 80 percent. Investments associated with tenure security include planting of perennial crops, installation of drainage systems, and adoption of soil conservation measures. In Honduras, López (1996) shows that increases in land and labor productivity associated with titling led to a 5 percent increase in farm income. Carter and Olinto (1998) shows similar results for Paraguay. See Feder (2002) for evidence in Honduras and in Brazil's frontier lands.

22. See Deininger, Castagnini, and González (2004). Recent experience in the region suggests that increasing the access of the poor to land through rentals tends to be less politically demanding and introduces fewer new economic inefficiencies than land reform based on expropriation, and it is cheaper for government than land reform with compensation to original owners (Macours, De Janvry, and Sadoulet 2004).

23. Past experiences, especially in Asia, suggest that to reap benefits, titling should be complemented by a fair and effective legal system; solid, consolidated cadastral surveys; and enforcement mechanisms. In their absence, receipt of a private land title may not provide much tenure security (Deininger 2003). Boucher, Barham, and Carter (2005) reports that in Nicaragua and Honduras, land rights continued to be contested even after major investments in titling and national land administration initiatives in the 1990s. Legal uncertainty was a major factor. In Nicaragua much of the newly titled land has been subjected to competing claims, especially since courts are still processing claims by large landowners whose holdings were expropriated by the government in the 1980s. In Honduras, the titling program unintentionally exacerbated land conflicts by creating multiple claims to land and undermining existing institutions for conflict resolution. Carter (2002) argues that land market activation policies on their own might not produce the fully beneficial productivity and distributional goals expected of them. Ensuring the efficacy of complementary factor markets is crucial—in particular, pairing land policies with programs and policies to improve financial

Increased Spending on Infrastructure in Rural Areas

This does not require expanding budgets. In most countries it requires reallocating public rural expenditures, from big private subsidies to investments in roads, transportation, water and energy distribution, and communications (see chapter 10).[24] Chile has spent more than US$30 million a year on an irrigation-drainage public subsidy scheme that targets a limited number of non-poor farmers. The lucky farmers are paid between 25 and 75 percent of their total investment, up to US$275,000.[25]

Active Policies Geared to Development

Employ active policies that target rural and agricultural development. Investment in agricultural research and development (R&D) and extension services, which is essential to boosting productivity and improving the competitiveness of rural sector activities in the region, would speed diffusion of new technologies and encourage farmers to adopt improved

---

markets. Land titling programs alone have had relatively weak effects on access to credit in developing countries, including in Latin America (Boucher, Barham, and Carter 2005, 2007). Macours, De Janvry, and Sadoulet (2004) finds that in the Dominican Republic lack of access to working capital constrains participation of the poor in land rental markets; the authors estimate that increasing both tenure security and tenant access to working capital would boost the number of poor families with access to land through rentals by 151 percent and the total land area rented by the poor by 310 percent. Removing the threat of government expropriation in the name of land reform is important (Deininger 2005, 2003). That was a key step in getting land rental markets going in Indonesia.

24. Expanding the coverage of paved roads in particular has been associated with enhanced productivity. A 1 percent increase in road density in the region is associated with an increase of 0.42 percent in agricultural productivity (Bravo-Ortega and Lederman 2004). López (2005) suggests that reallocating just 10 percent of subsidy expenditures in order to supply public goods could increase per capita agriculture income by about 2.3 percent in the region. By contrast, increasing total rural expenditure by 10 percent without changing its composition raises agricultural incomes by only 0.6 percent. In East Asia, the build-up of infrastructure—roads, bridges, transportation, electricity, water, and sanitation—was a key factor in the rapid growth of agricultural productivity and output in the 1970s and 1980s. During that time, countries in East Asia allocated a larger share of public investment to rural areas than did other low- and middle-income countries (World Bank 1993).

25. López (2005). The author finds evidence suggesting that most irrigation services in the region are completely or almost completely subsidized and that they benefit non-poor farmers only.

production and management techniques.[26] In Paraná, Brazil, the Fábrica do Agricultor program has helped small farmers and entrepreneurs to invest in equipment, management, technology, and commercial practices and to develop strong and efficient organizations to meet the requirements of specialized buyers (supermarkets).[27] R&D policies should include efforts to institutionalize agricultural research; support the development and strengthening of scientific institutions capable of training, supporting, and directing agricultural scientists; and help establish links between research systems and farmers.[28] Government support for R&D in Chile was a key ingredient in the country's agricultural success story. Active support from the government for agricultural research and extension services was also essential in East Asia.[29]

Urban land markets as well as rural markets need attention in Latin America. In urban areas, the economic logic of granting formal titles to squatters is becoming more and more clear. Hernando de Soto's work has emphasized how titling of poor people's property can unleash its otherwise suppressed value.[30] Titling offers security and facilitates investment in home improvements and community-based businesses. One recent study of titling in Buenos Aires found positive effects on housing investment, school achievement, and nutrition and a reduction in teenage pregnancy rates.[31]

26. Empirical studies suggest that average annual rates of return on investments in agricultural R&D are in the range of 40 to 60 percent. Agricultural research is also shown to have positive effects on the alleviation of poverty across a wide range of countries and technologies (Acquaye and others 2004).

27. Reardon and Berdegue (2002, 2006) and Del Grossi and Graziano da Silva (2001). In Paraná, the state government, with financial and technical support from multilateral development banks, has provided small local food processors with technical assistance, training in marketing, and commercial contacts to help them sell to supermarkets in intermediate-size cities. To facilitate commercial relations, a state-level licensing/certification program for businesses also was created.

28. Brazil alone accounts for 50 percent of total regional agricultural research spending (Argentina, Brazil, and Mexico together account for about 85 percent). Agricultural research organizations in the region are relatively new and most are small; the majority have less than 200 researchers. Brazil and Mexico, responsible for 50 percent of regional agricultural output in the 1990s, employ more than two-thirds of the region's agricultural researchers, while Central America, which produced 12 percent of total output, employs only 8 percent (Acquaye and others 2004).

29. De Ferranti and others (2005) and World Bank (1993).

30. See De Soto (2000).

31. See Galiani and Schargrodsky (2007, 2004).

To promote equality, countries should put a high priority on funding for urban land titling programs. The public sector needs to finance these programs, but experience has shown that they should be managed by private groups that are held accountable for results. In Peru, the COFOPRI (Comisión de Formalización de la Propiedad Informal) program regularized 1.6 million lots and registered more than 1.2 million titles in just over five years by streamlining administrative and legal procedures and adopting a large-scale approach to regularizing vast tracks of illegal housing.[32]

32. As a result of the reforms, roughly 80 percent of Peru's eligible residents became nationally registered property owners, affecting about 6.3 million individuals (Field 2004). Field and Torero (2006) provides evidence of the positive impact of Peru's titling program on beneficiaries' access to credit.

EIGHT

Tackling Corruption
Head On

Latin Americans are well aware of how corruption undermines their governments and societies. In Transparency International's latest surveys of local and international perceptions of government corruption, most countries in the region ended up in the bottom half of the 163 countries covered: Brazil, Mexico, and Peru ranked 70, Argentina 93, Bolivia 105, and Ecuador and Venezuela 138.[1] Only Chile and Uruguay did better, at 20 and 28 respectively. Latin America has democratic governments and considerable transparency. Yet in terms of corruption, Latin American countries rank consistently below the world average (table 8-1) and just above the poorest nations in Africa and Asia in international comparisons.[2] Low growth, limited access to information, the high dependence

1. Costa Rica ranked 55; El Salvador, 57; Colombia, 59; Guatemala, Nicaragua, and Paraguay, 111; and Honduras, 121 (Transparency International 2006a).
2. In the 2006 Corruption Perceptions Index (CPI) nearly all Latin American countries score below the world mean; Chile, Uruguay, and Costa Rica are the exceptions. The average score for Latin America excluding the three best performers is the same as that of Africa and just slightly ahead of the scores for Eastern Europe and Central Asia (Transparency International 2006a). The bribe index in Mocan (2004) suggests that corruption in Argentina and Bolivia—measured as the share of citizens surveyed who indicated that they had been asked for a bribe—is among the highest in the world (29 and 26 percent respectively), behind only Indonesia (30 percent). Data in Kaufmann, Kraay, and Mastruzzi (2006) measuring the quality of governance—including one indicator for control of corruption—show Latin America with a low rating, especially when compared with developed countries and East Asia. See also the ethics and corruption subindex in the World Economic Forum's Global Competitiveness Index 2006–2007 (Lopez-Claros and others 2006).

TABLE 8-1. Corruption Perceptions Index, 2006
Range 0–10, with 0 = most corrupt.

Region	Index score	Country	Index score	Country	Index score
Africa	2.9	Ecuador	2.3	Mexico	3.3
Latin America[a]	2.9	Venezuela	2.3	Colombia	3.9
East Asia	5.7	Paraguay	2.6	Costa Rica	4.1
OECD[b]	7.4	Bolivia	2.7	Uruguay	6.4
		Argentina	2.9	Chile	7.3
Global average	4.1	Brazil	3.3		

Source: Transparency International (2006a)
a. Excluding Chile, Uruguay, and Costa Rica.
b. Excluding Mexico and Turkey.

of civil society organizations on public funding, and a public sector that is still large despite a decade of privatization probably all contribute.

Despite an increase in awareness and visibility and the many small anti-corruption legislative and program initiatives that have appeared, at least on paper, it is difficult to document any real improvement. Attitude surveys suggest that improvements occurred in Colombia and Mexico over 1995–2005 but that the situation deteriorated in Argentina and Venezuela.[3] And, of course, such surveys may simply reflect general discouragement in countries that are suffering economic setbacks and optimism in countries that are doing better.

Corruption Poisons any Equity Strategy

One of the worst aspects of corruption in Latin America is its role in perpetuating inequality and undermining efforts to reduce poverty. How does that process work?

First, corruption undermines competition, and that hurts small businesses, consumers, and taxpayers. An obvious example is corruption in procuring government services.[4] If a few large firms with the right contacts

---

3. See Lambsdorff (2005) for analysis of the Corruption Perceptions Index and its component data and initial findings related to country trends in about sixty countries over 1995–2005.

4. Surveys of perceptions among Latin American business owners suggest that problems of capture and corruption in public procurement are more serious than administrative corruption (for example, the extent of bribery associated with access to public services, customs, and taxation) (Kaufmann 2003).

and the capacity to pay bribes get the inside track, the costs will be paid by others—in higher prices, wasted public money, poor-quality services, and lost opportunities for competitive, job-intensive small firms to expand. Less visible but also insidious are the effects on small businesses and consumers of delays at customs, excessive tax and health "inspections," and so on—in part the result of an environment that encourages ill-paid public servants to hope for side payments. In Peru, Colombia, Ecuador, and Honduras, small businesses report requests for bribes to obtain services more often than larger firms; they also report larger bribe payments to secure public contracts. A survey in Mexico estimates that in 2005, families paid nearly US$1.8 billion in bribes to obtain public services. For households earning the minimum wage or less, the cost of bribes represented almost 25 percent of income.[5]

Second, by undermining competition, corruption reduces the level of and the return to private investment, thereby reducing job creation and ultimately hurting the poor.[6]

Third, corruption undermines government. A weak and ineffective government hurts growth and cannot protect its most vulnerable citizens.[7] Public revenues are wasted on unproductive projects that line insiders' pockets. The benefits of public investments in roads and hospitals are lost

5. Anderson, Kaufmann, and Recanatini (2004); Transparencia Mexicana (2006). Surveys in Ecuador show that smaller firms are more likely to pay bribes than larger firms (46 percent and 29 percent respectively); they also report higher bribe payments to secure public contracts (10 percent of the contract value on average). Both larger firms and microenterprises report slightly lower bribe payments. After the number of inspections is normalized by firm size, smaller firms also receive a much higher number of visits per employee and their managers spend much more time (per employee) than large firms in dealing with government regulations (World Bank 2005d). In Brazil, bribes to secure government contracts place a heavier burden on microenterprises and small firms—costing them between 13 and 15 percent of the contract value compared with 5 percent of the contract on average for large firms (World Bank 2005e). In Mexico, the average cost of bribes in 2005 amounted to about US$16 per household claiming to have paid bribes, or 8 percent of household income (Transparencia Mexicana 2006). See also Kaufmann, Montoriol-Garriga, and Recanatini (2005) for evidence from Peru.

6. Mauro (1995, 1997) and Keefer and Knack (1995) show that corruption reduces total investment. Wei (2000) shows that corruption also reduces foreign direct investment.

7. See, for example, Kaufmann (2005); Kaufmann and Kraay (2002); Tanzi (1998a); Gupta, Davoodi, and Alonso-Terme (2002); Gupta, Davoodi, and Tiongson (2001); Anderson, Kaufmann, and Recanatini (2004).

to poor maintenance and corrupt procurement practices.[8] A discouraged civil service loses its sense of public service and responsibility.[9]

Fourth, corruption undermines confidence in government, with pernicious effects. One example: honest but alienated citizens feel justified in evading and minimizing their taxes; the resulting smaller tax base means lost opportunities to invest in education, health, and other public services on which the poor rely most.[10]

Analysis suggests that countries with less corruption spend more on education—presumably because more honest governments spend more on the poor. (It could also be that when governments spend more on education fewer opportunities exist for the more lucrative forms of corruption that more capital-intensive public spending provides.) [11]

What Can Be Done?

Most countries in the region took a critical step in fighting corruption when they opened their economies to global competition. There is nothing like outside competition to reduce the space for unproductive rent seeking by private firms and nothing like eliminating tariffs and quotas to eliminate the bureaucratic discretion that invites bribery.[12]

Today's high awareness of corruption—and sensitivity to it—also represents an important change. Over the past decade and a half, much

8. Mauro (1998); Tanzi and Davoodi (1998a); Keefer and Knack (2007, forthcoming). Tanzi and Davoodi (1998a) shows that corruption is likely to increase public investment but to reduce its productivity (as corrupt officials tend to invest in projects based on the opportunity for corruption and kickbacks and not on the basis of their intrinsic economic value). The authors also find that, other things being equal, higher levels of corruption are associated with lower expenditure on operations and maintenance and lower quality of public infrastructure (statistically, the impact of corruption is strongest on the quality of roads and power outages). A summary of their findings can be found in Tanzi and Davoodi (1998b).

9. In Paraguay, public servants surveyed in 2005 cited the lack of a merit-based promotion system and the many obstacles they face in bringing forward corruption allegations as the main reasons for their overall low morale and lack of motivation (CISNI 2006).

10. Tanzi and Davoodi (2001) finds that a one point increase in corruption is associated with a 2.7 percent decline in tax revenues as a share of GDP (and specifically with a 0.63 percent of GDP decline in individual income taxes collected). See also Tanzi (1998b).

11. Mauro (1998) shows that government spending on education as a ratio of GDP is negatively and significantly correlated with corruption. Specifically, a decline in corruption of one standard deviation is associated with an increase in government spending on education by 0.6 percentage point of GDP. See also De la Croix and Delavallade (2007).

12. See Ades and Di Tella (1999, 1997) for further discussion on these points.

progress has been made. Civil society organizations in Mexico, Panama, and Colombia have introduced national-level public perception surveys and corruption studies that provide key information on the nature, magnitude, and location of corruption within countries.[13] Similar initiatives exist in Brazil, Chile, Costa Rica, Ecuador, Paraguay, and Peru.[14] In most places, voters are insisting on more accountable government; in addition, the media are relatively free to criticize government policy and are actively doing so.[15]

But in terms of crackdowns on and effective prevention of corruption, the region's record is much less positive. While most countries have passed anticorruption legislation, it is rarely enforced (but see box 8-1 for signs of effort). Most governments use legal instruments as "window dressing" to comply with international conventions against corruption or to dodge domestic corruption allegations.[16] Bolivia, for example, has passed laws aimed at curbing abuse of authority and influence peddling

13. In 2001, 2003, and 2005 Transparencia Mexicana's National Index of Corruption and Good Governance assessed corruption levels in thirty-eight key public services through client responses. In Panama, an impunity index issued in 2003 by the Fundación para el Desarrollo de la Libertad Ciudadana revealed that of 110 cases of corruption that appeared in the media between 1997 and 2002, only four resulted in convictions. The Integrity Index for National Public Institutions developed by Transparencia por Colombia ranks more than 100 public entities according to indicators of transparency, efficiency, control, and punishment. See Transparencia Mexicana (2006); Transparencia por Colombia (2005, 2006); Fundación para el Desarrollo de la Libertad Ciudadana (2003).

14. For a mapping of nearly 100 corruption measurement tools (including opinion surveys, public sector diagnostics, and private sector surveys) being developed in Latin America at the national and local levels, see Transparency International (2006b).

15. In Latin America, three countries (Costa Rica, Chile, and Uruguay) were rated "free" in the 2007 Freedom of the Press global survey, fourteen countries were rated "partly free," and two (Cuba and Venezuela) were rated "not free." Of the 195 countries surveyed, Venezuela has registered the largest decline in media independence since 2002. Argentina has recently slipped in the ranking due to the misuse of official advertising, while in Bolivia and Peru political turmoil and polarization between state-run and privately owned media has weakened freedom of the press. Setbacks in other countries are mostly related to the rising violence against journalists covering drug trafficking and organized crime, which in turn reflects the general intensification of violence in the region (Freedom House 2007). See also Reporters Without Borders' Worldwide Press Freedom Index 2006 (www.rsf.org).

16. Governance indicators for 1996–2005 in Kaufmann, Kraay, and Mastruzzi (2006) show that Latin America has performed poorly on control of corruption over the last ten years. In two small opinion surveys in Argentina, respondents from the private sector, civil society, and government identified reducing corruption as the area where Argentina is doing the least well (World Bank 2006d). See also Parker and others (2004); Acción Ciudadana (2006); Proética (2006); and country reports in Transparency International (2007, 2006c) and Global Integrity (2007).

BOX 8-1. Cracking Down on Corruption

In Buenos Aires a newly elected city government carried out an effective corruption crackdown in public hospitals from September 1996 through December 1997 by using a mix of audit policies (sticks) and higher wages (carrots). The monitoring initiative required that the thirty-three Buenos Aires public hospitals report to the Health Secretariat the price, quantity, brand, supplier, and month of each purchase of a number of very basic supplies.[1] The information was summarized and sent regularly to all hospitals, highlighting those that paid the lowest and the highest prices. Evidence shows that prices fell by 15 percent following the introduction of the monitoring policy. After the initial nine months of the program, average prices paid by the procurement officers increased but were still 10 percent lower than the pre-crackdown levels.[2] Higher wages among procurement officers were associated with lower input prices in the last phase of the crackdown, when audit intensity could be expected to be moderate (that is, lower than in the initial phase of the crackdown, when audit probability was very high, but higher than in the pre-crackdown period).[3]

---

1. Hospital supplies were acquired through a decentralized procurement processes. The information was to be copied directly from the invoices for each purchase in a format that enabled auditing by including the invoice number. The method used by the government was to start with very homogeneous products whose price differences could not be explained in terms of quality, so as to make price comparisons as powerful as possible.
2. This confirms previous informal accounts of corruption crackdowns that estimate that effects of such policies tend to decrease over time.
3. Higher wages had no effect on input prices when audit probability was very high.

at all levels of government. But in practice, cases of unlawful enrichment by government representatives—which have risen in recent years, especially at the municipal level—are difficult to prosecute because there is no law in Bolivia allowing authorities to probe assets and earnings of public officials. Several drafts have been introduced in the country's congress, but all have been rejected.[17] In another example, Ecuador's national electoral tribunal is obligated by law to provide information on campaign finance to citizens upon request. But in practice, when accounting reports are filed, the electoral court ignores the law and makes the information inaccessible. In 2002, a nongovernmental organization, Participación

17. Serrano (2006).

In 2002, Mexico approved the comprehensive Federal Law of Transparency and Access to Public Government Information, unique in Latin America in terms of its depth and scope. It requires government agencies to publish routinely and make accessible all information concerning their functions, including budgets, operations, staff, salaries, internal reports, contracts, and concessions. An uncomplicated request process was established to obtain information not already in the public domain, granting citizens the right to appeal an agency's decision to deny information and take the case to court if the appeal is denied. The law includes the first clause prohibiting government from withholding under any circumstance information regarding crimes against humanity or gross human rights violations. There is a special budget provision for implementation and oversight; another key component provides for educating both the public on how to use the law and government bureaucrats on how to comply with it. The law legitimizes and encourages the role of civil society in monitoring compliance.

In 2000 Chile enacted the Law on Tender Offers and Corporate Governance. In 2001 Brazil approved reforms to the Corporation Law, strengthening minority shareholder rights and enhancing disclosure standards; a separate reform provided greater functional and financial independence to the Securities Commission. In 2001 in Colombia the Superintendencia de Valores enacted a resolution requiring all issuers who intend to be recipients of pension fund investment to disclose their governance practices in some detail.

Sources: Di Tella and Schargrodsky (2003); Sobel and others (2006); Banisar (2006); IFAI (2004); Villanueva (2003); Parker and others (2004); Capaul (2003); OECD (2003).

Ciudadana, requested copies of all campaign expenditure reports filed by presidential candidates and their parties that year. The electoral tribunal ruled that the information was to be deemed confidential until the tribunal finished revising it and issued its own report. Participación Ciudadana filed an appeal with the country's Constitutional Court, but lost.[18]

The watchdog agencies (for example, anticorruption institutions or commissions, ethics offices, ombudsmen) often set up by governments to ensure accountability in public institutions have the right form but little

18. Speck (2004); Dirani, Schied, and Voika (2004). In 2004, Ecuador's Congress approved a new access to information law, but so far there have been very few gains from it. Implementation of the law has been exceedingly slow, largely because of the lack of cooperation from public entities, federal agencies, and local governments (Banisar 2006).

substance. The agencies frequently lack the credibility, resources, power, and independence to enforce their anticorruption mandates; at worst, some may even extort rent.[19] Peru's Congressional Ethics Commission, created in 2003, failed to find fault with a single legislator in its first year, although dozens of complaints and corruption allegations were brought to its attention. A second, temporary, commission set up by the justice minister in 2004 to develop an anticorruption program collapsed less than a year later, after the minister resigned.[20]

One problem may be that "when corruption is widespread, individuals do not have incentives to fight it even if everybody would be better off without it."[21] Countries end up stuck in a bad equilibrium in which pervasive corruption and low investment and growth are common.[22] In most of the

---

19. Argentina, Costa Rica, Guatemala, Panama, Peru, and Venezuela are among the countries that have set up anticorruption agencies, offices, or commissions in recent years. Studies show that such watchdog agencies have achieved success only in countries where governance is generally good, such as Chile. Where institutional environments are weak and corrupt, strategies that rely heavily on anticorruption agencies have been largely ineffective (Huther and Shah 2000; Shaha and Schacter 2004). In many cases, anticorruption agencies are not empowered to enforce accountability directly; they can enforce it only indirectly by referring cases to judicial and legislative bodies, which in Latin America are mostly weak and corrupt themselves (Santiso 2006). (Svensgen 2005 also briefly discusses the problem with anticorruption agencies.) Moreover, focusing on internal control mechanisms falls far short of what is needed when corruption is not limited to administrative and bureaucratic circles (Kaufmann 2003).

20. Proética (2006); Castilla and Olivares (2006). Peru's Congressional Ethics Commission was restructured in 2004 to boost performance but managed to make only a single recommendation in 2004–05, calling for a 120-day suspension for a legislator who assaulted a government official. The length of the suspension was later reduced by Congress.

21. Mauro (2004, p. 16).

22. Mauro (2004) presents a model that embeds strategic complementarity—that is, if many people steal, then the probability of any one of them being caught will be low—into the Barro (1990) model of economic growth with government expenditure in the production function as an input. When other people are stealing from the government, an individual will base his or her decision not only on a lower marginal product of working in legal activities, but also on a higher marginal product of stealing, because the chances that he or she will be caught are lower. As a result, it will be profitable to allocate more time to rent seeking and less time to productive activities. The model obtains multiple equilibriums—a "good one" characterized by absence of corruption and high rates of investment and growth and a "bad one" by pervasive corruption and low investment and growth. Slow growth and low investment in the bad equilibrium result from the waste of labor hours spent on the unproductive transfer of resources and from a low marginal product of capital, because a lower proportion of government expenditure reaches the production processes of which it is an input. The model emphasizes the role of individuals stealing from the government and may be interpreted as allowing for both petty corruption (paying a bribe to obtain a driver's license) and grand corruption (paying a bribe to build a highway with substandard materials).

region, corruption is still rooted in institutions such as the police, justice, and health services systems, which have the greatest contact with the public.[23]

Unfortunately, evidence on which anticorruption programs and measures work best is scarce. But a serious anticorruption agenda would include

◆ An independent judicial system. This is part of institution-building reforms. Many countries in the region still lag behind in meeting the standards of due process observed in developed countries, and courts and judges often are vulnerable to political interference and bribery.[24] Accountability mechanisms are rarely in place. The same problem plagues other regulatory agencies—bank supervisors, for example, need to be protected from intimidation. Institutional safeguards that are needed to ensure judicial accountability and independence include security of tenure and improving conditions of service for judges; rigorous and transparent appointment and disciplinary procedures; transparent mechanisms of case allocation and case management; clear rules on conflict of interest; transparent and open hearings; right of appeal and publication of judicial decisions; and public information about the courts.[25] In Chile, reforms led by the judiciary have resulted in greater transparency, streamlined administrative procedures, and better-trained judges and court staff.[26]

23. See, for example, Hunt (2006); Herrera and Roubaud (2004); Seligson (2006); and, on corruption in the health sector, Lewis (2006).

24. Judicial systems in Latin America, which are mostly inefficient and ineffective, often are also corrupt, contributing to impunity. Public officials are rarely prosecuted, let alone convicted on corruption charges. Political influence in the judicial process remains a major problem in most countries. In Guatemala, for example, judges in the Supreme Court have talked about receiving "instructions" on how to resolve certain cases if they wished to remain in their posts (ICJ 2005; Melgar Peña 2007). In Brazil, public officials can be investigated and tried only in the country's superior courts, which are not designed or equipped to handle criminal cases. The result, according to a new study by the Association of Brazilian Magistrates (AMB 2007), is almost guaranteed impunity. Out of the 463 cases brought against public officials in the country's superior courts between 1988 and 2007, only five resulted in convictions. In some countries, there is a lack of resources and professional training for judges and court staff. In Mexico, local courts lack decent budgets and the means to handle their workload, while federal courts have good resources and their staff enjoy high salaries (Carbonell 2007). Systems everywhere are overwhelmed, and citizens, especially the poor, often lack access. See Transparency International (2007); CEJA (2007); Popkin (2004); Gargarella (2002); and Buscaglia (2001) for further discussion on these issues.

25. See Transparency International (2007) and World Bank (2005c) for further discussion.

26. Harasic (2007). Costa Rica also has undertaken reforms of the judicial sector with positive results (Salazar and Ramos 2007). See Treisman (2000) and Ades and Di Tella (1997) for evidence on the positive effects of an independent judiciary in curbing corruption.

◆ Measures to lock in governments' obligation to disclose and "voluntarily" disseminate key information.[27] Guaranteeing full public access to government information—about contracts, prices, and regulatory decisions—helps curb corruption. Advances in information technology have made the dissemination of public information much easier. Brazil has recently implemented innovative e-procurement mechanisms (making procurement web-based), which reportedly has led to significant cost savings and an increase in transparency and accountability in government agencies.[28] Greater transparency also means full access to the kind of information that can help the public identify corrupt public officials.[29] In most countries the constitution recognizes the right of citizens to free access to public information, but that right is not respected in practice. Mexico has made progress with the Federal Law of Transparency and Access to Public Government Information (box 8-1).[30]

27. Transparency "refers to the key characteristics of an effective flow of information—namely access; timeliness; relevance; and quality of economic, social, and political information—accessible to all relevant stakeholders" (Kaufmann 2003, p. 20). See Bellver and Kaufmann (2005) for a transparency index ranking 194 countries. The authors find that transparency is associated with lower corruption, increased competitiveness, and better socioeconomic indicators. Furthermore, transparency reforms do not cost much, and much progress can be achieved on a very low budget (Kaufmann 2005).

28. Evenett and Hoekman (2005). The Panama Canal Authority uses an e-procurement website with online tenders, a bid calendar, and the names of successful bidders for contracts and those suspended or debarred from receiving contracts (IMF 2006c). Mexico has recently introduced an electronic procurement portal for managing the bidding process in an effort to increase transparency and reduce corruption. But the system has not yet been adopted by all agencies. (World Bank 2006c).

29. Concrete reforms in this direction include public disclosure of assets and incomes of political candidates, public officials, politicians, legislators, judges, and their dependents; and public disclosure of political campaign contributions by individuals and firms and of campaign expenditures (Kaufmann 2005). It remains problematic that in most of the region, electoral courts and other oversight bodies have a monopoly on campaign information as well as regulatory responsibility (Walecki 2004).

30. Apart from Mexico, only five countries in the region have federal laws to regulate provision of or to facilitate access to information held by public institutions. Colombia first adopted a law on access in 1885, but its current law, from 1985, is largely unused. Laws have also been adopted in Panama, Peru, Ecuador, and the Dominican Republic (Banisar 2006). In most countries (especially those without specific laws), public requests for access to information are managed hastily and hazardously. In Guatemala, a study by civil society organizations in the country showed that between October 2002 and June 2004, six of every ten requests for public information were denied—and eight of every ten were denied during election periods (Acción Ciudadana 2006; Urizar 2006). In Honduras, a local nongovernment organization, Ética y Transparencia, has made more than eighty official information requests of government agencies over the last ten years, almost all of which have been ignored (Global Integrity 2007). See also Transparency International (2003); Inter-American Dialogue (2003).

♦ Legitimizing the watchdog role of civil society, the press, and independent analysts. Independently funded watchdogs that are analytically strong and savvy with respect to advocacy are the key to ensuring accountability and transparency, especially in environments in which corruption is relatively high and governance is weak.[31] In countries like Argentina and Chile, civil society groups have become increasingly involved in promoting better disclosure and transparency in political finance. In Central America, leading nongovernment organizations have launched several noteworthy monitoring and accountability initiatives to curb corruption in the judiciary. In Mexico, such groups have taken advantage of the access to information law to independently audit government contracts and hold officials accountable for corruption and misuse of public funds.[32] In most of the region, however, civil society organizations still lack the financial and technical capabilities to play an effective role in monitoring and oversight. The business sector also has a role to play in fighting corruption and improving overall governance.[33]

♦ Investing in civil service reform and upgrading of public bureaucracies. In some settings and countries, wage increases and audit policies could be employed as complementary tools. A combination of wage increases and audit policies was effective in curbing corruption in public hospitals in Buenos Aires, Argentina, in 1996–97 (box 8-1). Ecuador's tax administration office and the Canal Authority in Panama improved their performance by raising wages as part of a comprehensive package of organizational reforms.[34] Because incompetence and lack of training in public administration often open the door to

---

31. See discussion in Kaufmann (2003). On the association between greater freedom of the press and lower corruption, see Brunetti and Weder (2003).

32. Maldonado and others (2004); Transparency International (2004); Salazar and Gramont (2007); Popkin (2004); and Hofbauer (2006).

33. Research discussed in Kaufmann (2003) shows that the corporate responsibility and ethics strategies that powerful businesses (including foreign investors) choose to implement can further improve or undermine national governance within a country.

34. Drosdoff (2002); Parker and others (2004). Huther and Shah (2000) suggests that a system of performance measurement that ties wage increases to increases in public satisfaction with government services could encourage officials to trade income from corrupt sources for legitimate income—especially if the probability of paying penalties also increases (as a result, say, of greater judicial independence). However, Shah and Schacter (2004) suggests that in environments where governance is weak, wage-based strategies are not likely to have a significant impact on civil service corruption.

corruption, frequent training programs to enhance enforcement and improve overall job performance—including efforts that target public officials—also are warranted.

◆ Reducing the scope of public sector activities, including through more privatization.[35] Despite large-scale privatization in the 1990s (see chapter 11), the public sector in Latin America remains large and has a strong presence in the markets, including through full ownership of businesses or through shares or participation in key privatized businesses. That opens the way for greater corruption. In Brazil, congressional investigations and the press have uncovered wide misuse of public funds and corruption by high-level officials in public companies (including Petrobrás and Banco do Brasil) who were appointed by President Lula.[36]

◆ Evaluating the impact of anticorruption programs and policies. Few countries in the region have any form of evaluation to determine what impact, if any, their anticorruption efforts are having. Information and documents about actual effects, if they exist, have not been made public, so no lessons can be drawn from them.[37]

35. Privatization is controversial. But the evidence shows that privatization of water, electric, telecommunications, and other services has worked for the poor in Latin America. See Birdsall and Nellis (2003) and Nellis and Birdsall (2005) for examples. Also see chapter 11 in this volume.

36. See, for example, Procuradoria-Geral da República, Ministério Público Federal, "Denúncia no Inquérito n° 2245" (www.pgr.mpf.gov.br/pgr/asscom/mensalao.pdf [March 2006]); Elizabeth Lopes and Ricardo Brandt, "Petrobrás deu R$ 8,7 mi a ONG ligada ao PT," *O Estado de S. Paulo*, January 4, 2006, p. A07; and Diego Escosteguy, "Acusados por mensalão ainda controlam cargos mais cobiçados," *O Estado de S. Paulo*, March 12, 2006. In Brazil, the size of activities by nonfinancial public enterprises remains large despite extensive privatization in the 1990s. After discounting the oil sector (Petrobrás), on the assumption that its operations are largely commercial in nature, the expenditures by the remaining nonfinancial state-owned enterprises reach around 9 percent of GDP (World Bank 2007a). Evidence in Tanzi (1998a) suggests that a large public sector and pervasive government intervention may be associated with greater corruption. Comparative static exercises in Mauro (2004) suggest that, other things being equal, countries are more likely to end up in a bad equilibrium with low growth and widespread corruption when they have low productivity and a large public sector. Goel and Nelson (1998) finds that the scope of government activities rather than the size of government affects the incidence of corruption. See also Gurgur and Shah (2005).

37. Huther and Shah (2000) discusses four key criteria for evaluating anticorruption programs: relevance, efficacy, efficiency, and sustainability. See also Shah and Schacter (2004).

NINE

Schools for
the Poor, Too

here is little (or no) consensus on the tools in our equity kit, with one
exception: education. Just, fair, and democratic societies can be con-
structed only if good-quality education is available to all. The same is
true for constructing more efficient and faster-growing economies.
And other tools in our kit rely on education for their success.

Given its income, Latin America has extraordinarily poor-quality education. The majority of children who finish primary school fail to achieve
basic skills in reading, writing, and arithmetic. In 2003, students in Mexico, Uruguay, and Brazil scored far below the OECD mean and below the
poorest-performing major OECD country, Greece, on internationally
comparable tests of learning; they also lagged far behind the top performers in two other developing regions, eastern Europe and East Asia.[1]
In addition, the distribution of education is unequal, with five to eight
years' difference between years of schooling for rich and for poor children,

1. In the 2003 PISA (Program for International Student Assessment), which surveyed students in forty-one countries, fifteen-year-olds in the three participating Latin American countries (Uruguay, Mexico, and Brazil) scored near the bottom in reading, math, and science.
On an earlier PISA exam (2000), students from Argentina, Brazil, Chile, Mexico, and Peru
performed just as poorly, scoring considerably lower than the OECD mean and below what
would be expected given the countries' level of per-student investment (PREAL 2006). In
both PISA exams (for 2000 and 2003), Latin American countries performed consistently
below what would be expected given their GDP, whereas all countries in East Asia and the
Pacific region performed above what would be expected (Di Gropello 2006). See also Filmer,
Hasan, and Pritchett (2006).

and in most countries that gap increased over the past decade.[2] The gap in quality between the schools that rich and poor children attend is much greater than the gap in distribution of education.[3] Latin American families that can afford to send their children to private schools do so. Even middle-income households use private schools—often assuming an onerous financial burden for schooling of a quality that is only slightly better than that in public schools.

Average education levels have improved since the 1960s, but progress has been much slower than in East Asia and levels remain considerably lower than in developed countries (figure 9-1). Adults now average six years of schooling in Latin America, four years less than in South Korea, where the rich-poor gap is much smaller.[4] High drop-out and repetition rates that are almost twice the developing country average impede progress in raising average schooling levels and reinforce persistent educational divides.[5]

2. The educational Gini coefficients fell for most Latin American countries in the 1990s, but the gap (absolute difference) in years of education between the richest and poorest quintiles increased. For most countries (Chile and Mexico are notable exceptions), the gap in years of education between rich and poor is wider for younger adults (ages thirty-one through forty) than for older ones (ages fifty-one through sixty), suggesting that the problem of educational inequality may have worsened in the last few decades (De Ferranti and others 2004).

3. This is true whether measured by school infrastructure, teacher education, or spending per student. Outcomes, not surprisingly, also are unequal, with poor students from Brazil, Peru, Mexico, and Chile scoring sharply lower than their richer peers on the PISA exam in reading (Malkin 2006; PREAL 2006).

4. In 1960 the adult populations of Latin America and South Korea had basically the same level of schooling, 3.2 years on average (Barro and Lee 2000). In 1960 the education Gini coefficient for South Korea (population age 15 or older) was 0.55, compared with 0.34 in Argentina and 0.41 in Chile. Forty years later, South Korea had successfully lowered its education Gini by more than half, to 0.19, while Argentina and Chile saw little progress, displaying education Gini coefficients of 0.27 and 0.37 in 2000 (Thomas, Wang, and Fan 2003). Recent analysis shows that overall, Latin American workers have almost 1.5 years less schooling than do workers in countries with similar incomes, while workers in the East Asian tigers have almost one year more (PREAL 2006).

5. While primary repetition rates declined from 29 percent in 1988 to 11 percent in 2002, they remained almost double the world average (5.6 percent) and significantly higher than the average for even low-income countries (6.7 percent). Although most Latin American children, with the exception of those in some rural areas, now complete primary school, fewer children enroll in secondary school, and even fewer finish. Secondary repetition rates are in line with world trends, but they are significantly higher than in Asian countries like Indonesia, the Philippines, and Vietnam. Secondary school graduation rates also are low, around

F I G U R E   9-1. Average Years of Schooling of the Labor Force, 1960–2000ᵃ

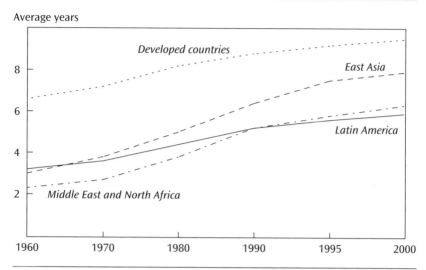

Source: Adapted from PREAL (2006), with data from Barro and Lee (2000).
a. Simple averages. Labor force is defined as those age twenty-five and over.

Across developing countries, the unequal distribution of schooling—as well as the low overall level of schooling—reduces average income growth, and it reduces income growth of poor households even more decisively.[6] In many countries, the wage gap between educated (skilled) and less-educated (unskilled) workers is rising. That seems to be a global phenomenon, but in Latin America the wage gap is especially large, perhaps as a result of some combination of skill-biased technological change and the integration of goods and capital markets through trade and international capital

---

60 percent or less in most countries. Argentina and Mexico have rates below those in Malaysia and Thailand, countries with similar or lower GDP per capita. In all Latin American countries, poor children continue to fall behind, displaying the lowest enrollment rates in primary and secondary school as well as the highest drop-out and repetition rates (PREAL 2006; WDI 2006).

6. Statistical analysis of the effects of the distribution of schooling measured at the country level suggests that income growth of the poorest 20 percent of households is about twice as sensitive to an unequal distribution as average income growth, controlling for the average level of schooling (Birdsall and Londoño 1997).

flows.[7] An unusually limited supply of educated workers results in an unusually large wage premium for those with higher education.[8] That premium, which increased dramatically in the 1990s, has been a major contributor to the sustained high overall wage (and thus income) inequality in the region, and the problem is only likely to get worse.[9] To the extent that technological change is skill biased, open economies in Latin America will struggle with huge pockets of unemployment given the region's uneducated, low-skilled workforce and the huge pool of low-wage workers in China and India, many with better schooling.

If Latin America's school systems can be upgraded and reformed, the region will have an opportunity to reap substantial benefits;[10] getting poor children into better schools can bring both faster overall growth and faster

7. See De Ferranti and others (2003); Rodrik (1997); Sánchez-Páramo and Schady (2003). Behrman, Birdsall, and Székely (2003) notes the likelihood that capital and skilled labor are complements to explain the finding of a statistically significant effect of the opening of capital markets on the rising gap in returns to skilled and unskilled labor.

8. In Latin America, less than 20 percent of the population has thirteen years of schooling or more, compared with 55 percent in the United States. The region's gross enrollment rates at the tertiary level average 29 percent, compared with an average of 70 percent in the OECD countries (91 percent in South Korea, 83 percent in the United States, and 62 percent and 67 percent in Canada and Spain, respectively). Tertiary enrollment rates in Colombia (29 percent), and Mexico and Brazil (24 percent) are lower than in Thailand (43 percent) and Malaysia (32 percent), but they are higher than in China and India (20 and 11 percent respectively)—although China is catching up fast, despite starting at lower levels in 1990, with 3 percent tertiary enrollment compared with 15 percent in Mexico (World Bank EdStats Data Query). Workers with postsecondary education in Mexico, Brazil, and Colombia earn on average 3.3, 3.7, and 4.3 times, respectively, the labor earnings of workers with incomplete primary education; in the United States the differential is 2.5 (Vélez, Barros, and Ferreira 2004). In Brazil, 60 percent of the increase of the skill premium to tertiary education for 1981–99 could be attributed to supply shortage (Blom and Vélez 2004).

9. Wages are the major component of income, so rising wage inequality translates into rising income inequality. Wage gaps may well be magnified as globalization and technological change increase the demand for skilled workers and as inequality in tertiary education continues to rise in Latin America.

10. Good schooling is the keyword here, especially at the primary school level, where quality is a bigger concern than access. In most countries enrollment rates at primary school level have increased across all quintiles, and enrollment gaps between the rich and poor have been shrinking among children under twelve years of age. But while gaps in attendance, especially at primary school, are narrowing, gaps in quality may be growing larger. The increase in primary school enrollment in many countries may have come at the cost of better-quality education, since the increase in education spending at the primary level (to hire more teachers, provide school materials, improve school infrastructure) has not been sufficient to accommodate the increase in the number of students.

reductions in poverty.[11] Now is the ideal time to jump-start education. Fertility declines mean that for the next twenty years or so there will be fewer young people to educate relative to the still rapidly growing tax-paying labor force—and a comparably small contingent of elderly dependents. And ever-cheaper access to distance learning technologies like radio, television, and the Internet can eliminate geographical barriers to knowledge, allowing all countries to exploit opportunities for world-class teaching and learning. Radio in particular has huge cross-border potential, given that Spanish is a common language for so many students and that in several settings, radio's success has been demonstrated.[12]

There are signs of progress. Countries in the region substantially increased their public spending on education, by 27 percent between 1996 and 2002 alone (figure 9-2 shows some evidence on the incidence of spending in selected countries).[13] Some countries whose primary and secondary

11. IDB (1997) estimates that growth could increase by as much as 1 percent a year if the average education of the workforce were to rise by one year (above trend) over the previous decade. That increase could also reduce the Gini coefficient of inequality by about 2 points over that period. Krueger and Lindahl (2001) shows that after correcting for errors in measuring years of education, changes in education positively affect GDP growth. Hanushek and Wößmann (2007) finds that the quality of education (measured by students' PISA scores)— rather than mere school attainment—has a significantly strong positive effect on individual earnings, on the distribution of income, and on economic growth. See also Hanushek and Kimko (2000) and Barro (2001).

12. Bolivia implemented a very successful interactive radio education program in the 1990s at a cost of one dollar per student. Mexico and Brazil have had generally positive experiences using relatively more expensive television programs for mass education (Anzalone and Bosch 2005; Moura Castro 2002). But it is important that countries use distance learning technologies as part of an overall strategy that ensures availability of materials and trains teachers and other support personnel in how to use and maintain equipment. In Mexico, telesecundarias (based on distance learning through satellite communications) now account for about 20 percent of total secondary enrollment, with a particularly strong presence in rural areas. But quality is an urgent challenge—telesecundaria students performed significantly worse on the 2003 PISA exam than students in other types of schools, even after relevant school and individual characteristics were controlled for (Hagerstrom 2006).

13. Public education spending in Latin America increased from 3.4 percent of GDP in 1996 to 4.3 percent of GDP in 2001–02 (World Bank EdStats Data Query). Spending allocation varies across countries: Chile has seen a large, equalizing convergence across the primary, secondary, and tertiary levels; Mexico has experienced steady growth at all levels, thereby maintaining unequal patterns; and Brazil has a large bias toward tertiary education, which receives seven times more funding than does secondary education (De Ferranti and others 2004). Lindert, Skoufias, and Shapiro (2006) shows that in seven countries (Brazil, Dominican Republic, Ecuador, Guatemala, Mexico, Peru, and Uruguay) public spending on primary education is somewhat progressive (55 percent of expenditures go to the poorest

FIGURE 9-2. Percent of Total Public Education Spending on the Richest and Poorest 20 Percent of the Population

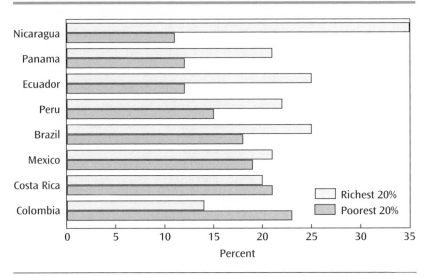

Source: PREAL (2006).

school completion rates are among the lowest in the region began to give priority to raising those rates among the poor and have significantly raised schooling levels across all income groups.[14] Colombia, El Salvador, and Nicaragua are giving more autonomy to rural schools—in the case of Nicaragua, to all public schools. A few countries are starting to evaluate teacher performance and experimenting with programs designed to pay good teachers more. Programs in Brazil and Mexico that provide cash

two quintiles), largely because richer families opt to send their children to higher-quality private schools. Secondary education spending benefits mostly the middle quintiles, with the poor largely uncovered (since most drop out or do not enroll in secondary school) and, again, with the rich for the most part sending their children to private schools. Public spending on tertiary education is regressive in all seven countries. Most countries spend more heavily on secondary and tertiary education, which tends to make the overall effect of education spending regressive. In six of the nine Latin American countries for which data are available, the poorest fifth of the population receives less than a fifth of all education spending (PREAL 2006).

14. Brazil raised the proportion of rural and urban youth with six years of schooling by almost 20 percent between 1990 and 2002. Guatemala and El Salvador also have made important gains, especially since 1995 (PREAL 2006).

transfers to families on the condition that they keep their children in school are proving effective in increasing levels of schooling among the poor (see chapter 3). Chile made valiant efforts to rationalize public spending on higher education by introducing fees in public universities— and the fact that students are now contributing to the costs may help explain their June 2006 protests over the poor quality of education.[15]

But the politics of education reform in the region are difficult (box 9-1). Despite years of positive rhetoric, progress where it counts—better schools for poor students—has been halting. Even where there is political will, the institutional constraints are daunting. We call attention to four important areas for the education reform agenda.

Performance-Based School Reform

Success would be measured by how much children learn rather than by increases in enrollment and spending. Performance-based systems begin with a widely shared vision of what society expects of its schools and map out the resources needed to attain that vision. Regular monitoring shows how far a country has come in meeting its goals and where policy adjustments may be needed. Unfortunately, the most important performance indicator, national achievement tests, are a relatively new phenomenon in most countries and do not play a central role in policy design or evaluation.[16] It will be a sign of real commitment to better education when governments regularly measure and report on student learning through national and international tests.[17] National test results that are broken down by school level and subgroup (for example, poor students, male and

15. Chile also has created incentives for quality improvement by tying a fraction of public subsides to each student admitted whose score on the national university entrance exam is among the best 27,000 (Thorn, Holm-Nielsen, and Jeppesen 2004; Bernasconi and Rojas 2004).

16. In Chile, national tests are well established and used for policy purposes. In Brazil, two national evaluation tests were introduced in the last decade, but they do not yet play a central role in policy design or evaluation.

17. Only eight Latin American countries (Argentina, Brazil, Belize, Chile, Colombia, Mexico, Peru, and Uruguay) have participated in internationally comparable achievement tests (not counting the UNESCO/OREALC regional test). Most governments claim tests are too expensive, but considering how much they invest in education, it is difficult to see why they would not want to measure results.

BOX 9-1. Politics and Public Schools

Politics may be the biggest obstacle to improving education in Latin America today, and few governments have figured out how to deal with it.

The political challenges that reformers face are daunting. Governments have a virtual monopoly in designing and delivering public education. They face little competition, and they are subject to only minimal oversight by civil society. The consumers of public education—most of them poor—have little information and almost no influence on education policy. Influential elites, who send their children to private schools, are not directly affected by the failings of public schools.

As a result, public education is "captured" by informed, well-organized interest groups—primarily teacher unions and universities—that can engage decisionmakers. Governments, realizing that they have few allies against these groups, tend to give in to their demands, leading to ironclad job security for teachers, regardless of performance, and free university tuition for the rich. The poor lack such power. They seldom have a seat at the negotiating table and rarely take to the streets to protest poor school quality. Because they lose out to groups with more political muscle, their children are left with third-rate educations in underfunded and poorly managed public primary schools.

To be sure, governments have taken the politically popular decision to expand enrollments, thereby putting more poor children in school. But few have successfully tackled the politically difficult reforms that would improve the quality, equity, and accountability of schools, largely because powerful vested interests oppose them.[1] The lack of reform is due largely to failure of leadership and the absence of strong demand for policy reform. As part of

---

The text of this box was written by Jeffrey Puryear and Tamara Ortega Goodspeed of Partnership for Educational Revitalization in the Americas (PREAL).

1. One can imagine political parties that, in the name of the poor, stand up to special interests and demand the hard decisions needed to improve public schools. That seldom happens, however, perhaps because party leaders perceive that doing so will cause them more trouble than doing nothing, at least in the short term. And, of course, presidential leadership could help energize state bureaucracies and party leaders and craft political strategies for change. But presidents realize that unions and universities are strong and well-organized while the poor are not, making the political payoff from pushing through difficult reforms smaller than the payoff from capitulating to those who benefit from the status quo.

their strategy to confront political obstacles head on, leaders from all sectors need to strengthen demand. Doing so requires three inputs: information, involvement, and empowerment. Governments should inform consumers of public education by providing them with reliable, timely, and user-friendly information on the education system. They should involve consumers by soliciting their input during the design and evaluation of reforms, thereby giving them an ownership stake that they would be more likely to defend. And they should empower consumers by delegating significant decisionmaking authority, particularly on financial issues, to local entities so that they can more easily participate. These steps will not guarantee success. But they will begin to tip the political balance away from the powerful groups that currently dominate education policy, giving the poor a better chance of having their interests served.

There have been a few successes. In the early 1990s, Nicaragua implemented an innovative and ambitious program to ensure school accountability and parental participation that public schools can choose to join if they wish. Championed by strong ministerial leadership—and with support from international organizations and donors—the Autonomous Schools Program established a system of school-based management, creating local school councils controlled by parents and responsible for hiring and firing principals and allocating resources derived in part from fees paid by parents.

Reformers bypassed unions—already weakened by divisions and infighting—by appealing directly to teachers with pay incentives tied to the autonomous project. Earlier changes in the Education Ministry bureaucracy and the establishment of ministry delegates at the municipal level also helped overcome political barriers. At the macro level, the program benefited from strong links to broader goals related to the process of democratization and market reform. By 2000, more than 50 percent of primary school students and nearly 80 percent of secondary students were enrolled in autonomous schools. The success of the program, which initially was implemented through a ministerial directive, helped it survive years of legislative battles later.[2]

---

2. For more on Nicaragua's Autonomous Schools Program, see Gershberg (2004) and Arcia and Belli (2002). For more on the politics of education reform, see Kaufman and Nelson (2004); Grindle (2004); Navarro (2005); Corrales (2006, 1999).

female students, students from ethnic and racial minorities) should be widely publicized in an easy-to-understand format.[18]

Genuine Accountability: Voice and Choice

Schools should be accountable to citizens for achieving educational objectives. Schools in Latin America are accountable to almost no one. Their goals are poorly specified, and attainment is difficult to measure. Teachers are seldom evaluated, never dismissed, and paid the same amount whether they perform well or poorly. Parents and communities have little information on how schools are doing and almost no power to effect change. Citizens should demand that the central government make accountability a central component of education policy by setting clear objectives; holding ministries, schools, and teachers accountable for achieving those objectives; and giving them the authority to do so.

In most countries accountability requires voice. There should be a radical decentralization of education services in order to involve parents and local communities in governing and running schools. Hiring and payroll should be done at the local level, with the central government allocating funds to schools on the basis of the number of enrolled students and compensating for low family income.

Accountability also requires choice. There should be some mechanism to ensure greater competition; options include allowing parents to choose among public schools and, through vouchers and other child-based subsidies, between public and private schools.[19]

Preschool for the Poor

Investment in early childhood education benefits all children, especially those from poor and disadvantaged families.[20] It costs less and produces

18. Parents and local communities should receive regular updates on teacher qualifications, teaching materials, and school budgets in a clear and understandable format. And all actors need to know which policies show promise under what conditions.

19. The central government's key roles are in quality control and financing to minimize inequity across geographical areas. See PREAL (2006) for guidelines.

20. Research shows that poorer children reach school age with a significantly greater disadvantage in cognitive and social abilities than better-off children. Paxson and Schady

more dramatic and lasting results than investment in education at any other level.[21] Poor children also benefit indirectly, because their parents, single mothers in particular, have more flexibility to join the labor force.[22] Preschool enrollment has increased over the past decade, especially among the poor in countries where programs target disadvantaged rural populations; however, even though poor children are most likely to benefit from preschool, they are least likely to attend.[23] Governments need to increase public funding for both public and private childcare and preschool programs that reach the poor, complementing them with programs to help parents improve their child-rearing practices. Programs need to account for the needs of working women by extending their hours and the number of children and parents covered.

Fewer Subsidies for Better-off Students at Public Universities and New Post-secondary Options for More Students

In most countries, public systems of higher education subsidize the rich and are accountable to almost no one for the quality of their services.[24] The relatively few students from poor families who manage to finish high

---

(2007) shows substantial differences related to socioeconomic status and parental education among six-year-old children in Ecuador. Early deficits are associated with weaker future academic performance and lower adult economic and social outcomes (Grantham-McGregor and others 2007; Rutter, Giller, and Hagell 2000). Evidence from internationally comparable tests of student learning in developed regions suggests that countries with universal preschool programs have been able to enhance the equity of the education system by attenuating the impact of family background on student performance without sacrificing average levels of educational attainment (World Bank 2005c).

21. World Bank (2005c); Heckman and Masterov (2007); Carneiro and Heckman (2003).

22. A study in Brazil in the mid-1990s found that access to affordable childcare in the slums of Rio de Janeiro was associated with higher female labor force participation and earnings (Deutsch 1998). See Attanasio and Vera-Hernández (2004) for evidence from Colombia.

23. In Latin America, 40 percent of children still do not enroll in preschool; the proportion is even higher (around 70 percent) in countries with high poverty rates, such as Guatemala, Honduras, Nicaragua, and Paraguay (PREAL 2006; World Bank EdStats Data Query).

24. Because most poor children in Latin America never finish secondary school, public funds spent on higher education almost automatically favor the rich (about 80 percent of resources go to the two richest quintiles on average). Although ratios are generally declining, on average, Latin America still spends more than three times as much per student at the university level than at the primary level; in several countries, the ratio is much higher (PREAL 2006).

school are ill-prepared for further study and often are unable to pass difficult entrance exams at free public universities. They are left with few choices, which usually involve paying for education in private institutions that put less emphasis on initial test scores or forgoing higher education altogether. In Brazil, students from the poorest 40 percent of the population make up just 3 percent of the student body at public universities.[25] Countries need to introduce fees at public universities for those who are able to pay and give an increasing share of public funds directly to needy students, rather than to institutions, in the form of merit-based loans and scholarships that they can use at the institution of their choice.[26] The public needs to demand that independent national accreditation agencies generate and analyze data on the performance of institutions of higher learning. Institutions that receive public funding can be broadened to include non-university, postsecondary programs, such as two-year colleges and postsecondary technical training, augmenting both the equity and efficiency of public spending on postsecondary education.[27] Governments

25. Mexico, Colombia, Chile, and Argentina fare somewhat better, but access to higher education is still highly unequal (Holm-Nielsen and others 2005). In Mexico, only 3 percent of the eighteen- to twenty-four-year-olds from the poorest quintile of households attend a tertiary education institution, while 26 percent from the wealthiest quintile do so (Brunner and others 2006). In Colombia in 2002, the enrollment rate in tertiary education was less than 20 percent among the low-income population (defined as strata 1 and 2 of six socioeconomic strata) but close to 60 percent for high-income students (Cerdán-Infantes and Blom 2007).

26. Increased financial aid to students enrolled in the fields of science and engineering would help increase the supply of trained, highly qualified professionals and contribute to the region's innovative capacity.

27. Experience in East Asia suggests that institutions such as two-year junior colleges can produce graduates with the skills needed on the labor market. In Taiwan, more than 90 percent of exports are produced by junior college graduates in small and medium-size businesses, which together employ about 80 percent of the workforce. Non-university tertiary institutions also have made a positive contribution in South Korea, where junior colleges enroll about 25 percent of the students in tertiary education—preparing them for careers in vocational fields such as health care, business, and engineering—and often set up partnerships with local businesses, especially SMEs, offering customized training financed by the businesses and adapted to their needs (Grubb and others 2006). In 2002, there were as many as 3,000 non-university tertiary institutions in Latin America, of which roughly 60 percent were private. In countries like Peru, Argentina, Brazil, and Chile these institutions account for more than 35 percent of total enrollment in tertiary institutions while in most of Central America they still account for less than 5 percent (Schwartzman 2003; World Bank 2002a; Bernasconi and Moura Castro 2005). Many countries have invested heavily in publicly managed systems of vocational training. But for the most part, those systems are expensive and irrelevant to the constantly changing demands of private industry; in addition, they often do not reach the poor, who barely finish primary school.

should subsidize demand through voucher-like systems, thereby encouraging small entrepreneurs to develop and supply training and broadening access for eligible students.

Fixing the supply of education is of course only one part of the solution. Demand for education, particularly beyond primary school, is low among the poor, not only because public schools are so ineffective (reducing the "return" to schooling), but because poor job prospects and discrimination in employment mean staying in school just may not seem worth it. We address demand-side issues in other chapters.

TEN

Dealing Openly with Discrimination

Data on racial and ethnic minorities in Latin America are poor, and the criteria for classification of minorities vary. Estimates suggest that indigenous groups account for about 10 percent (50 million) of the region's population and groups of African descent for 30 percent (150 million). Indigenous people constitute a majority of the population in Bolivia and Guatemala, and they are a significant minority in Ecuador and Peru. Afro-descendents are a majority in the Dominican Republic and Panama, and they form 45 percent of the population in Brazil and more than 10 percent of the population in Colombia, Venezuela, and Nicaragua (figure 10-1).[1]

In Latin America, the contours of inequality run broadly along racial and ethnic lines. Compared with "whites," indigenous and Afro-descendent people are, as a rule, less educated and less healthy and they have less access to such basic institutions as the justice system. They face greater difficulties in transforming educational and occupational achievement into income, generally earning considerably less for the same number of years of schooling (see box 10-1).

1. We exclude observations for the rest of the Caribbean, where Afro-descendents represent the vast majority of the population. Busso, Cicowiez, and Gasparini (2005) shows three different estimates of the size of indigenous and Afro-descendent populations in Latin American countries. Hall and Patrinos (2006) provides a lower-bound estimate of the indigenous population in Latin America of close to 30 million.

F I G U R E   10-1. Indigenous and Afro-Descendent Populations[a]

Percent of total population

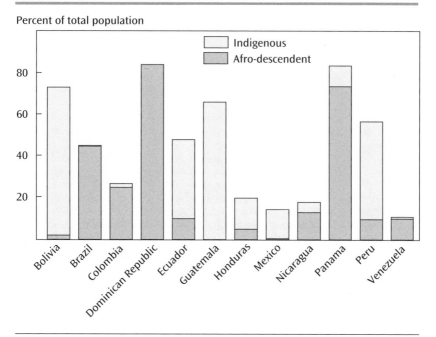

Source: De Ferranti and others (2004).
a. Includes countries where indigenous or Afro-descendent groups or both represent more than 10 percent of the population. Estimates of indigenous and Afro-descendent populations in Latin America vary widely. See note 1.

Yet until very recently, racial and ethnic issues have not been central to social and political discourse in the region. That neglect has contributed to and reinforced the myth that Latin American societies are color blind.

A Double Burden for Girls and Women

Indigenous girls' poor performance in school contrasts sharply with the general rule that, on average, girls throughout the region do as well as—and in some countries better than—boys.[2] In Guatemala, indigenous girls

2. Boys and girls start and complete schooling at similar rates in almost every country; in some (for example, Argentina, Brazil, Panama, Uruguay, and Venezuela) girls do better (PREAL 2006). See also Duryea and others (2007).

BOX 10-1. Lagging Behind: Selected Indicators on Afro-Descendent and Indigenous Groups in Latin America

Included are only those countries that have accessible and reliable data on significant indigenous and Afro-descendent populations. The omission of Venezuela, Dominican Republic, Honduras, and Nicaragua as well as the limited number of references to Panama are due to lack of reliable data.

Poverty

◆ In Peru, Bolivia, and Mexico, after other factors are accounted for, being indigenous increases the probability of being poor by 11, 13, and 30 percent respectively.

◆ In Ecuador, members of indigenous groups are almost twice as likely to live in poverty as non-indigenous groups and 4.5 times more likely to be extremely poor. In Guatemala, seven of every ten indigenous people are poor; the figure is fewer than four for every ten non-indigenous people.

◆ In the Pacific coast region of Colombia, where 90 percent of the population is Afro-Colombian, 85 percent live in poverty; the national average is 32 percent.

◆ In Brazil in the 1990s, after other factors were accounted for, racial differences accounted for one-fourth of poverty and inequality.

Education

◆ In Mexico, net secondary enrollment rates for indigenous peoples are 40 percent below the national average. The primary school drop-out rate of students in predominantly indigenous municipalities is twice that of students in non-indigenous municipalities.

◆ Brazil's 1990s education reforms extended schooling rates for Afro-descendents between seven and thirteen years of age more than for whites. But Afro-descendent students continue to record higher repetition and drop-out rates. While at school, they also record worse exam results than whites, even when the analysis controls for socioeconomic variables.[1] In Paraguay, close to 80 percent of indigenous youth (ages 15 to 19) did not finish primary school compared to less than 20 percent of non-indigenous teens.

---

1. Between one-third and one-half of the deficit in test results for Afro-descendent students is associated with differences in socioeconomic status or condition of schools. A slightly higher proportion of the deficit is attributable to both socioeconomic and school conditions taken together.

◆ In Ecuador, virtually all children start primary school, but completion rates of whites continue to exceed those of indigenous and Afro-descendent minorities. These groups also lag behind whites in test scores for language and math. The achievement scores of predominantly Afro-descendent schools are especially low—behind those of indigenous and Hispanic schools.[2]

◆ Panama has made significant progress in increasing alphabetization levels, including in poor areas. However, among indigenous groups less than two-thirds of children older than nine years of age can read or write.

◆ In Bolivia and Guatemala, more than half of indigenous girls have dropped out of school by age fourteen. At age seven, only half of Guatemala's Mayan (indigenous) girls have enrolled in school; the corresponding figures are 75 percent for non-indigenous girls and 71 percent for indigenous boys. In Bolivia, one of every four indigenous women more than thirty-five years of age is illiterate.

◆ In Ecuador, more than 80 percent of indigenous girls ages fifteen to seventeen are out of school, a rate more than double that of nonindigenous boys and girls—and 20 percent higher than the rate for indigenous boys.

◆ In Peru, rural indigenous girls are particularly prone to enter primary school late, and in recent years, drop-out rates among girls who speak a native language have increased. The illiteracy rate among indigenous women is 65 percent; it is 26 percent among non-indigenous women.

Labor market

◆ In Ecuador, indigenous workers earn 21 percent less on average than non-indigenous workers with the same amount of schooling. In Bolivia, non-indigenous workers receive on average an earnings gain of 85 percent for nine years of schooling, while the gain is about 59 percent for indigenous workers for the same amount of schooling.

◆ In urban Peru, predominantly white workers have higher access to human capital and physical capital assets and earn higher wages than predominantly indigenous workers in an analysis controlling for individual and household characteristics.

---

2. Fifth graders in Afro-descendent schools score 80 to 85 percent below indigenous and Hispanic schools in math and 20 to 35 percent below them in language.

(continued)

BOX 10-1. Lagging Behind: Selected Indicators on Afro-Descendent and Indigenous Groups in Latin America (*continued*)

- Afro-Brazilians with a secondary education earn 16 percent less on average than whites in an analysis controlling for workers' schooling, parents' education, and school quality. Pay discrimination is greater at the higher salary jobs for any skill level.
- In Guatemala, while 65 percent of urban non-indigenous workers have waged employment, less than 50 percent of urban indigenous workers do. In urban Ecuador, more than 50 percent of nonindigenous workers but only 28 percent of indigenous laborers are formally employed.

Health

- In Guatemala, maternal mortality among indigenous women is almost double that of non-indigenous women. In Honduras, maternal mortality ranges from 190 to 255 per 100,000 in communities with a high concentration of indigenous people; the national average is 147 per 100,000. In Peru and Bolivia, the corresponding rates are between 270 and 390 per 100,000 in indigenous areas. The average rate for the region is 125 per 100,000.
- In Mexico, infant mortality levels are higher in the states with a high concentration of indigenous residents (43 per 1,000 live births) than in non-indigenous states (26 per 1,000 live births). In Ecuador, infant mortality among indigenous peoples (68 per 1,000 live births) is more than twice that of non-indigenous people (30 per 1,000 live births).
- In the predominantly Afro-descendent Pacific coast region of Colombia, infant mortality rates are almost four times higher than the national average.
- Brazil shows differentials in infant mortality rates by race and ethnicity even when the analysis controls for socioeconomic variables, including education and income, and the racial disparities have been accentuated over time. While according to the 1980 census the differential between the infant mortality rate of Afro-descendents and of whites was 21 percent, twenty years later it reached 40 percent.

Sources: Patrinos and Skoufias (2007); ECLAC (2006a); Hall and Patrinos (2006); PREAL (2006); Lewis and Lockheed (2006); Perry and others (2006); De Ferranti and others (2004); Arias, Yamada, and Tejerina (2004); McEwan and Trowbridge (2007); McEwan (2004); Garcia Aracil and Winkler (2004); Barbosa (2004); Rosemberg (2004); Hall and Humphrey (2003); Henriques (2002); Ñopo, Saavedra, and Torero (2004).

complete fewer than two years of schooling on average; the rate is (an also miserable) three years for indigenous boys and five and six years for non-indigenous girls and boys respectively. Indigenous girls start school later and drop out earlier than indigenous boys and non-indigenous boys and girls.[3] In Mexico, illiteracy rates of women are systematically greater than those of men in municipalities with a higher share of indigenous people.[4]

Women of all minority groups suffer a kind of double discrimination. For Afro-Brazilian women in urban labor markets in São Paulo in the 1990s, a lower return on their education and age, compared with white men, accounted for 50 percent of their lower overall wages.[5]

As a group, all women still suffer discrimination in some arenas. Although that is true even in OECD countries, there is evidence that in one area—domestic violence—the situation in Latin America may be especially bad.[6]

A Visible Attack on Discrimination

The region has made some progress in the last fifteen years. Ecuador and Chile have created special secretariats dedicated to indigenous matters.[7]

3. World Bank (2003a); Lewis and Lockheed (2006).

4. Hall and Patrinos (2006). Illiteracy among indigenous women in Mexico is 43 percent—far above the national average of about 10 percent.

5. Silva (2000). Data refer to the city of São Paulo.

6. World Health Organization surveys in 1999 and 2000 show that in Nicaragua around 27 percent of adult women reported having been physically assaulted by a partner in an intimate relationship. In Quito, about 37 percent of women said that they had experienced domestic violence. In Lima, 31 percent of women reported experiencing physical violence by an intimate partner. In Colombia, a survey conducted in the mid-1990s found that one of every five women in some kind of union in 1995 had suffered physical violence inflicted by her spouse or partner. Among those, only 27 percent reported the violence to authorities, although the majority of respondents were aware of at least one institution that provided recourse against domestic violence. Estimates based on a social survey for urban households in 1999 found that poor women and younger women with fewer years of completed schooling were much more likely to be victims of domestic violence than wealthier, older, and more educated women. Each year of schooling reduced the probability of victimization by as much as 1.4 percentage points. Women who worked also were more likely to report experiencing incidents of domestic violence (World Bank 2007b).

7. Peru and Honduras have established similar mechanisms for the promotion of racial and ethnic equality. Panama, Venezuela, and the Dominican Republic, which have significant Afro-descendent populations, have failed to advance policies that address racial discrimination (IAC 2003). At the international level, the World Bank, Inter-American Development Bank (IDB), and the Inter-Agency Consultation on Race in Latin America have

Argentina has a minimum number of electoral seats reserved for women in the national and local assemblies;[8] Peru and Paraguay also have gender quotas.[9] But progress has been limited on many practical issues, including bilingual education, affirmative action, outright discrimination, police violence, and domestic violence. While there are no easy answers, changing attitudes toward discrimination is at least one area in which leadership is far more critical than increased public spending.

What is the right agenda?

◆ Recognize the problem of racial and ethnic differences and sponsor assessment of racial and ethnic issues through data collection (censuses, household surveys, and periodic surveys) and social science research.[10] Such efforts are best undertaken with the participation of

---

engaged in efforts to research and raise awareness of racial and ethnic inequalities in the region. Indigenous peoples have notably increased their presence in the legislatures of a number of countries: In Bolivia, indigenous representation in Congress rose from 1 percent in 1998 to 27 percent in 2001; similar growth occurred in Ecuador and, to a lesser extent, in Argentina and Colombia (Deruyttere 2006).

8. In early 2007, women headed 25 percent of the ministries in Latin America; in Peru, Nicaragua, and Ecuador, that number was 35 percent (Blanco 2007). Between 1990 and 2006, the proportion of seats held by women in national parliament rose, on average, from 6 to 35 percent in Argentina, 11 to 35 percent in Costa Rica, 12 to 26 percent in Mexico, and 6 to 18 percent in Peru (ECLAC 2007a). Most countries have a parliamentary commission on women's issues, and all countries have created special women's bureaus to monitor and implement public policies related to women, some at the ministerial level (Buvinic and Roza 2004; Buvinic and Mazza 2005). In Brazil, civil society organizations have been active in developing programs and services with gender-specific objectives.

9. By 2004, eleven countries in the region had instituted quotas establishing a minimum level of representation (between 20 and 40 percent) for women in party lists for legislative elections. Colombia also has defined a minimum quota of 30 percent for women's representation in the executive branch. Overall, quotas increased women's presence in legislatures by an average of 9 percent between 1990 and 2003, but there is significant variation in the success of quota laws across countries. Success in getting more women elected depends on the law—for example, whether it is obligatory; whether it only reserves a slot, as in Brazil, or requires the slot to be filled by a woman; or whether the woman must be placed in an electable position, as in Argentina, or merely at the bottom of the list. It also depends on the nature of the country's electoral system (closed versus open lists) (Buvinic and Roza 2004; Buvinic and Mazza 2005; Htun, 2003).

10. More than fifteen Latin American countries collect information on ethnicity through their census, but only a few—most notably Brazil and Colombia—collect data on Afro-descendents. In all countries, there are still significant gaps for almost every indicator and extensive problems in relevance, accuracy, consistency, and reliability of data. Only three countries compile an extensive bibliography on race and ethnic inequality issues: Brazil for Afro-descendents and Peru and Guatemala for indigenous groups (ECLAC 2006a; Urrea 2006; Del Popolo and Avila 2006).

the affected groups, especially in designing and implementing questionnaires. The availability of disaggregated data by race and ethnicity provides a necessary starting point not only for political and social recognition of diversity, but also for the analysis of and legal redress for discrimination.

◆ Take steps to encourage minority groups to exercise their political and social rights and to push for their own advancement. Colombia assigns seats in its house of representatives to Afro-Colombians. Brazil recently introduced affirmative action programs that include the use of quotas in the public university system and in a new scholarship program designed to encourage low-income students to enroll in private universities.[11]

◆ Establish and strengthen programs to protect women against domestic violence. Gender-based violence reflects deep-seated attitudes, and governments can use the bully pulpit to help change those attitudes and legitimize civil society and community group efforts to combat violence.[12] Laws and policies should strengthen victims' rights, making violent behavior costlier to the abuser. Where laws and policies to protect women already exist, governments should improve the judicial process, strengthen programs that provide women with access to legal services, and step up awareness campaigns. In Guatemala, community-based programs

---

11. Between 2001 and 2005, sixteen public universities in Brazil (nine at the state level and seven at the federal level) implemented affirmative action programs with admission quotas for low-income and Afro-descendent and indigenous students. In a few states (including Rio de Janeiro, Mato Grosso, and Minas Gerais) the program is mandated by law. In others, the decision is made at the university level. By 2006, nearly thirty universities, both public and private, had adopted affirmative action programs (Dias da Silva 2006; Paiva 2004). Through its ProUni program, the Brazilian government encourages private universities to offer scholarships to low-income students—with a share reserved for Afro-descendent and indigenous students—in exchange for tax breaks. Around 163,000 scholarships were offered in 2007. The share allotted to each minority group is proportional to its representation in the population of each state. In the 2006 National Student Achievement Test, ProUni students performed better than their paying colleagues in nearly all university courses covered by the test, including law, business, and medicine (Brazil, Ministry of Education, "ProUni: Programa Universidade para Todos" (http://prouni-inscricao.mec.gov.br/prouni [July 2007]). In 2004, Colombia approved plans to implement short-term affirmative action policies for Afro-Colombians, although these policies have yet to be defined (Stubbs 2007).

12. Community-based initiatives are shown to be especially effective in preventing gender-based violence and offering services to victims (Bott, Ellsberg, and Morrison 2004, 2005).

inform abused women of their rights and help them navigate the legal system. In Cali, Colombia, the Consejerías de Familia monitor cases and provide support and counseling (and in some cases temporary shelter) to abused women, who are referred to them by the city's judicial centers.[13]

13. Several countries in the region have enacted key legislative reforms addressing gender-based violence over the last two decades, including Argentina, Brazil, Peru, Mexico, Nicaragua, Costa Rica, and Honduras. Other noteworthy initiatives include establishing police stations for women, staffed and directed by women, a practice that was pioneered in Brazil and later adopted in Argentina, Colombia, Costa Rica, Ecuador, Nicaragua, Peru, and Uruguay. In Rio de Janeiro, nongovernment organizations (such as CEPIA) are implementing training programs on gender issues for judicial personnel, police, and health sector professionals. The Nicaragua Network of Women against Violence engages in annual awareness campaigns. In Peru's Defensorías Comunitarias, grassroots women act as community monitors to provide support and assistance to victims of domestic violence and abuse—helping to change deep-seated attitudes toward gender-based violence in some of the country's poorest areas, which are mostly rural and indigenous. Projusticia in Ecuador was relatively effective in providing legal aid services for poor women to deal with issues such as domestic violence and lack of child support (Bott, Ellsberg, and Morrison 2004, 2005; World Bank 2002b, 2003a; ECLAC 2007b).

ELEVEN

Consumer-Driven Public Services

What traditionally are called "public services," although some are provided by private, usually regulated firms, are critical to the smooth functioning of a market economy. In Latin America, services to provide public transportation, roads, water, electricity, and telecommunications and to enforce government standards regarding sanitation, pollution and other environmental issues, food and drug safety and other consumer concerns, and public health, including control of endemic diseases, have all been plagued by problems of funding, access, and quality. With their buying power and privileged access to bureaucrats and regulators, higher-income households have never felt the need to use the democratic process to insist on the political accountability of those in charge of public service provision. One result has been the low overall coverage and poor quality of these services, on which poor and middle-income households are so dependent.

1990–2005: Top-Down Reforms

Access to infrastructure-based services—such as water, sanitation, electricity, and telecommunications—has improved in the region over the past fifteen years, particularly in urban areas. But public investment has been on a persistent decline since the 1980s, and the increase in private investment in the 1990s following the establishment of privatization programs had collapsed by 2002, as investors became weary of the uncertainties caused by political fallout and unreliable government regulatory arrange-ments.[1] (In the case of utilities, the implosion of the power sector in core OECD markets, including the United States, forced many investors to pull out.) Overall, progress in providing infrastructure has been slow and uneven—especially when compared with that in East Asia and, more recently, in other middle-income countries and China, which once trailed the region (box 11-1). Poor infrastructure has been a key factor in the low ranking of most Latin American countries in indexes of global competi-tiveness.[2] It takes five days at the most for exports to pass through ports in Malaysia, compared with seventeen days in Brazil.[3] Logistics costs in

1. Electrical service reaches about 87 percent of the population in Latin America. In 2004, just over nine of every ten Latin Americans had access to an improved water source (up from eight in 1990) and 77 percent of the region's population had access to improved sanitation (up from 68 percent a decade earlier). There were close to fifty telephone lines (including fixed and mobile) for every 100 inhabitants in Latin America (up from six in 1990) (WDI 2006). At the same time, total infrastructure investment in telecommunications, power, and land transportation declined by 1.5 percent of GDP on average from the early 1980s to the late 1990s, with a sharp decline in public investment (from 3 percent of GDP in 1980 to less than 1 percent of GDP in 2001). Public infrastructure investment fell in all countries, with Argentina posting the largest drop, 2.7 percent of GDP, and Colombia the smallest, 0.3 percent, during that period. The substantial expansion of private investment post privatization (from US$12 billion in 1990 to US$74 billion in 1998) was not enough to offset the fall in public investment, except in Colombia and Chile. Moreover, by 2003–04, total private investments in infrastructure in the region had dropped to US$16 billion (Calderón and Servén 2004a; WDI 2006).

2. See, for example, the World Economic Forum's Global Competitiveness Index 2006–2007 (Lopez-Claros and others 2006) and the Latin American Competitiveness Report (Vial and Cornelius 2002).

3. World Bank (2005e); reference is to total time needed for cargo to pass through port, from ship call to the port exit gate. In China, exports take at most eight days to ship out and in India, about nine days. The delays in transport and delivery caused by inadequate infra-structure in the region erode the benefits of geographic proximity to the U.S. or other mar-kets (Limão and Venables 2001). Clark, Dollar, and Micco (2004) finds that on average having bad ports is equivalent to being 60 percent farther away from markets. Across the region, ports are a key bottleneck for export firms. Brazil, Argentina, Chile, Colombia, and Panama all privatized port operations in the 1990s. Some have taken important steps to reduce inefficiency. In Brazil's Santos port, the average container handling cost dropped by 40 percent between 1997 and 2000 as a result of a reform to cut labor costs, remove excess staff, and streamline operations. But overall, port tariffs and time delays caused by transit problems, poor infrastructure, and inefficient customs services are still too high in the region. In the case of Brazil, reforms have stalled largely because of the lack of an appropriate reg-ulatory framework or clear guidelines from the government to see reforms to completion; slow progress in undertaking major public investment works associated with port reform also is to blame (World Bank 2007c). In Colombia, port infrastructure also needs consider-able investment in upgrading and expansion, especially port terminals and nearby facilities (Reis and others 2007).

the region are two to three times the costs in industrialized countries, largely because—given the region's difficult geography and relatively sparse population—the roads are inadequate.[4] Fifty-five percent of private sector entrepreneurs in Latin America rank infrastructure as a serious problem—the highest level in the world, shared only by the Middle East and North Africa—while only 18 percent do so in East Asia and the Pacific.[5]

Rural areas still lag substantially behind urban areas in access to basic services, and the poor are ill served everywhere or not served at all.[6] The

4. Part of the logistics cost gap reflects the higher value relative to weight of OECD products, but much of it reflects the region's poor transport infrastructure and resulting higher losses in transit, higher transport costs, and the need to maintain larger inventories, tying up capital (Fay and Morrison 2007; Guasch and Kogan 2005). In Brazil, transportation costs are very high, comprising one-third of firms' average operational costs, and mostly reflect the extremely poor conditions of the country's federal paved road network. Overall, of the 58,000 kilometer network—which handles more than 70 percent of the country's total goods—90 percent are single-lane roads with two-direction traffic and only 25 percent are considered to be in good condition. There has been no rehabilitation or maintenance work done for at least ten years and no investment for at least fifteen years. The rundown road system adds about a half-billion dollars each year to vehicle operational costs, mostly paid by the private sector (World Bank 2007c, 2005e; Beath 2006). In a 2005 study by the U.S. International Trade Commission, Mexico was shown to fall far short on a number of indicators of logistics quality, especially when compared with East Asia. Mexico's roads were found to be slow, expensive, and unsafe; railroads to be limited and costly; and airports and ports to lack the capacity to handle high volumes (World Bank 2006d). During the 1990s, Mexico spent almost double the amount spent by the United States on transport as a share of GDP. Escribano and others (2005) finds for a sample of Latin American countries that transport and energy deficiencies (measured as shipment losses and duration of power outages) hurt productivity and the probability of exporting.

5. World Bank (2004b). Firms surveyed in Latin America report waiting an average of twenty-six days to obtain an electrical connection; the average is twelve days in the East Asia and Pacific region and eight days in OECD countries. Latin American firms also report experiencing twice the number of electrical outages and nearly five times the number of water supply failures as do firms in the East Asia and Pacific region; they also wait almost thirty days longer to obtain a mainline telephone connection (World Bank Enterprise Surveys).

6. Access to electricity has become nearly universal in Latin American urban areas (the share of the urban population with access rose from 92 percent in 1986 to 97 percent a decade later) but reaches only some 60 percent of the rural population. In urban and rural areas of Peru, 92 and 28 percent of the population, respectively, had access to electricity in 2000. In Mexico's largely rural southern states (Chiapas, Guerrero, Oaxaca, Veracruz), electricity reaches between 50 and 65 percent of the population, while coverage is nearly universal in urban areas across the country (World Bank 2006d). The gap in access to water and sanitation in the region has narrowed in the last decade but remains large: 96 percent of Latin Americans in urban areas but only 70 percent in rural areas have a connection to safe water, while almost twice as many people in urban areas as in rural areas have access to improved sanitation (WDI 2006).

BOX 11-1. **Latin America's Infrastructure Gap**

In 1980, the coverage of productive infrastructure in Latin America was similar to or higher than coverage in East Asia. Today, East Asia's capacity to generate electricity is more than double that of Latin America, and its telecommunications network is nearly three times denser (figure 11-1). East Asia also leads in total road length, despite starting at lower levels in 1980. In addition, Latin America has lost ground to China and middle-income countries (MICs) in electrical power, roads, and telephone lines, despite being wealthier in per capita terms; only in terms of access to safe water and sanitation does Latin America perform comparatively well (table 11-1).[1]

TABLE 11-1. **Latin America's Infrastructure Gap**[a]

Category	Road network (km/km²)	Paved roads (percent)	Telephone lines, total (per 1000 persons)	Access to electricity (percent of population)	Access to water (percent of population)	Access to sanitation (percent of population)
	2002	1997–02	2004	2000	2004	2004
Latin America	0.008	27	497	87	91	77
China	0.189	91	499	99	77	44
MICs	0.062	54	485	90	88	71
East Asia	0.203	78	979	n.a.	96	n.a.

Sources: WDI (2006); Fay and Morrison (2007); ADB/JBIC/WB (2005).
a. East Asia data exclude Taiwan; for road network and paved roads, they exclude also Hong Kong and Singapore. Total telephone lines include mainlines and mobile phone subscribers per 1,000 people.

To catch up to the infrastructure levels of East Asia's median country, South Korea, the region would need to invest at least 2.4 to 5.0 percent of GDP a year over twenty years—which is at least twice the level that it invests in infrastructure today.[2] Calderón and Servén (2004b) estimates that eliminating the infrastructure deficit could increase GDP per capita growth rates in the region by almost 4 percent a year on average and cause decreases across countries of 0.05 to 0.13 in the Gini coefficients of inequality.

---

1. Latin America is also ahead of China and MICs in mobile phone subscribers per 1,000 people.
2. Total infrastructure spending in the region is currently less than 2 percent of GDP a year; it is 7 percent of GDP in China (up from 3 percent in 1998) and 15 percent of GDP in Thailand (up from 5 percent in 1998).
Sources: Fay and Morrison (2007); ADB/JBIC/WB (2005); Calderón and Servén (2004a, 2004b); Calderón, Easterly, and Servén (2003b).

F I G U R E   11-1. Latin America's Infrastructure Gap

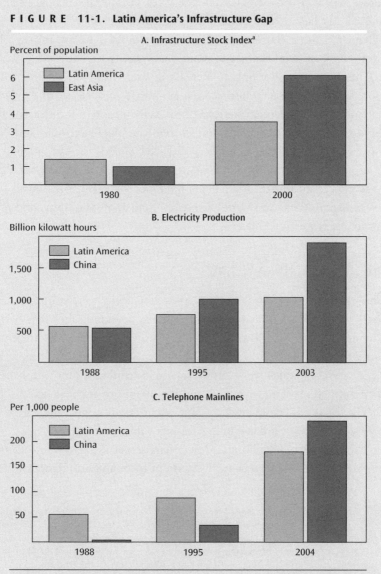

A. Infrastructure Stock Index[a]

B. Electricity Production

C. Telephone Mainlines

Sources: WDI (2006); Fay and Morrison (2007).

a. The infrastructure stock index includes paved roads, electricity production, and telephones (mainlines and mobile) per worker. The index is calibrated so that East Asia had a value of 1 in 1980.

rich suffer least when public infrastructure services are deficient—their neighborhoods usually are the best served in the first place, and they can resort to private providers for some services. For middle-income and poor households, lack of access and low quality are much more costly, in terms of higher health and occupational risks and time and income lost, as when electricity is unreliable and roads and bus systems are bad.

The challenge is not only to increase investment in infrastructure. It is more fundamental: to create and sustain public competence in regulating the nonfinancial sector. There has been some progress in infrastructure services regulation since the 1990s in countries like El Salvador and Peru, but an unstable, unpredictable (politicized and capricious) regulatory environment is still a problem in many large markets, including Brazil and Argentina. And most governments have not yet tackled seriously such issues as pollution control, public health, food and road safety, and other consumer protection concerns.[7]

Privatization: Also a Victim

Until the late 1980s infrastructure services typically were state run—supplied at subsidized rates by large public sector monopolies that had no commercial incentive to price services adequately or to serve their consumers well. Most state-run telecommunications, water, sanitation, and electricity companies were left unable to expand and innovate because they charged inadequate prices, and the quality of services deteriorated visibly. That ended up undermining social welfare and the lot of the poor—who always are last in line for any subsidized service.

Privatization of telephone and electricity services (and to a lesser extent of road, ports, and airport services) swept through Latin America in the

7. An IDB study (2004b) ranked enforcement of consumer protection laws in Brazil as excellent; in Mexico, Argentina, Panama, and Peru as satisfactory; and in Ecuador, Venezuela, El Salvador, Nicaragua, and Paraguay as largely ineffective. Bolivia and Honduras lacked a consumer protection system altogether. In examining data for Europe and Latin America, Gilardi, Jordana, and Levi-Faur (2006) finds that the tendency to establish regulatory agencies is much weaker in social sectors (pharmaceutical, food safety, environment, and so forth) than in economic sectors (utilities, finance, competition), especially in Latin America.

1990s.[8] Privatization has been less extensive in water, sanitation, urban public transportation, and public health services.[9] In many respects privatization has been a success, resulting in improved financial and operating performance in most firms and better quality and enhanced availability of services to consumers.[10] It also has relaxed the bottlenecks

8. We use the term "privatization" to refer to both privatization and public works concession schemes. The accumulated revenues from privatization in eighteen Latin American countries reached 6 percent of gross domestic product in the 1990s. By the end of the decade, the region accounted for fully 56 percent of total privatization revenues across the developing world (more than half of all the privatizations were of high-value infrastructure or utility firms, in contrast to those in other regions outside the OECD states). From 1990 to 2001, private investment in the region in infrastructure alone totaled US$360.5 billion, US$150 billion more than the next most attractive region, the East Asia–Pacific area (Nellis 2003; Harris 2003).

9. Public ownership remains the norm in most of the region in the water and sanitation sectors but not in the electric sector. In most countries, privatization of water services has been less successful technically and still less politically than privatization of other services. Violent protests erupted against the privatization of water services in Cochabamba, Bolivia, where the concession was cancelled. Popular unrest also led to the cancellation in 2005 of Bolivia's La Paz and El Alto water concessions. By 2005, more than one-third of Argentina's water and sanitation concessions had been cancelled or were in the process of being cancelled (World Bank Privatization Database, http://rru.worldbank.org/privatization). In the state of São Paulo, Brazil, sharp increases in rates, poor service, and complaints of corruption in the privatization process prompted the government to try to reverse the shift toward water concessions back to state delivery of services (IDB 2003b). More successful water concession arrangements in recent years have involved small-scale providers under contract to municipal governments, as in Paraguay and parts of Bolivia. Cartagena, Colombia, has adopted innovative mixed capital firms in which the city government has the majority stake in utilities companies, with responsibility for securing financing for infrastructure projects, while private operators, with a minority stake, are responsible for the management and operation of the company, working under a contract with clear performance and expansion targets (Luis Alberto Moreno, "Water Works," *Wall Street Journal,* March 9, 2006, p. A19; Guasch 2004; Kariuki and Schwartz 2005).

10. Case studies in Chong and López-de-Silanes (2005) based on a large sample of privatized firms in Argentina, Brazil, Chile, Colombia, Mexico, and Peru show a median gain in firm profitability after privatization of around 14 percent, efficiency gains of almost 70 percent, and output increases of more than 40 percent. In Argentina, the number of phone lines more than doubled after privatization. In Chile, the waiting time for a new fixed phone line dropped from 416 days in 1993 to fewer than six days in 2001, while the waiting list dropped from a peak of 314,000 people in 1992 to only 32,000 by 2001 (Fischer, Gutiérrez, and Serra 2005). In more cases than not, privatization also freed the state from a heavy administrative and unproductive financial burden, closing the door to widespread corruption and mismanagement by publicly appointed state company employees (Nellis 2003). Andres, Foster, and Guasch (2006) analyzes the impact of privatization on the electricity sector in the region, separating the short-term from the long-term results. The study finds that changes in ownership generate significant improvements in labor productivity, efficiency, and product and service quality—and that most of those changes occur in the transition

that service supply shortages used to create. Furthermore, enhanced access resulting from privatization often has benefited the poor.[11] In Argentina the privatization of water services in poorer areas was associated with a reduction in child mortality of as much as 24 percent. The poor have benefited even in sectors, such as telephone services, in which privatization has led to price increases, because often they had no previous access to services at all (the pre-privatization price was, in effect, infinite). Increasing access made them better off.[12]

Nonetheless, privatized infrastructure programs have been plagued by corruption and the failure of regulatory agencies to protect consumers from price gouging in some cases and in other cases to protect newly private firms from government restriction of legitimate price increases.[13] As a result, privatization has been an especially unpopular reform.[14] Also to

---

period around the privatization process. The improvements in the post-privatization period—beyond two years after the change in ownership—are much more modest.

11. Birdsall and Nellis (2003); Nellis and Birdsall (2005). Analyzing results from the water sector in Colombia, Barrera-Osorio and Olivera (2007) finds that in addition to increasing the frequency of service, privatization in urban areas increases access to and quality of service and also improves health outcomes for the lower quintiles. But in rural areas, the positive effects of privatization on the frequency of service and on health indicators are outweighed by negative impacts on access and prices.

12. Galiani, Gertler, and Schargrodsky (2005) finds that in Argentina, child mortality fell 8 percent on average in municipalities that privatized their water services. The effect was largest in the poorest municipalities that privatized, where child mortality fell 26 percent. Evidence of a pro-poor impact of private sector services also was found in Chile and Bolivia, where 25 to 30 percent of network expansion targeted the lowest 20 percent of the income profile (World Bank 2003b). In Argentina, Gonzalez-Eiras and Rossi (2007) finds some evidence of lower child mortality related to food poisoning and lower frequency of low birth weight in provinces that privatized their electricity service than in provinces with public distribution networks—though the evidence is less conclusive (possibly due to the low number of cross-section observations). Instances of price increases in privatized firms often are necessary if the firm is to modernize, meet demand, and operate without subsidies. Under state ownership, many Latin American governments set utility prices so low that they did not cover costs, which led to scarcity, rationing, and starving firms of investment capital.

13. In Colombia, scandals and allegations of corruption followed the privatization of the electricity sector (TermoRío case). In Argentina, the obscure bidding process in privatization programs raised suspicions of corruption and political favoritism (Ayala and Millán 2002; Chong and López-de-Silanes 2003). In Argentina's Tucuman province, opportunistic behavior by the local government, popular protests, and poor performance led to cancellation after two years of a thirty-year private concession for water and sanitation provision (Nellis 2003; Guasch 2004).

14. Latinobarómetro (2006) shows that between 1998 and 2003, support for privatization among Latin Americans surveyed dropped from 46 percent to 21 percent (falling across all countries and income groups). Satisfaction with privatized services rose 12 percentage

blame are a few cases that have gone very wrong, such as the privatization of water services in Cochabamba, Bolivia.[15] Along with instances of price increases, job losses—even when small relative to overall employment—have added to the sense of frustration, reinforcing the perception among Latin Americans that privatization has been unfair, generally making the rich richer and the poor poorer.[16]

A central problem was that the region's approach to privatization was shaped heavily by fiscal considerations, since sales help shore up government revenues and may permit retirement of government debt.[17] Often that meant that insufficient emphasis was placed on ensuring that markets would be competitive after privatization and that consumers would be protected from abuse. Sales were made to single firms, for example, or regulation of natural monopolies became inadequate after they were in private hands.[18] The lack of accountability reflected the reality that privatization policies were never embedded in a broader vision of social policy. In most cases it meant that opportunities to share the gains of privatization more fairly with the broader public were lost or ignored.[19]

---

points among respondents in 2004–06 as economies picked up steam, but the average figure, 30 percent, remains low. For an overview of the arguments and evidence on the unpopularity of privatization in Latin America, see Nellis (2003); Nellis, Menezes, and Lucas (2004).

15. See Nickson and Vargas (2002) and Kohl (2004) on the case of Cochabamba, Bolivia.

16. Privatization often had a short-term effect on employment—labor had to be shed for the privatized enterprises to restore efficiency and profitability. But in most cases the number of workers laid off due to privatization was small relative to the entire workforce and tended to be offset in the medium term by the increased job creation produced in part by privatization and liberalization (McKenzie and Mookherjee 2005).

17. Privatization has brought a positive flow of funds and reduced public debt to governments in Latin America through price rationalization, retirement of accumulated debt, elimination of subsidy flows, and increased tax revenues from more profitable and productive private firms (Nellis 2003; Macedo 2000).

18. Privatization of public utilities has in many cases left consumers defenseless vis-à-vis the new owners of the formerly state-run enterprise. Typically, consumers have been poorly represented, creating a lack of transparency and the perception of abuse, which work against the long-term sustainability of privatization reforms. There have been instances, as in Argentina, in which the privatized firms did not honor some of the commitments that they made to the government, such as investing a percentage of their profits in modernizing infrastructure, improving customer service, shortening service installation times, or extending coverage to certain areas. Uruguay's energy sector regulatory body, Unidad de Regulación de Energía y Electricidad, was established only in 2000, five years after the start of sector reform and the establishment of a services concession system (IDB 2003a, 2003b).

19. Nellis and Birdsall (2005) includes a number of country studies that illustrate this point. They note that when distributional issues have been considered, it has generally been in the context of greasing the wheels of the process to make it politically more palatable (as

An exception, for a while, was Bolivia. There some of the expected benefits of privatization were initially distributed to citizens in the form of future pension benefits or stock holdings, creating more shareholders in the market economy through a kind of popular capitalism. But that program fell afoul of Bolivia's fiscal problems in the late 1990s. Meanwhile, privatization in Brazil, though clearly leading to more efficient and competitive production, failed to provide for any improvement in the distribution of wealth and income (box 11-2).

The perception of unfairness has slowed privatization and even begun to reverse its contributions to improving efficiency and the access of the poor to services. In Mexico, energy remains a state-run business, limiting the new investment that private owners would bring. In Argentina, the current government has limited tariff increases to well below inflation, putting a stop to new investment and continued extension of services to poorer neighborhoods.

What's Needed Now: A Bottom-Up Approach

The key reform for the future is a radical rethinking of the culture of service delivery. In infrastructure services, continuing private involvement and ownership are essential if a government hopes to secure adequate investment and avoid the past problems of state-owned enterprises. But to avoid corruption and guarantee a good regulatory environment also requires the government to make an active commitment to ensuring transparency and providing information to consumers regarding privatized firms.

In some countries, improving infrastructure and other consumer services may require expanding public budgets.[20] But above all, it is a matter

---

when employees of enterprises to be privatized are given special deals on obtaining shares in the new firm or when the sellers oblige the new owners to accept post-privatization conditions such as service guarantees for less-profitable markets or to commit to maintaining certain levels of investment or numbers of employee for a specified time). See also Birdsall and Nellis (2003).

20. Recent research by the World Bank estimates that the annual financing requirement for infrastructure in the region for the next ten years is about 3 percent of regional GDP (Fay and Morrison 2007; Fay and Yepes 2003). Assuming that the public sector supplies half of that amount, it would need to devote 1.5 percent of GDP a year to infrastructure. That would be an increase of 0.7 percent of GDP from the average level of public infrastructure spending in the region from 1996 to 2001.

BOX 11-2. **Privatization and Popular Capitalism**

Letting Taxpayers Hold the Bag in Brazil

Since the early 1990s, Brazil has privatized more than 115 state-owned enterprises, transferring more than US$71 billion worth of equity capital to private owners. From an efficiency point of view, reflected in the improved profitability of privatized firms, privatization has been a success. But its impact on income and asset distribution has been less positive.

To be sure, equity concerns were never at the heart of the program's objectives. Although democratization of capital was initially stated as a goal, the Brazilian government—facing a fiscal crisis when the program peaked in 1997 and 1998—focused instead on using privatization to promote foreign investment and maximize revenue from sales. To get higher prices, it auctioned most of the state-owned enterprises in large, controlling blocks of shares to big foreign and national corporations. In the few cases in which room was made for democratization of capital, the beneficiaries were mostly middle-income workers of former state-owned enterprises participating in manager-employee buyouts and workers covered by pension funds of former state-owned enterprises that participated in the auctions. Worse, the program did not reduce public debt, which actually increased sharply from 1994 to 1999, due in part to external shocks. Taxpayers, including the poor, are now bearing the costs of higher public debt.

Creating Stakeholders in Bolivia: A Good Idea Run Aground

Bolivia's privatization program in the 1990s put income redistribution at the heart of its objectives. Under the model adopted in 1995, private purchasers of state-owned firms committed themselves to doubling the net worth of the companies in exchange for half the shares. The government distributed the remaining half to the Bolivian people in the form of life annuities (initially set at US$250), beginning at age sixty-five. (The annuity represented 27 percent of Bolivia's per capita income.) The idea was to create stakeholders in the future of the firms and the market economy. Subsequent fiscal pressures eventually prompted the government to lower the annuity amount and to decree that only citizens who were fifty-five years old or older at that time would qualify for a life annuity when they reached age sixty-five. All others would receive shares in the privatized firms instead. In 2002, then President Sanchez de Lozada promised to return Bonosol to its initial level, but lower-than-expected dividend flows from capitalized firms made that impossible. The performance and popularity of the program was further undermined by inadequate regulation, prolonged economic recession, and

(continued)

BOX 11-2. Privatization and Popular Capitalism (*continued*)

a couple of high-profile failures among foreign firms (like Brazil's VASP). By 2006, the idea of "capitalization" was being eclipsed in the key energy sector by the newly elected president's decision to renegotiate contracts with foreign holders of privatized entities.[1]

---

1. It is not clear whether the Bolivian state enterprise YPFB (Yacimientos Petrolíferos Fiscales Bolivianos), which took a majority stake in the countries' main gas and oil production companies, will maintain pension payments. The government has claimed that it does not have sufficient funds to pay the existing yearly pension to the elderly beyond 2007 ("Out of Gas," *Economist*, August 17, 2006; Matthew Cowley, "Gas, Oil Takeover Pits Bolivia against Brazil, Foreign Cos," *Wall Street Journal*, May 2, 2006; "Bolivian May Day Brings Higher Hydrocarbons Revenues and Higher Expectations," Andean Information Network/Red Andina de Información, May 4, 2007).

Sources: Barja, McKenzie, and Urquiola (2005); Birdsall and Nellis (2005); Macedo (2005, 2000); Barja and Urquiola (2001); Graham (1998); Valdez (1998).

of creating a market in which public financing is combined with a radical new style of management, one that focuses on greater consumer choice and voice. The government then assumes two major roles. The first is to empower citizens and community groups with effective regulation and information about standards and prices. The second is to ensure, through voucher-like subsidies and cash grants, that the poor have the buying power to demand good-quality services. User participation and voice and firm accountability are crucial in particular for sustaining an adequate quality of services at the local level. In the end, however, civil society and grassroots advocacy cannot substitute for the fundamental role of government.[21]

We set out below policies and programs to look for in infrastructure services; the same logic and spirit can be applied to all regulatory services.[22]

---

21. See Fiszbein (2005) for more on this point.

22. The general benefits of the policies and practices that we suggest depend heavily on well-functioning legal and economic institutions that promote and monitor transparent market operations. The more careful and extensive the preparation devoted to the institutional underpinnings of private participation, the better the results, in terms of both efficiency and equity (Nellis 2003). See also the discussion in Guasch and Straub (2006).

First, Focus on Competition and Information

◆ In designing privatization and concession contracts and transactions, avoid the mistakes of the 1990s. Maximize competition wherever and whenever possible. When the lack of exclusive rights or other forms of monopoly privilege look like a deal breaker, negotiate hard to make the period of exclusion as short as possible.

◆ Build more transparency into privatization operations by opening bids on television and using independent monitors to vet transactions and certify their openness and honesty. Make full disclosure regarding access, pricing, user rights, and performance benchmarks a legal part of contract provisions with private providers.[23] Encourage monitoring and publication of information on service quality by consumer groups, nongovernmental organizations, and the press.[24]

Second, Make Special Efforts to Reach the Poor

◆ When auctioning service contracts, obligate private operators to extend access to poor neighborhoods.[25]

◆ Use connection subsidies, given directly to poor households.[26]

◆ Include provisions in contracts that give service operators incentives to tap the labor of the poor in delivering services. In Argentina, the low-income population in some neighborhoods is providing the

23. A review of urban water utilities in Latin America in the early 2000s concluded that giving consumers little information about the process of reform and tariff setting while limiting their opportunity for comment weakens the regulatory process and the credibility of reform, thereby making rate changes, however justified, difficult to implement (World Bank 2003b).

24. In some cases having a modern, technically savvy ombudsman or agency might make sense. The person or agency would be a watchdog for poor and working-class consumers, and it would accountable to an elected body.

25. On this point, see Estache, Foster, and Wodon (2002); Estache and Quesada (2001); Briceno-Garmendia, Estache, and Shafik (2004).

26. See Komives and others (2006); Nellis (2003); Estache, Foster, and Wodon (2002). Latin America has a long history of distortive, poorly targeted subsidy programs, which have tended to benefit mostly the urban middle class rather than the poor (Estache, Gomez-Lobo, and Leipziger 2001). In Mexico in 2003, subsidies for electricity consumption absorbed 1.1 percent of GDP, about the same amount as total public investment in infrastructure that year, with the bulk of subsidies going to non-poor consumers and more economically developed regions (World Bank 2006d).

labor to establish and maintain water connections. By involving consumers in poor communities in setting standards and mapping infrastructure networks, one of Manila's water concessionaires has
helped reduce the costs of providing water to the communities by
25 percent.[27]

◆ Eliminate regulations that undercut what would be viable markets
in poor communities.[28] In Yemen, the government now allows poor
communities to tap into already available electrical lines and to manage service distribution and pricing. In other developing countries,
eliminating the state telephone monopoly has created a good rental
market for mobile phones in poor neighborhoods. In Paraguay,
independent small-scale water providers are reaching poor households in isolated neighborhoods at prices that are competitive with
those of public utilities.[29]

Some of these "pro-poor" contractual obligations have costs, which
governments must allow private providers to recover through the rates
that they charge.

Third, a Political Strategy

◆ Minimize the losses of laid-off workers. Make special provisions in
privatization schemes to compensate laid-off workers without com-
promising the government's fiscal position or generating excessive
political pressure. This step is politically important. Although the
number of job losses due to privatization in Latin America has been
small relative to the total number of jobs, job loss has a high political

27. World Bank (2003b).
28. See Trémolet and Hunt (2006) for an in-depth discussion on this point based on case
studies from Bolivia, Vietnam, South Africa, and Zambia in which existing regulations were
eliminated or adapted to facilitate the expansion of water services to poor consumers.
29. Small-scale water providers serve about 25 percent of the urban population in
Argentina, Bolivia, Colombia, Guatemala, Paraguay, and Peru. They range from fixed networks (piped delivery) to mobile providers (tanker trucks) serving individual households and
institutions. In Santa Cruz, Bolivia, cooperatives are the only water suppliers for the city's 1
million people. The aguateros in Asunción, Paraguay, have invested more than US$30 mil-
lion to provide service to 75,000 households, and they have fully recovered both operating
and investment costs (Solo 2003; Kariuki and Schwartz 2005).

cost and helps fuel much of the opposition to reform. During Uruguay's state restructuring and modernization program in the early 1990s, special funds were set aside to cover the costs of severance, early retirement, or transfer of redundant employees. The reforms took place without strikes or labor protests.[30]

◆ Develop a strategy to deal with public opinion. In some settings it may be necessary to minimize the negative public perception of privatization in order to preserve the political possibility of deepening or extending privatization or other efficiency- and growth-oriented reforms.[31] In Peru, a campaign to inform the public that privatization of electrical service would be undertaken through a transparent process and that rate increases would be regulated increased support among citizens from 21 to 60 percent.[32]

Governments will always have fundamental responsibilities to protect the environment, public health, and consumers as well as to provide the infrastructure and services necessary to run a modern state. In all these areas, public policy and practice need to become more consumer driven and the government must become more accountable to citizens than to bureaucracies and interest groups. At the same time, the constant scrutiny of citizens is critical if the government is to be held to account for its performance.

30. The approach in Uruguay emphasized incentives and voluntary participation instead of job cuts. The special funds also helped provide limited technical support, business training, and small loans for civil servants who opted to start their own businesses in the private sector. Many of the laid-off employees received training and assistance in finding private sector employment, and many now provide services to the government—at lower cost—as private contractors (Constance 2002).

31. Public campaigns should explain choices; detail the government's priorities within sectors, between sectors, and between policy instruments; and address concerns regarding privatization strategy, regulatory strategy, and social policy. To ensure public perception of transparency, sales of state-run enterprises could be addressed separately in public campaigns. Too often, impending privatizations have been used by political rivals to create dissension and confusion among the population, as in Bolivia.

32. World Bank (2003b).

TWELVE

How the United States Can Help: Opening Markets and More

Our fair-growth tools depend largely on domestic policies and practices in Latin America. But what happens at the global level and what rich countries do also matter. Some rich countries show a stronger commitment to development than others. The United States, whose policies and practices probably matter most for most countries in Latin America, ranks in the middle of the twenty-one OECD countries whose "commitment to development" is assessed annually by the Center for Global Development.[1] The United States has been increasing its spending on aid since 2001, in particular to help Colombia cope with its civil conflict, and along with the United Kingdom and other OECD donors, it has financed a major program of debt relief for Nicaragua, Honduras, and Bolivia. But beyond aid and debt relief, the support of the United States and the rest of the outside world for increasing opportunities for Latin America's poor and middle-income majority has been sparing.[2]

---

1. See CGD's Commitment to Development Index online at www.cgdev.org.

2. Periodic financial crises, for example, have been a special problem in Latin America because of its open capital markets, and the costs have been especially high for the region's poor and middle-income households in terms of jobs, school drop-out rates, and even infant mortality. In the subsequent good years of low global interest rates and high commodity prices, the collective international effort to reform the international financial architecture has focused almost solely on stepped-up programs of IMF surveillance and increased transparency and reporting by developing countries of their financial, debt, and banking situation.

To illustrate the potential for outsiders to make a difference, we concentrate in this chapter on concrete examples of how the United States could advance the ideas and the reality of fair growth in Latin America.[3]

Trade Agreements with Help for the Losers

Most Latin American governments have made progress in reducing policy biases that in past decades undermined agricultural growth, hurting the rural poor especially.[4] In the process, Latin American economies have generally become more export-oriented and open to competition from international trade. Meanwhile, however, the industrial countries, including the United States, continue to protect their own "sensitive" markets, especially in agriculture—a sector in which Latin America has comparative advantages and therefore has the potential to create more jobs for the poor and less educated.[5] Protection and subsidies are greatest (as a share of farm receipts) for nongrain crops such as sugar, fruits, and vegetables and for milk and meat products—all labor-intensive commodities in which Latin American countries could specialize more than they do if rich

---

3. Many of the proposals for what the United States can do are from Birdsall and Hakim (2007).

4. Forty percent of poor Latin Americans live in rural areas. Past policies penalized agriculture and other labor-intensive sectors in favor of heavy industry, thereby hurting the poor. Protectionism, price controls, and overvalued exchange rates, among other interventions, meant high effective taxes on agriculture, with resulting urban income gains more than offset by income losses in the generally poorer rural areas.

5. OECD countries spend about $100 billion a year in trade-distorting support to their own agricultural sectors, although farm producers and workers make up less than 5 percent of their labor force. When the gains of OECD farmers from the price-raising effect of tariff and tariff rate quotas are added to direct government support (in order to calculate the so-called total support estimate), the transfers to agriculture in high-income OECD countries are estimated to have amounted to US$337 billion a year in 2002–04. Actual government payouts—for example, subsidies and other trade-distorting payments as defined in Roodman (2005)—averaged about US$89 billion a year in 2002–04 (OECD 2005b). Agriculture in particular has been the sticking point between the developing and advanced economies in the Doha round—and it still is as this book goes to press in late 2007. On agriculture in the Doha round, see Elliott (2006). Estimates indicate that the OECD countries and the developing world would be US$120 billion better off from free trade in agriculture alone. Cline (2004) estimates that agricultural liberalization would generate developing country gains of about US$40 billion and industrial country gains of around US$80 billion. Industrial country protection in agriculture is far higher than protection of textiles and apparel, making agriculture the most important sector to liberalize.

country markets were more open.[6] In addition, the U.S. is protecting its corn-based ethanol producers who cannot compete with more energy efficient sugar-based ethanol producers in Brazil and elsewhere in the region. Indeed, given the region's agricultural assets, the potential is tremendous for production of biofuels, and thus of agriculture-based energy exports, to meet increasing global demand for nonfossil energy sources.

With the multilateral Doha trade round and the Free Trade for Americas Agreement stalled, bilateral and plurilateral free trade agreements have become the only recourse for Latin American governments that are eager to lock in better access to the U.S. market. Eleven such agreements had been signed as of late 2007 (three requiring congressional approval in the United States). They are spurring exports and investment and encouraging better economic management in the region. But according to even their strongest supporters, the terms of the agreements have been inflexible and tight-fisted, undermining rather than supporting inclusive growth. The United States, for instance, over the objections of every government in Latin America, continues to restrict exports of agricultural products, especially sugar, and to limit apparel exports through burdensome rules of origin.[7] At the same time, the United States resists any reduction in its support for its hugely subsidized grain products, which are displacing the corn and rice sold by Latin America's unsubsidized and unmechanized peasant producers.[8]

With a fair growth agenda, the United States would worry more explicitly about whether Latin America's poor and middle-income majority benefits (and by how much relative to the rich) from the trade agreements it negotiates.[9] A better U.S. trade policy would focus on increasing the

6. In the United States, estimates show that the support provided to sugar, as a percent of farm receipts, is higher than for any other major product. A small number of sugar cane and beet growers (less than one-half of 1 percent of all U.S. farms) benefit by as much as US$1 billion a year from the artificially high sugar prices maintained by the government through sharp restrictions on imports (Elliott 2005; General Accounting Office 2000).

7. Bhattacharya and Elliott (2005).

8. Papademetriou and others (2003).

9. Estimates of the actual impact of completely free trade on reducing poverty in the region are modest, from declines in the number of the poor by 2015 of between just 5 million and more than 15 million. The 5 to 15 million is relative to a base of 120 million poor, calculated by using the international poverty line of US$2 a day. The estimates of fewer people living in poverty take into account static and dynamic productivity effects (the 15 million includes also a dynamic induced-investment effect). See Andersen, Martin, and van der

number of winners and compensating and helping potential losers. For example, to increase the number of winners, agreements could include U.S. financing for the training of workers and technical assistance to small firms—a form of trade adjustment assistance to trading partners. Reducing the number of losers would require that the U.S. government stand down big agribusiness, pharmaceutical, and other interest groups that traditionally have hijacked trade negotiations, often disregarding the real long-term interests of even U.S. producers and consumers.[10]

The United States also could do more to explicitly ensure that its foreign aid programs reach small farmers in the region (who, without resources and technical inputs, have been losing out on trade opening) by using aid to compensate them for the competitive advantage U.S. farmers get from subsidies, tariffs, and other barriers. Aid programs also could support trading partners' efforts to increase agricultural productivity. In addition, trade-related aid programs could be extended to countries that have not yet signed bilateral trade agreements with the United States, as long as they show a commitment through their own expenditures to education, health, and other programs that help ensure that the benefits of more open trade markets reach their poor and middle-income majorities.

Helping Migration Help Those Left Behind

Migration from a relatively poor to a relatively rich country is without question the single best route out of poverty for the millions of people who face limited prospects in their home country. Opening its U.S. labor market to more people from Latin America (and other developing countries), especially poor and middle-income people with relatively limited skills, would be good not only for the additional immigrants themselves. It

---

Mensbrugghe (2006) and Cline (2004). Those estimates refer to completely free trade, including among the countries of the region, and not just to access to other markets, as envisioned in the current Doha round of multilateral negotiations. They are relatively modest estimates because of the fact that completely open trade would create losers as well as winners, in the absence of complementary domestic safety net, education, and other development programs and policies.

10. Though politically contentious, it can be done, as suggested by the recent agreement between the congressional leadership and the administration to loosen strong intellectual property protections if they impede policies to promote public health.

would trigger an increase in many benefits for those left behind, including remittances from relatives who have emigrated, greater incentives for families to invest in their children's education ("induced human capital"), and a greater likelihood of emigrant-financed local investments.[11] The potential for change at home through remittances from abroad is illustrative.

Remittances from low-income migrants in the United States are now Latin America's largest source of external capital. The $60 billion-plus in annual remittances is forty times the amount of U.S. aid in the region, and it is making a huge dent in rural and urban poverty.[12] Remittances improve the living conditions of poor families and help them reduce the risks that they face. And unlike foreign aid, remittances often go directly to families in places that are difficult to reach with development assistance.

The United States government could make it official policy to enhance the social impact of remittances. One step would be for the U.S. Treasury to use its bully pulpit to press the financial community to encourage U.S.-based senders and Latin America–based receivers to open bank accounts to facilitate the process.[13] The immediate payoff would be lower costs for

11. See Prichett (2006) and Kapur and McHale (2005) for discussion of these potential benefits and a broader investigation of international migration and labor mobility issues.

12. ECLAC-CELADE (2006); IOM (2005); World Bank (2005a); ECLAC (2006a). In some places (for example, Honduras, Nicaragua, and El Salvador) remittances more than double the incomes of the poorest 20 percent of the population, significantly increasing their purchasing power and standard of living (Inter-American Dialogue 2004). In many small countries, as many as half of those in receiving households would be living under the poverty line without that support. Remittances also are shown to improve income distribution in receiving households in Mexico, El Salvador, Ecuador (urban areas), Guatemala, Nicaragua, and the Dominican Republic. Acosta and others (2007) finds that the flow of remittances to Latin America tends to have an equalizing effect on income distribution in the home country because remittances are directed to a larger extent to households in the lower quintiles of the income distribution. Adams (2005) finds that households receiving remittances in Guatemala tend to spend more on investment goods such as education, health, and housing than do households receiving no remittances. See López-Córdova (2006) for evidence from Mexico. Edwards and Ureta (2003) finds that in El Salvador higher remittance income seems to help keep children in school longer than other types of income. And while capital flows fluctuate, remittances have increased even during recessions, providing a vital safety net for the region's poorest citizens. In addition to remittances, migrants also send donations collectively through hometown associations—organizations formed by immigrants abroad to raise funds to help the development of their hometowns (see Orozco 2006b). For a less rosy view on remittances, see López and Fajnzylber (2007).

13. In Mexico a commercial alliance between the National Savings and Financial Services Bank (BANSEFI) and dozens of savings and credit institutions—called L@Red de la Gente—provides remittance transfer services in low-income rural and urban areas not covered by the

sending remittances, putting more money in the hands of recipients. Bank accounts would open the way for new financial opportunities (direct deposit, free cash checking, credit) for Latin Americans, further expanding their ability to save, borrow, and invest.[14] The U.S. Treasury could also target its technical assistance in the region to help Latin American bank regulators and banks find ways to end the long-standing presumption that banking is only for the well-heeled.[15]

From a War against Drugs to a War against Poverty: Land and Jobs in Coca-Growing Regions

More than half of all U.S. "aid" to Latin America (about $750 million of $1.4 billion in 2006) supports Washington's antidrug campaign in the Andean region, predominantly in Colombia. The eradication of coca plants has long been the mainstay of that effort, but eradication by itself cannot produce lasting results; no matter how much of the coca crop is eliminated, small coca-growing farmers will return to coca cultivation when they cannot find other sources of employment. The failures of U.S. policy are most obvious in Bolivia, where the singular focus on coca eradication contributed to loss of employment and livelihoods and to growing resentment in rural areas, thereby helping in 2006 to elect President Evo Morales, whom voters saw as a champion of resistance to unjust U.S. programs.

In Colombia, the United States has finally begun to shift a share of its anti-drug support away from the single (and unrealistic) goal of coca eradication

---

financial system. The clients of L@Red de la Gente are encouraged to open regular bank accounts once their remittance has been paid. But such initiatives are the exceptions rather than the norm. Orozco (2006a).

14. In Latin America fewer than two of every ten people report having an account in a financial institution. Among remittance recipients, the share of bank accounts is larger. In El Salvador, 31 percent of recipients have bank accounts, while only 19 percent of the general population does (Orozco 2006a). López and Fajnzylber (2007) shows that at the microeconomic level, remittances increase access to deposit accounts, but that the use of credit by recipient households remains unchanged. Converting more remittance senders into bank account holders would further reduce transfer costs, with the added benefit of offering wider access to financial services (see Orozco 2006a).

15. Remittance-receiving countries also can help by removing legal and other barriers to competition, for example, by allowing a wider range of savings and credit institutions to provide money transfer services (Mexico has made progress in this area), and they can motivate banks through tax and other incentives to reach out to remittance senders and recipients, further enhancing links between remittances and financial services.

and toward development and job creation. But much more could be done, there and in Bolivia, including establishing comprehensive land distribution programs (see chapter 7) and encouraging rural enterprise development that targets indigenous and other landless peoples.

In Middle-Income Countries, Help Engage Poor Minorities

Most of Latin America's poor live in middle-income countries that no longer receive large infusions of foreign aid from any major donors. For example, the Millennium Challenge Account, an innovative U.S. foreign assistance program established by the Bush administration in 2004, serves no more than five or six of Latin America's smallest and poorest countries, which together account for less than 5 percent of the region's poverty-stricken families. In other countries, U.S. aid need not be massive; it just needs to be smart. In southern Mexico and northeast Brazil, for example, U.S. aid programs could concentrate on developing and supporting local innovations designed to reach and engage the poor, especially members of Afro-descendant and indigenous groups.[16]

Support Reform and Innovation in Hidebound School Systems

The dismal quality of education remains the Achilles' heel of economic and social development virtually everywhere in Latin America, despite significantly increased spending on schooling in the last two decades. In country after country, local and national governments are struggling with hidebound regulations, rigid educational bureaucracies, self-serving

16. Some of this already is being done. For example, the Inter-American Foundation, a small and little-known U.S. government program, provides small grants directly to the poor in nearly every Latin American country. Such programs generate knowledge about what works that local governments can then use to imitate and extend successful programs. Given the foundation's success over many years, the United States should scale up its funding and activities. Senator Robert Menendez has proposed legislation to establish a Latin America–wide social development fund that would pool resources from the countries of the region with those of the United States and Canada and the multilateral development agencies. For example, such a fund could be used to engage vulnerable populations in efforts to educate girls. See Lewis and Lockheed (2006) for evidence that girls in indigenous communities in Latin America are far less likely than boys in their communities and other girls to attend school. They find that nearly three-quarters of the 60 million girls not in school in developing countries belong to ethnic, religious, linguistic, racial, and other minorities. For case studies of girls' poor access to education in Guatemala, see Hallman and others (2007).

unions, and regressive expenditure patterns. U.S. funding for education is tiny compared with government spending. It should go to the champions of serious reform in the region to help catalyze the changes discussed in chapter 9. In addition, the United States could expand financing, and reduce barriers such as visas, for Latin American students and scientists seeking access to the country's university-based research and training.

Help Latin America Deal with its Wave of Crime and Violence

Crime is as devastating to the poor in Latin America as unemployment and discrimination. Latin America leads the world in kidnappings. Its homicide rate is twice the global average. Youth gangs have thrown several Central American countries into turmoil. Mexico is using its army to battle narcotics dealers and corrupt police. Brazil's two largest cities, São Paulo and Rio de Janeiro, have been terrorized by drug gangs. Everywhere, it is the poor that bear the brunt of Latin America's pervasive and escalating criminal violence, which is aggravated in many places by the corruption, disorganization, and inadequate financing of police forces and judicial systems.

The United States can best help Latin American countries stem the tide of crime by pushing the World Bank and the Inter-American Development Bank to work with countries on police reform. Signing on to the U.N. protocol on small arms trafficking would also help, at least by signaling serious concern. Finally, the United States could end its practice of deporting convicted felons to their country of origin, regardless of how long they have resided in the United States. Such deportees today are leading the vicious youth gangs that have become so destructive in parts of Latin America.[17]

A concluding note: The main front in the battle for equitable growth in Latin America must form inside each of the countries in the region. Outside measures can complement but not substitute for a fair growth agenda within the region. Today more than ever, the most important outcome of a robust U.S. strategy to support inclusive growth may not be what it accomplishes, but what it encourages those countries themselves to do.

17. United Nations (2007).

References

Acción Ciudadana. 2006. "Estudio sobre el Sistema Nacional de Integridad en Guatemala." Ciudad Guatemala: Acción Ciudadana.

Acevedo, Germán, Patricio Eskenazi, and Carmen Pagés. 2006. "Unemployment Insurance in Chile: A New Model of Income Support for Unemployed Workers." Social Protection Discussion Paper 0612. Washington: World Bank.

Acosta, Olga Lucia, and Richard M. Bird. 2003. "The Dilemma of Decentralization in Colombia." ITP Paper 0404. University of Toronto, Joseph L. Rotman School of Management.

Acosta, Pablo, and others. 2007. "What Is the Impact of International Remittances on Poverty and Inequality in Latin America?" Policy Research Working Paper 4249. Washington: World Bank.

Acquaye, Albert, and others. 2004. "Productivity and Innovation in the Latin American Agricultural Sector." Paper presented at the Tenth Annual World Bank Conference on Development in Latin America and the Caribbean. San José, Costa Rica, November 3.

Adams, Richard H. 2005. "Remittances, Household Expenditure, and Investment in Guatemala." Policy Research Working Paper 3532. Washington: World Bank.

Addis Botelho, Caren, and Lara Goldmark. 2000. "Paraguay Vouchers Revisited: Strategies for the Development of Training Markets." Paper presented at the conference "Business Services for Small Enterprises in Asia: Developing Markets and Measuring Performance." U.S. Agency for International Development. Hanoi, Vietnam, April 3–6.

Ades, Alberto, and Rafael Di Tella. 1997. "National Champions and Corruption: Some Unpleasant Interventionist Arithmetic." *Economic Journal* 107 no. 443: 1023–42.

———. 1999. "Rents, Competition, and Corruption." *American Economic Review* 89, no. 4: 982–93.

Agosin, Manuel R., and others. 2005. "Panorama Tributario de los Países Centroamericanos y Opciones de Reforma." In *Recaudar para Crecer: Bases para la Reforma Tributaria en Centroamérica,* edited by Manuel R. Agosin, Alberto Barreix, and Roberto Machado. Washington: Inter-American Development Bank.

Ahmad, Ehtisham, and Mercedes García-Escribano. 2006. "Fiscal Decentralization and Public Subnational Financial Management in Peru." Working Paper 06/120. Washington: International Monetary Fund.

Alesina, Alberto, Alberto Carrasquilla, and Juan José Echavarría Soto. 2002. "Descentralización en Colombia." In *Reformas Institucionales en Colombia,* edited by Alberto Alesina. Bogotá: Fedesarrollo and Alfaomega.

Alwang, Jeffrey, and others. 2004. "Drivers of Sustainable Rural Growth and Poverty Reduction in Central America: Guatemala Case Study." Paper presented at the Tenth Annual World Bank Conference on Development in Latin America and the Caribbean. San José, Costa Rica, November 3.

Anderson, James E., Daniel Kaufmann, and Francesca Recanatini. 2004. "Service Delivery, Poverty, and Corruption: Common Threads from Diagnostic Surveys." Background paper for the 2004 World Development Report, *Making Services Work for Poor People.* Washington: World Bank.

Anderson, Kym, Will Martin, and Dominique van der Mensbrugghe. 2006. "Global Impacts of the Doha Scenarios on Poverty." In *Poverty and the WTO: Impacts of the Doha Development Agenda,* edited by Thomas W. Herter and L. Alan Winters. World Bank and Palgrave Macmillan.

Andres, Luis, Vivien Foster, and J. Luis Guasch. 2006. "The Impact of Privatization on the Performance of the Infrastructure Sector: The Case of Electricity Distribution in Latin American Countries." Policy Research Working Paper 3936. Washington: World Bank.

Angelelli, Pablo, Rebecca Moudry, and Juan José Llisterri. 2006. "Institutional Capacities for Small Business Policy Development in Latin America and the Caribbean." Sustainable Development Department Technical Paper Series MSM-136. Washington: Inter-American Development Bank.

Angelelli, Pablo, and Alejandro Solís. 2002. "Políticas de Apoyo a la Pequeña Empresa en 13 Países de América Latina." Informe de Trabajo. Washington: Inter-American Development Bank, Sustainable Development Department, Micro, Small and Medium Enterprise Unit.

Anzalone, Stephen, and Andrea Bosch. 2005. "Improving Educational Quality with Interactive Radio Instruction: A Toolkit for Policymakers and Planners." Working Paper Series 52, Africa Region Human Development. Washington: World Bank.

Arcia, Gustavo, and Humberto Belli. 2002. "La Autonomía Escolar en Nicaragua: Restableciendo el Contrato Social." Documento 21. Washington and Santiago, Chile: Partnership for Educational Reform in the Americas (PREAL).

Arenas de Mesa, Alberto. 2005. "Fiscal and Institutional Considerations of Pension Reform: Lessons Learned from Chile." In *A Quarter Century of Pension Reform in Latin America and the Caribbean: Lessons Learned and Next Steps,* edited by Carolin A. Crabbe. Washington: Inter-American Development Bank.

Arenas de Mesa, Alberto, and others. 2007. "The Chilean Pension Reform Turns 25: Lessons from the Social Protection Survey." In *Lessons from Pension Reform in the Americas,* edited by Stephen J. Kay and Tapen Sinha. Oxford University Press.

Arias, Omar, Gustavo Yamada, and Luis R. Tejerina. 2004. "Education, Family Background, and Racial Earnings Inequality in Brazil." *International Journal of Manpower* 25, no. 3–4: 355–74.

Artana, Daniel, Ricardo López Murphy, and Fernando Navajas. 2003. "A Fiscal Policy Agenda." In *After the Washington Consensus: Restarting Growth and Reform in Latin America,* edited by Pedro-Pablo Kuczynski and John Williams. Washington: Institute for International Economics.

Asian Development Bank, Japan Bank for International Cooperation, and World Bank (ADB/ JBIC/WB). 2005. "Connecting East Asia: A New Framework for Infrastructure." Manila, Tokyo, and Washington.

Association of Brazilian Magisterials/Associação dos Magistrados Brasileiros (AMB). 2007. *Juízes Contra a Corrupção: Diagnóstico do Problema da Impunidade e Possíveis Soluções Propostas pela AMB.* Brasília, Brazil: AMB.

Attanasio, Orazio P., and Miguel Székely. 2001. "Going beyond Income: Redefining Poverty in Latin America." In *A Portrait of the Poor: An Asset-Based Approach,* edited by Orazio Attanasio and Miguel Székely. Johns Hopkins University Press.

Attanasio, Orazio P., and Marcos Vera-Hernández. 2004. "Medium- and Long-Run Effects of Nutrition and Child Care: Evaluation of a Community Nursery Programme in Rural Colombia." Working Paper EWP04/06. London: Institute for Fiscal Studies, Centre for the Evaluation of Development Policies.

Ayala, Ulpiano, and Jaime Millán. 2002. "Sustainability of Power Sector Reform in Latin America: The Reform in Colombia." Working Paper. Washington: Inter-American Development Bank.

Baca-Campodónico, Jorge, Luiz de Mello, and Andrei Kirilenko. 2006. "The Rates and Revenue of Bank Transaction Taxes." Economics Department Working Paper 494. Geneva: Organization for Economic Co-Operation and Development.

Baer, Katherine. 2006. "La Administración Tributaria en América Latina: Algunas Tendencias y Desafíos." In *Tributación en América Latina: En Busca de Una Nueva Agenda de Reformas,* edited by Oscar Cetrángolo and Juan Carlos Gómez Sabaini. Santiago, Chile: United Nations, Economic Commission for Latin America and the Caribbean (ECLAC).

Bakker, Marie, Leora Klapper, and Gregory Udell. 2004. "Financing Small and Medium-Size Enterprises with Factoring: Global Growth in Factoring and Its Potential in Eastern Europe." Policy Research Working Paper 3342. Washington: World Bank.

Balassone, Fabrizio, and Manmohan S. Kumar. 2007 (forthcoming). "Addressing the Procyclical Bias." In *Promoting Fiscal Discipline.* Washington: International Monetary Fund.

Banisar, David. 2006. *Freedom of Information around the World 2006: A Global Survey of Access to Government Information Laws.* London: Privacy International.

Barbosa, Maria Ligia. 2004. "Diferencias de Género y Color en las Escuelas de Brasil: Los Maestros y la Evaluación de los Alumnos." In *Etnicidad, Raza, Género, y Educación en América Latina,* edited by Donald R. Winkler and Santiago Cueto. Washington and Santiago, Chile: Partnership for Educational Revitalization in the Americas (PREAL).

Barja, Gover, David McKenzie, and Miguel Urquiola. 2005. "Bolivian Capitalization and Privatization: Approximation to an Evaluation." In *Reality Check: The Distributional Impact of Privatization in Developing Countries,* edited by Nancy Birdsall and John Nellis. Washington: Center for Global Development.

Barja, Gover, and Miguel Urquiola. 2001: "Capitalization, Regulation, and the Poor: Access to Basic Services in Bolivia." WIDER Discussion Paper 2001/34. United Nations University.

Barrera-Osorio, Felipe, and Mauricio Olivera. 2007. "Does Society Win or Lose as a Result of Privatization? Provision of Public Services and Welfare of the Poor: The

Case of Water Sector Privatization in Colombia." Research Network Working Paper R-525. Washington: Inter-American Development Bank.

Barro, Robert J. 1990. "Government Spending in a Simple Model of Endogenous Growth." *Journal of Political Economy* 98, no. 5: S103–S125.

———. 2000. "Inequality and Growth in a Panel of Countries." *Journal of Economic Growth* 5, no. 1: 5–32.

———. 2001. "Human Capital and Growth." *American Economic Review* 91, no. 2: 12–17.

Barro, Robert J., and Jong-Wha Lee. 2000. "International Data on Educational Attainment: Updates and Implications." CID Working Paper 42, appendix data tables. Harvard University, Center for International Development (CID).

Batra, Geeta, Daniel Kaufmann, and Andrew H. W. Stone. 2003. *Investment Climate around the World: Voices of the Firms from the World Business Environment Survey*. Washington: World Bank.

Beath, Andrew. 2006. "The Investment Climate in Brazil, India, and South Africa: A Contribution to the IBSA Debate." Working Paper. Washington: World Bank.

Bebczuk, Ricardo. 2004. "What Determines the Access to Credit by SMEs in Argentina?" Documento de Trabajo 48. La Plata, Argentina: Universidad Nacional de La Plata, Facultad de Ciencias Económicas, Departamento de Economía.

———. 2007. "Access to Credit in Argentina." Serie Financiamiento del Desarrollo 188. Santiago, Chile: United Nations, Economic Commission for Latin America and the Caribbean (ECLAC).

Beck, Thorsten, and Augusto de la Torre. 2007. "The Basic Analytics of Access to Financial Services." *Financial Markets, Institutions and Instruments* 16, no. 2: 79–117.

Beck, Thorsten, Asli Demirgüç-Kunt, and Vojislav Maksimovic. 2003. "Bank Competition, Financing Obstacles, and Access to Credit." Policy Research Working Paper 2996. Washington: World Bank.

———. 2005. "Financial and Legal Constraints to Firm Growth: Does Firm Size Matter?" *Journal of Finance* 60, no. 1: 137–77.

Beck, Thorsten, and Ross Levine. 2005. "Legal Institutions and Financial Development." In *Handbook of New Institutional Economics,* edited by Claude Ménard and Mary M. Shirley. Dordrecht, Netherlands: Springer.

Behrman, Jere R., Nancy Birdsall, and Gunilla Pettersson. 2008 (forthcoming). "Inequality Has Slowed Reform in Latin America." In *Helping Reforms Deliver Growth in Latin America,* edited by Liliana Rojas-Suarez and Simon Johnson. Washington: Center for Global Development.

Behrman, Jere R., Nancy Birdsall, and Miguel Székely. 2001. "Pobreza, Desigualdad, y Liberalización Comercial y Financiera en América Latina." In *Liberalización, Desigualdad, y Pobreza: América Latina y el Caribe en los 90s,* edited by Enrique Ganuza and others. Buenos Aires: Editorial Universitaria de Buenos Aires and United Nations Development Program.

———. 2003. "Economic Policy and Wage Differentials in Latin America." Working Paper 29. Washington: Center for Global Development.

Behrman, Jere R., Susan W. Parker, and Petra E. Todd. 2007. "Do School Subsidy Programs Generate Lasting Benefits? A Five-Year Follow-Up of Oportunidades Participants." Working Paper. University of Pennsylvania.

Behrman, Jere R., and Emmanuel Skoufias. 2006. "Mitigating Myths about Policy Effectiveness: Evaluation of Mexico's Antipoverty and Human Resource Investment Program." *Annals of the American Academy of Political and Social Science* 606, no.1: 244–75.

Behrman, Jere R., and others. 2006. "The Impact of an Experimental Nutritional Intervention in Childhood on Education among Guatemalan Adults." FCND Discussion Paper 207. Washington: International Food Policy Research Institute, Food Consumption and Nutrition Division.

Bellver, Ana, and Daniel Kaufmann. 2005. "Transparenting Transparency: Initial Empirics and Policy Applications." Preliminary draft, September. Washington: World Bank Institute.

Berdegué, Julio A., and others. 2005. "Central American Supermarkets' Private Standards of Quality and Safety in Procurement of Fresh Fruits and Vegetables." *Food Policy* 30, no. 3: 254–69.

Berger, Allen N., and W. Scott Frame. 2007. "Small Business Credit Scoring and Credit Availability." *Journal of Small Business Management* 45, no.1: 5–22.

Berger, Marguerite. 2006. "The Latin American Model of Microfinance." In *An Inside View of Latin American Microfinance*, edited by Marguerite Berger, Lara Goldmark and Tomás Miller-Sanabria. Washington: Inter-American Development Bank, Multilateral Investment Fund.

Bernasconi, Andrés, and Claudio de Moura Castro. 2005. "Los Institutos Técnicos Superiores Norteamericanos y América Latina: Clonación, Inspiración, o Rechazo?" In *Modernización de la Educación Técnica Post-Secundaria: Opciones y Desafíos para América Latina y El Caribe,* edited by Viola Espínola and Norma García. Washington: Inter-American Development Bank.

Bernasconi, Andrés, and Fernando Rojas. 2004. "Informe sobre la Educación Superior en Chile: 1980–2003." Santiago, Chile: Editorial Universitaria.

Berstein, Solange, Guillermo Larraín, and Francisco Pino. 2006. "Chilean Pension Reform: Coverage Facts and Policy Alternatives." *Economía* 6, no. 2: 227–79.

Bertola, Giuseppe. 1990. "Job Security, Employment, and Wages." *European Economic Review* 34, no. 4: 851–79.

Besley, Timothy, and Robin Burgess. 2004. "Can Labor Regulation Hinder Economic Performance? Evidence from India." *Quarterly Journal of Economics* 119, no. 1: 91–134.

Bhattacharya, Debapriya, and Kimberly Elliott. 2005. "Adjusting to the MFA Phase-Out: Policy Priorities." Policy Brief. Washington: Center for Global Development.

Bird, Robert. 2003. "Taxation in Latin America: Reflections on Sustainability and the Balance between Equity and Efficiency." ITP Paper 0306. Toronto, Canada: Joseph L. Rotman School of Management, International Tax Program.

Birdsall, Nancy. 2001. "Why Inequality Matters: Some Economic Issues." *Ethics and International Affairs* 15, no. 2: 3–28.

———. 2002. "From Social Policy to an Open Economy Social Contract in Latin America." Working Paper 21. Washington: Center for Global Development (www.cgdev.org/content/publications/detail/2769 [May 2006]).

———. 2007. "The World Is Not Flat: Inequality and Injustice in our Global Economy." In *Advancing Development: Core Themes in Global Economics,* edited by George Mavrotas and Anthony Shorrocks. London: Palgrave Macmillan.

Birdsall, Nancy, and Augusto de la Torre with Rachel Menezes. 2001. *Washington Contentious: Economic Policies for Social Equity in Latin America.* Washington: Carnegie Endowment for International Peace and Inter-American Dialogue (www.cgdev.org/content/publications/detail/2923/ [May 2006]).

Birdsall, Nancy, Carol Graham, and Stefano Pettinato. 2000. "Stuck in the Tunnel: Have New Markets Muddled the Middle Class?" Center on Social and Economic Dynamics Working Paper 14. Washington: Carnegie Endowment for International Peace.

Birdsall, Nancy, Carol Graham, and Richard Sabot, eds. 1998. *Beyond Trade-Offs: Market Reforms and Equitable Growth in Latin America.* Brookings and Inter-American Development Bank.

Birdsall, Nancy, and Peter Hakim. 2007. "Poverty and Inequality in Latin America: How the U.S. Can Really Help." Policy Brief. Washington: Center for Global Development.

Birdsall, Nancy, and Juan Luis Londoño. 1997. "Asset Inequality Matters: An Assessment of the World Bank's Approach to Poverty Reduction." *American Economic Review* 87, no. 2: 32–37.

Birdsall, Nancy, and Rachel Menezes. 2005. "Toward a New Social Contract in Latin America." Policy Brief. Washington: Center for Global Development and Inter-American Dialogue.

Birdsall, Nancy, and John Nellis. 2003. "Winners and Losers: Assessing the Distributional Impact of Privatization." *World Development* 31, no. 10: 1617–33.

Birdsall, Nancy, and Miguel Székely. 2003. "Bootstraps, not Band-Aids: Poverty, Equity, and Social Policy." In *After the Washington Consensus: Restarting Growth and Reform in Latin America,* edited by John Williamson and Pedro-Pablo Kuczynski. Washington: Institute for International Economics.

Blanchard, Olivier, and Justin Wolfers. 1999. "The Role of Shocks and Institutions in the Rise of European Unemployment: The Aggregate Evidence." Working Paper 7282. Cambridge, Mass.: National Bureau of Economic Research.

Blanco, Eglé Iturbe. 2007. "Participación de la Mujer en los Gabinetes Latinoamericanos." In "Mujer y Política en América Latina," *Boletín Electrónico Prolead*, segunda edición. Washington: Inter-American Development Bank, Gender Equality in Development Unit, Program for the Support of Women's Leadership and Representation (Prolead).

Blanco, Federico, and Cristina A. Valdivia. 2006. "Child Labour in Venezuela: Children's Vulnerability to Macroeconomic Shocks." UCW Working Paper. Understanding Children's Work (UCW) Project. Rome: International Labor Organization, United Nations Children's Fund–UNICEF, and World Bank.

Blázquez-Lidoy, Jorge, Javier Rodríguez, and Javier Santiso. 2006. "Ángel o Demonio? Los Efectos del Comercio Chino en Los Países de América Latina." *Revista de la CEPAL* 90: 17–43.

Blom, Andreas, and Carlos Eduardo Vélez. 2004. "The Dynamics of the Skill-Premium in Brazil: Growing Demand and Insufficient Supply?" In *Inequality and Economic Development in Brazil.* World Bank Country Study. Washington: World Bank.

Borensztein, Eduardo, and Paolo Mauro. 2004. "The Case for GDP-Indexed Bonds." *Economic Policy* 19, no. 38: 165–216.

Botero, Juan, and others. 2003. "The Regulation of Labor." Working Paper 9756. Cambridge, Mass.: National Bureau of Economic Research.

Bott, Sarah, Mary Ellsberg, and Andrew Morrison. 2004. "Addressing Gender-Based Violence in the Latin American and Caribbean Region: A Critical Review of Interventions." Policy Research Working Paper 3438. Washington: World Bank.

———. 2005. "Preventing and Responding to Gender-Based Violence in Middle- and Low-Income Countries: A Global Review and Analysis." Policy Research Working Paper 3618. Washington: World Bank.

Boucher, Stephen, Bradford Barham, and Michael Carter. 2005. "The Impact of Market Friendly Reforms on the Operation of Credit and Land Markets in Honduras and Nicaragua." *World Development* 33, no. 1: 107–28.

———. 2007. "When Land Titles Are Not the Constraint: Complementary Financial Policies to Enhance Agricultural Productivity." Working Paper. University of Wisconsin, Madison, Agricultural and Applied Economics.

Bouillon, César Patricio, and Luis Tejerina. 2006. "Do We Know What Works? A Systematic Review of Impact Evaluations of Social Programs in Latin America and the Caribbean." Draft Working Paper, September 15. Washington: Inter-American Development Bank, Sustainable Development Department.

Bourguignon, François, Francisco Ferreira, and Phillippe Leite. 2003. "Conditional Cash Transfers, Schooling, and Child Labor: Micro-Simulating Brazil's Bolsa Escola Program." *World Bank Economic Review* 17, no. 2: 229–54.

Brasil, Ministério do Desenvolvimento Social (Brasil-MDS). 2007. "Sistema de Informações da SENARC." Online database. Brasília: Ministério do Desenvolvimento Social, Secretaria Nacional de Renda e Cidadania (SENARC) (www.mds.gov.br/adesao/mib/matrizsrch.asp [June 2007]).

Brasil, Ministério do Planejamento, Orçamento, e Gestão (Brasil-MP). 2007. "Orçamentos da União - Exercício Financeiro de 2007: Lei No. 11.451, de 07 de fevereiro de 2007." Brasília: Ministério do Planejamento, Orçamento e Gestão, Secretaria de Orçamento Federal.

Braun, Miguel, and Luciano di Gresia. 2003. "Towards Effective Social Insurance in Latin America: The Importance of Countercyclical Fiscal Policy." Working Paper 487. Washington: Inter-American Development Bank.

Bravo, David, and Dante Contreras. 2000. "The Impact of Financial Incentives to Training Providers: The Case of Chile Joven." Paper presented at the Thirteenth Annual Inter-American Seminar on Economics: Micro-Data Research in Latin America, organized by the National Bureau of Economic Research. Santo Domingo, Costa Rica, November 16–17.

Bravo-Ortega, Claudio, and Daniel Lederman. 2004. "Agricultural Productivity and Its Determinants." Background paper prepared for the Tenth Annual World Bank Conference on Development in Latin America and the Caribbean. San José, Costa Rica, November 3, 2004.

Briceno-Garmendia, Cecilia, Antonio Estache, and Nemat Shafik. 2004. "Infrastructure Services in Developing Countries: Access, Quality, Costs, and Policy Reform." World Bank Policy Research Paper 3468. Washington: World Bank.

Brunetti, Aymo, and Beatrice Weder. 2003. "A Free Press Is Bad News for Corruption." *Journal of Public Economics* 87, no. 7: 1801–24.

Brunner, José J., and others. 2006. "Thematic Review of Tertiary Education: Mexico." Country Note. Paris: Organization for Economic Co-operation and Development (OECD).

Buscaglia, Edgardo. 2001. "An Analysis of Judicial Corruption and Its Causes: An Objective Governing-Based Approach." *International Review of Law and Economics* 21, no. 2: 233–49.

Busso, Matías, Martín Cicowiez, and Leonardo Gasparini. 2005. *Ethnicity and the Millennium Goals*. Bogotá: United Nations Development Program (UNDP).

Buvinic, Mayra, and Jacqueline Mazza. 2005. "Gender and Social Inclusion: Social Policy Perspective from Latin America and the Caribbean." Presented at the World Bank Conference "New Frontiers of Social Policy: Development in a Globalizing World." Arusha, Tanzania, December 12–15.

Buvinic, Mayra, and Vivian Roza. 2004. "Women, Politics, and Democratic Prospects in Latin America." Technical Papers Series WID-108. Washington: Inter-American Development Bank, Sustainable Development Department.

Caballero, Jose Maria, and others. 2007. "Rural Competitiveness and Poverty Reduction: A Contribution to the Construction of the Internal Agenda for Agriculture and the Rural Economy in Colombia." In *Colombia 2006-2010: A Window of Opportunity*. Bogotá, Colombia: World Bank

Caballero, Ricardo J., and others. 2004. "Effective Labor Regulation and Microeconomic Flexibility." Working Paper 10744. Cambridge, Mass.: National Bureau of Economic Research.

Caccia Bava, Silvio, and others. 1998. *Programas de Renda Mínima no Brasil: Impactos e Potencialidades*. Revista Pólis. São Paulo: Instituto de Estudos, Formação, e Assessoria em Políticas Sociais (Pólis).

Calderón, César, and Luis Servén. 2004a. "The Effects of Infrastructure Development on Growth and Income Distribution." Working Paper Series 3400. Washington: World Bank.

———. 2004b. "Trends in Infrastructure in Latin America, 1980–2001." Working Paper Series 3401. Washington: World Bank.

Calderón, César, William Easterly, and Luis Servén. 2003a. "Latin America's Infrastructure in the Era of Macroeconomic Crises." In *The Limits of Stabilization: Infrastructure, Public Deficits, and Growth in Latin America*, edited by William Easterly and Luis Servén. Stanford University Press and World Bank.

———. 2003b. "Infrastructure Compression and Public Sector Solvency in Latin America." In *The Limits of Stabilization: Infrastructure, Public Deficits, and Growth in Latin America*, edited by William Easterly and Luis Servén. Stanford University Press and World Bank.

Calvo, Guillermo A. 2005. "Crises in Emerging Market Economies: A Global Perspective." Working Paper 11305. Cambridge, Mass.: National Bureau of Economic Research.

Calvo, Guillermo A., and Carmen M. Reinhart. 2002. "Fear of Floating." *Quarterly Journal of Economics* 107, no. 2: 379–408.

Capaul, Mierta. 2003. "Corporate Governance in Latin America." Background paper for the LAC regional study "Whither Latin American Capital Markets?" Washington: World Bank, Latin America and the Caribbean Region, Office of the Chief Economist.

Carbonell, Miguel. 2007. "Judicial Corruption and Impunity in Mexico." In Transparency International, *Global Corruption Report 2007: Corruption in Judicial Systems*. Cambridge University Press.

Cardoso, Eliana, and André Portela Souza. 2004. "The Impact of Cash Transfers on Child Labor and School Attendance in Brazil." Paper 04-W07. Vanderbilt University, Department of Economics.

Carneiro, Pedro, and James J. Heckman. 2003. "Human Capital Policy." Working Paper 9495. Cambridge, Mass.: National Bureau of Economic Research.

Carstens, Agustín, and Luis I. Jácome H. 2005. "Latin American Central Bank Reform: Progress and Challenges." Working Paper 05/114. Washington: International Monetary Fund.

Carter, Michael R. 2002. "Land and Other Factor Markets in Latin America." Moderator Comments for the World Bank Regional Workshop on Land Issues in Latin American and the Caribbean. Preliminary draft. Hidalgo, Mexico, May 19–22, 2002.

Carter, Michael, and Pedro Olinto. 1998. "Do the 'Poor but Efficient' Survive in the Land Market? Capital Access and Land Accumulation in Paraguay." Paper prepared for the XXI International Congress of the Latin American Studies Association. Chicago, September 24–26, 1998.

Castañeda, Tarcisio, and others. 2005. "Designing and Implementing Household Targeting Systems: Lessons from Latin America and the United States." Social Protection Discussion Paper 0526. Washington: World Bank.

Castilla, Samuel R., and Leonardo N. Olivares. 2006. "Peru." Country report in Transparency International, *Global Corruption Report 2006: Corruption and Health*. London and Ann Arbor, Mich.: Pluto Press.

Castro Forero, Mauricio. 2007. "Avances de la Política de Reducción de Trámites: Trámites Empresariales." Presentation at the II Foro de la Microempresa, "Como Enfrentar los Nuevos Desafíos." Corporación para el Desarrollo de las Microempresas. Barranquilla, Colombia, February 7–9.

Center for Global Development. 2005. "The Hardest Job in the World: Five Crucial Tasks for the New President of the World Bank." Center for Global Development Working Group, Nancy Birdsall and Devesh Kapur, co-chairs. Washington (www.cgdev.org/content/publications/detail/2868 [January 2006]).

———. 2006. "A New Era at the Inter-American Development Bank: Six Recommendations for the New President." Center for Global Development and Latin American Shadow Financial Regulatory Committee (www.cgdev.org/content/article/detail/5825/ [January 2006]).

———. 2007. "Does the IMF Constrain Health Spending in Poor Countries? Evidence and an Agenda for Action." Report of the CGD Working Group on IMF Programs and Health Spending.Washington.

Centro de Estudios de Justicia de las Américas (CEJA). 2007. *Reporte sobre el Estado de la Justicia en las Américas 2006–2007*. Santiago, Chile: CEJA

Cerdán-Infantes, Pedro, and Andreas Blom. 2007. "Colombia: Assisting Talented Students from Low-Income Families Attend Tertiary Education." *En Breve* 100 (January).

Chamon, Marcos, and Paolo Mauro. 2006. "Pricing Growth-Indexed Bonds." *Journal of Banking and Finance* 30, no. 12: 3349–66.

Chile Emprende. 2005. "La Situación de la Micro y Pequeña Empresa en Chile." Santiago, Chile: Gobierno de Chile, Chile Emprende and Servicios de Cooperación Tecnológica para Empresas de Menor Tamaño (Sercotec).

Chong, Alberto, and Florencio López-de-Silanes. 2003. "The Truth about Privatization in Latin America." Research Network Working Paper R-486. Washington: Inter-American Development Bank.

———. 2005. *Privatization in Latin America: Myths and Reality.* Inter-American Development Bank and Stanford University Press.

Christen, Robert P., and Jared Miller. 2006. "Future Challenges in Latin American Microfinance." In *An Inside View of Latin American Microfinance*, edited by Marguerite Berger, Lara Goldmark, and Tomás Miller-Sanabria. Washington: Inter-American Development Bank, Multilateral Investment Fund.

Clark, Ximena, David Dollar, and Alejandro Micco. 2004. "Port Efficiency, Maritime Transport Costs, and Bilateral Trade." *Journal of Development Economics* 75, no. 2: 417–50.

Clarke, George R. and others. 2005. "Bank Lending to Small Businesses in Latin America: Does Bank Origin Matter?" *Journal of Money, Credit, and Banking* 37, no.1: 83–118.

Clarke, George R., Robert Cull, and María S. Martínez Pería. 2001. "Does Foreign Bank Penetration Reduce Access to Credit in Developing Countries? Evidence from Asking Borrowers." Working Paper 2716. Washington: World Bank.

Clements, Benedict, Christopher Faircloth, and Marijn Verhoeven. 2007. "Public Expenditure in Latin America: Trends and Key Policy Issues." Working Paper 07/21. Washington: International Monetary Fund.

Cline, William. 2002. "Financial Crises and Poverty in Emerging Market Economies." Working Paper 8. Washington: Center for Global Development.

———. 2004. *Trade Policy and Global Poverty.* Washington: Center for Global Development and Institute for International Economics.

Coady, David, Margaret Grosh, and John Hoddinott. 2004. *Targeting of Transfers in Developing Countries: Review of Lessons and Experience.* Washington: World Bank and the International Food Policy Research Institute.

Cohen, Ernesto, and Rolando Franco. 2006. "Los Programas de Transferencias con Corresponsabilidad en América Latina: Similitudes y Diferencias." In *Transferencias con Corresponsabilidad: Una Mirada Latinoamericana,* edited by Ernesto Cohen and Rolando Franco. Mexico City: FLACSO-México and Secretaría de Desarrollo Social (SEDESOL).

Cohen, Ernesto, Rolando Franco, and Pablo Villatoro. 2006. "México: El Programa de Desarrollo Humano Oportunidades." In *Transferencias con Corresponsabilidad: Una Mirada Latinoamericana,* edited by Ernesto Cohen and Rolando Franco. Mexico City: FLACSO-México and Secretaría de Desarrollo Social (SEDESOL).

Conning, Jonathan, and Michael Kevane. 2002. "Community-Based Targeting Mechanisms for Social Safety Nets: A Critical Review." *World Development* 30, no. 3: 375–94.

Consejo Impulsor del Sistema Nacional de Integridad (CISNI). 2006. "Patrones de Comportamiento y Desempeño Institucional, Gobernabilidad, y Corrupción en el Sector Público en Paraguay, 2005: Resumen Ejecutivo." Washington: World Bank Institute.

Constance, Paul. 2002. "Just Don't Call It Downsizing." *IDBAmérica* (March 2002). Washington: Inter-American Development Bank.

Cont, Walter. 2006. "Evasión del Impuesto al Valor Agregado en Argentina en el Año 2004." In *Presión Tributaria sobre el Sector Formal de la Economía*. Buenos Aires: Fundación de Investigaciones Económicas Latinoamericanas (FIEL).

Cont, Walter, and Nuria Susmel. 2006. "Evasión Impositiva en Impuestos Directos Personales: Ganancias de las Personas y Seguridad Social." In *Presión Tributaria sobre el Sector Formal de la Economía*. Buenos Aires: Fundación de Investigaciones Económicas Latinoamericanas (FIEL).

Corbacho, Ana, and Gerd Schwartz. 2007 (forthcoming). "Fiscal Responsibility Laws." In *Promoting Fiscal Discipline over the Business Cycle*. Washington: International Monetary Fund.

Cornejo Azzarri, Rafael A., Mauricio Mesquita, and Matthew Shearer. 2006. "Integration and Trade in the Americas: A Preliminary Estimate of 2006 Trade." Periodic Note, November 30. Washington: Inter-American Development Bank, Integration and Regional Programs Department.

Corrales, Javier. 1999. "The Politics of Education Reform: Bolstering the Supply and Demand; Overcoming Institutional Blocks." Education Reform and Management Series, vol. 2, no.1. Washington: World Bank.

———. 2006. "Political Obstacles to Expanding and Improving Schooling in Developing Countries." In *Global Educational Expansion: Historical Legacies and Political Obstacles*, edited by Aaron Benavot, Julia Resnik, and Javier Corrales. Cambridge, Mass.: Academy of Arts and Sciences.

Council of Economic Advisers. 2004. "Growth-Indexed Bonds: A Primer." White Paper. Washington.

Cruz, Carlos, Rodolfo de la Torre, and César Velázquez. 2006. *Evaluación Externa de Impacto del Programa Oportunidades 200–2006: Informe Compilatorio*. Cuernavaca, México: Instituto Nacional de Salud Pública.

Cueva, Simón. 2007. "La Transparencia del Presupuesto del Estado Ecuatoriano." Temas de Economía y Política. Quito: Corporación de Estudios para el Desarrollo (Cordes).

Cuevas, Alfredo. 2003. "Reforming Intergovernmental Fiscal Relations in Argentina." Working Paper 03/90. Washington: International Monetary Fund.

Curi, Andréa Z., and Naércio A. Menezes-Filho. 2006. "Os Efeitos da Pré-Escola sobre os Salários, a Escolaridade, e a Proficiência Escolar." Anais do XXXIV Encontro Nacional de Economia Series 92. São Paulo: Associação Nacional dos Centros de Pósgraduação em Economia (ANPEC).

Damiani, Octavio. 2007. "Rural Development from a Territorial Perspective: Case Studies in Asia and Latin America." Working Paper RUR-07-01. Washington: Inter-American Development Bank, Sustainable Development Department, Rural Development Unit.

De Ferranti, David, and others. 2000. *Securing Our Future in a Global Economy*. Washington: World Bank.

———. 2003. *Closing the Gap in Education and Technology*. Washington: World Bank.

———. 2004. *Inequality in Latin America: Breaking with History?* Washington: World Bank.

———. 2005. *Beyond the City: The Rural Contribution to Development*. Washington: World Bank.

Deininger, Klaus. 2003. *Land Policies for Growth and Poverty Reduction.* World Bank and Oxford University Press.

———. 2005. "Land Policy Reforms." In *Analyzing the Distributional Impact of Reforms: A Practitioner's Guide to Trade, Monetary and Exchange Rate Policy, Utility Provision, Agricultural Markets, Land Policy, and Education,* edited by Aline Coudouel and Stefano Paternostro. Washington: World Bank.

Deininger, Klaus, Raffaella Castagnini, and María A. González. 2004. "Land Reform and Land Markets in Colombia: Impacts on Equity and Efficiency." Policy Research Working Paper 3258. Washington: World Bank.

Deininger, Klaus, and Juan Sebastian Chamorro. 2002. "Investment and Income Effects of Land Regularization: The Case of Nicaragua." Policy Research Working Paper 2752. Washington: World Bank.

Deininger, Klaus, and Pedro Olinto. 2000. "Asset Distribution, Inequality, and Growth." Policy Research Working Paper 2375. Washington: World Bank.

De Janvry, Alain, Frederico Finan, and Elizabeth Sadoulet. 2006. "Evaluating Brazil's Bolsa Escola Program: Impact on Schooling and Municipal Roles." Working Paper. University of California, Berkeley.

De Janvry, Alain, and Elisabeth Sadoulet. 2004. "Toward a Territorial Approach to Rural Development." Paper prepared for the World Bank Forum "Harvesting Opportunities: Rural Development in the 21st Century." San José, Costa Rica, October 19–21, 2004.

———. 2005. "Conditional Cash Transfer Programs for Child Human Capital Development: Lessons Derived from Experience in Mexico and Brazil." Paper presented at the GRADE 25th anniversary conference, "Investigación, Politicas, y Desarrollo." Grupo de Análisis para el Desarrollo/Group for the Analysis of Development (GRADE). Lima, Peru, November 15–17.

———. 2006. "Making Conditional Cash Transfer Programs More Efficient: Designing for Maximum Effect of the Conditionality." *World Bank Economic Review* 20, no. 1: 1–29.

De Janvry, Alain, and others. 2005. "Brazil's Bolsa Escola Program: The Role of Local Governance in Decentralized Implementation." Social Protection Discussion Paper 0542, Social Safety Nets Primer Series. Washington: World Bank.

De Janvry, Alain, and others. 2006. "Can Conditional Cash Transfer Programs Serve as Safety Nets in Keeping Children at School and from Working When Exposed to Shocks?" *Journal of Development Economics* 79, no. 2: 349–73.

De la Brière, Bénédicte, and Laura B. Rawlings. 2006. "Examining Conditional Cash Transfer Programs: A Role for Increased Social Inclusion?" Social Protection Discussion Paper 0603, Social Safety Net Primer Series. Washington: World Bank.

De la Croix, David, and Clara Delavallade. 2007. "Growth, Public Investment and Corruption with Failing Institutions." Working Paper 61. Palma de Mallorca, Spain: Society for the Study of Economic Inequality (ECINEQ).

De la Torre, Augusto. 2002. "La Reforma Económica y la Nueva Legitimidad." *Economía Exterior* 22 (Fall 2002).

De la Torre, Augusto, Juan Carlos Gozzi, and Sergio L. Schmukler. 2006. "Innovative Experiences in Access to Finance: Market Friendly Roles for the Visible Hand?" Latin America Regional Study. Washington: World Bank.

———. 2007a. "Capital Market Development: Whither Latin America?" Policy Research Working Paper 4156. Washington: World Bank.

————. 2007b. "Financial Development: Maturing and Emerging Policy Issues." *World Bank Research Observer* 22, no. 1: 67–102.

De la Torre, Augusto, Eduardo Levy-Yeyati, and Sergio L. Schmukler. 2002. "Financial Globalization: Unequal Blessings." *International Finance* 5, no. 3: 335–57.

De la Torre, Augusto, and Sergio L. Schmukler. 2004. *Whither Latin American Capital Markets?* Washington: World Bank.

Del Grossi, Mauro Eduardo, and José Graziano da Silva. 2001. "Fábrica do Agricultor do Estado do Paraná, Sul do Brasil." Best Practices and Strategies for Interventions to Promote Rural Nonfarm Employment in Latin America. Santiago, Chile: Department for International Development (DFID) and Rimisp–Centro Latinoamericano para el Desarrollo Rural.

Del Popolo, Fabiana, and Magally Avila, eds. 2006. *Pueblos Indígenas y Afrodescendientes de América Latina y el Caribe: Información Sociodemográfica para Políticas y Programas.* Santiago, Chile: United Nations, Economic Commission for Latin America and the Caribbean (ECLAC).

DeNavas-Walt, Carmen, Bernadette D. Proctor, and Cheryl Hill Lee. 2006. *Income, Poverty, and Health Insurance Coverage in the United States: 2005.* U.S. Census Bureau, Current Population Reports, P60-231. Washington: U.S. Government Printing Office.

Deruyttere, Anne. 2006. "Operational Policy on Indigenous Peoples and Strategy for Indigenous Development." Sector Strategy and Policy Papers Series 111. Washington: Inter-American Development Bank, Sustainable Development Department.

Dervis, Kemal, and Nancy Birdsall. 2006. "A Stability and Social Investment Facility for High-Debt Countries." Working Paper 77. Washington: Center for Global Development (www.cgdev.org/content/publications/detail/5853 [April 2006]).

De Soto, Hernando. 2000. *The Mystery of Capital: Why Capitalism Triumphs in the West and Fails Everywhere Else.* New York: Basic Books.

Deutsch, Ruthanne. 1998. "Does Child Care Pay? Labor Force Participation and Earnings Effects of Access to Child Care in the Favelas of Rio de Janeiro." Working Paper 384. Washington: Inter-American Development Bank, Office of the Chief Economist.

Di Gropello, Emanuela, ed. 2006. *Meeting the Challenges of Secondary Education in Latin America and East Asia: Improving Efficiency and Resource Mobilization.* Washington: World Bank.

Di Tella, Rafael, and Ernesto Schargrodsky. 2003. "The Role of Wages and Auditing during a Crackdown on Corruption in the City of Buenos Aires." *Journal of Law and Economics* 46, no. 1: 269-92.

Dias da Silva, Graziella M. 2006. "Ações Afirmativas no Brasil e na áfrica do Sul." *Tempo Social* 18, no. 2: 131–65.

Dirani, Valeria M., Michael Schied, and Inese Voika. 2004. "NGO Monitoring Efforts: Latvia, Ecuador, and India." In Transparency International, *Global Corruption Report 2004: Political Corruption.* London and Ann Arbor, Mich.: Pluto Press.

Djankov, Simeon, Caralee McLiesh, and Andrei Shleifer. 2007. "Private Credit in 129 Countries." *Journal of Financial Economics* 84, no. 2: 299–329.

Dos Reis, Laura, Paolo Manasse, and Ugo Panizza. 2007. "Targeting the Structural Balance." Working Paper 598. Washington: Inter-American Development Bank, Research Department.

Draibe, Sônia M. 2006. "Brazil: Bolsa-Escola y Bolsa-Família." In *Transferencias con Corresponsabilidad: Una Mirada Latinoamericana,* edited by Ernesto Cohen and Rolando Franco. Mexico City: FLACSO-México and Secretaría de Desarrollo Social (SEDESOL).

Drosdoff, Daniel. 2002. "Tax Cheats Beware." *IDB América* (September). Washington: Inter-American Development Bank.

Duryea, Suzanne, Olga Jaramillo, and Carmen Pagés. 2003. "Latin American Labor Markets in the 1990s: Deciphering the Decade." Working Paper 486. Washington: Inter-American Development Bank, Research Department.

Duryea, Suzanne, David Lam, and Deborah Levison. 2007. "Effects of Economic Shocks on Children's Employment and Schooling in Brazil." *Journal of Development Economics* 84, no.1: 188–214.

Duryea, Suzanne, and Carmen Pagés. 2002. "Human Capital Policies: What They Can and Cannot Do for Productivity and Poverty Reduction in Latin America." Working Paper 468. Washington: Inter-American Development Bank, Research Department.

Duryea, Suzanne, and others. 2007. "The Educational Gender Gap in Latin America and the Caribbean." Working Paper 600. Washington: Inter-American Development Bank, Research Department.

Easterly, William, and Stanley Fischer. 2001. "Inflation and the Poor." *Journal of Money, Credit, and Banking* 33, no. 2: 160–78.

Easterly, William, Timothy Irwin, and Luis Servén. 2007. "Walking Up the Down Escalator: Public Investment and Fiscal Stability." Policy Research Working Paper 4158. Washington: World Bank.

Easterly, William, and others. 1993. "Good Policy or Good Luck? Country Growth Performance and Temporary Shocks." *Journal of Monetary Economics* 32, no. 3: 459–83.

Economic Commission for Latin America and the Caribbean (ECLAC). 2000. *Preliminary Overview of the Economies of Latin America and the Caribbean: 2000.* Santiago, Chile: United Nations.

———. 2001. *Panorama Social de América Latina: 2000–2001.* Santiago, Chile: United Nations.

———. 2004a. *Latin America and the Caribbean in the World Economy: 2002–2003.* Santiago, Chile: United Nations.

———. 2004b. *Economic Survey of Latin America and the Caribbean: 2003–2004.* Santiago, Chile: United Nations.

———. 2005. *Panorama Social de América Latina: 2005.* Santiago, Chile: United Nations.

———. 2006a. *Panorama Social de América Latina: 2006.* Santiago, Chile: United Nations.

———. 2006b. *Shaping the Future of Social Protection: Access, Financing, and Solidarity.* Santiago, Chile: United Nations.

———. 2006c. *Preliminary Overview of the Economies of Latin America and the Caribbean: 2006.* Santiago, Chile: United Nations.

———. 2006d. *Economic Survey of Latin America and the Caribbean: 2005–2006.* Santiago, Chile: United Nations.

———. 2006e. *Latin America and the Caribbean in the World Economy: 2005–2006.* Santiago, Chile: United Nations.

————. 2007a. *Statistical Yearbook for Latin America and the Caribbean: 2006.* Santiago, Chile: United Nations.

————. 2007b. "Defensorías Comunitarias: Una Respuesta Comunitaria a la Violencia Familiar, Cusco (Perú)." Experiencias en Innovacion Social, Ciclo 2005–2006. Santiago, Chile: ECLAC and W.K. Kellogg Foundation.

Economic Commission for Latin America and the Caribbean, Latin American and Caribbean Demographic Center. (ECLAC-CELADE). 2006. Migración Internacional, Derechos Humanos, y Desarrollo. Santiago, Chile: Economic Commission for Latin America and the Caribbean, Population Division.

Economic Commission for Latin America and the Caribbean, Instituto Latinoamericano y del Caribe de Planificación Económica y Social (ECLAC-ILPES). Estadísticas de las Finanzas Públicas de América Latina. Online database. Santiago, Chile: United Nations (www.eclac.org/ilpes [April 2007]).

Economic Commission for Latin America and the Caribbean, Sistema Interactivo Gráfico de Datos de Comercio Internacional (ECLAC-SIGCI). 2007. Online database. Santiago, Chile: United Nations, Economic Commission for Latin America and the Caribbean, Division of International Trade and Integration (www.eclac.cl/comercio/ [April 2007]).

Edwards, Alejandra Cox, and Manuelita Ureta. 2003. "International Migration, Remittances, and Schooling: Evidence from El Salvador." *Journal of Development Economics* 72, no. 2: 429–61.

Eichengreen, Barry, Ricardo Hausmann, and Ugo Panizza. 2005. "The Mystery of Original Sin." In *Other People's Money: Debt Denomination and Financial Instability in Emerging Market Economies,* edited by Barry Eichengreen and Ricardo Hausmann. University of Chicago Press.

Elliott, Kimberly A. 2005. "Big Sugar and the Political Economy of U.S. Agricultural Policy." Policy Brief. Washington: Center for Global Development.

————. 2006. *Delivering on Doha: Farm Trade and the Poor.* Washington: Center for Global Development and Institute for International Economics.

Engel, Eduardo, Alexander Galetovic, and Claudio Raddatz. 1999. "Taxes and Income Distribution in Chile: Some Unpleasant Redistributive Arithmetic." *Journal of Development Economics* 59, no. 1: 155–92.

Engerman, Stanley, and Kenneth Sokoloff. 2002."Factor Endowments, Inequality, and Paths of Development among New World Economies." *Economia* 3, no. 1: 41–109.

Engle, Patrice L., and others. 2007. "Strategies to Avoid the Loss of Developmental Potential in More than 200 Million Children in the Developing World." *Lancet* 369, no. 9555: 229–42.

Escaith, Hubert, and Samuel Morley. 2001. "The Impact of Structural Reforms on Growth in Latin America and the Caribbean: An Empirical Estimation." Serie Macroeconomía del Desarrollo 01. Santiago, Chile: United Nations, Economic Commission for Latin America and the Caribbean (ECLAC).

Escobal, Javier, and Maximo Torero. 2005. "Measuring the Impact of Asset Complementarities: The Case of Rural Peru." *Cuadernos de Economía* 42, no.125: 137–64.

Escribano, Álvaro, and others. 2005. "The Impact of Infrastructure on Competitiveness in Latin America: A Firm-Level Analysis Based on Investment Climate Assessments." Washington: World Bank.

Estache, Antonio, Vivien Foster, and Quentin Wodon. 2002. *Accounting for Poverty in Infrastructure Reform: Learning from Latin America's Experience.* Studies in Development Series. Washington: World Bank Institute

Estache, Antonio, Andres Gomez-Lobo, and Danny Leipziger. 2001. "Utilities Privatization and the Poor: Lessons and Evidence from Latin America." *World Development* 29, no. 7: 1179–98.

Estache, Antonio, and Lucia Quesada. 2001. "Concession Contract Renegotiations: Some Efficiency versus Equity Dilemmas." Policy Research Working Paper Series 2705.Washington: World Bank.

Evenett, Simon J., and Bernard M. Hoekman. 2005. "International Cooperation and the Reform of Public Procurement Policies." Policy Research Working Paper 3720. Washington: World Bank.

Fajnzylber, Pablo and J. Humberto López. 2007. *Close to Home: The Development Impact of Remittances in Latin America.* Washington: World Bank.

Fay, Marianne, and Mary Morrison. 2007. *Infrastructure in Latin America and the Caribbean: Recent Developments and Key Challenges.* Washington: World Bank.

Fay, Marianne, and Tito Yepes. 2003. "Investing in Infrastructure: What Is Needed From 2000 to 2010?" Policy Research Working Paper 3102. Washington: World Bank.

Feder, Gershon. 2002. "The Intricacies of Land Markets: Why the World Bank Succeeds in Economic Reform through Land Registration and Tenure Security." Paper presented at the Conference of the International Federation of Surveyors. Washington, April 19–26.

Fenochietto, Ricardo. 1999. "Economía Informal y Evasión Impositiva en la República Argentina: Distintos Mecanismos de Medición, Sus Objetivos." Séptimo Congreso Tributario de San Martín de los Andes del CPCECF. San Martín de los Andes, Argentina, September, 4–8.

Ferreira Savoia, José Roberto. 2007. "Pension Reform in Brazil: The Challenge of Labor Inclusion." Paper presented at the Fifth International Research Conference on Social Security, "Social Security and the Labor Market: A Mismatch?" International Social Security Association. Warsaw, Poland, March 5–7.

Field, Erica. 2004. "Property Rights, Community Public Goods, and Household Time Allocation in Urban Squatter Communities: Evidence from Peru." *William and Mary Law Review* 45, no. 3: 837–87.

Field, Erica, and Maximo Torero. 2006. "Do Property Titles Increase Credit Access among the Urban Poor? Evidence from a Nationwide Titling Program." Working Paper. Cambridge, Mass.: Harvard University, Economics Department.

Filmer, Deon, Amer Hasan, and Lant Pritchett. 2006. "A Millennium Learning Goal: Measuring Real Progress in Education." Working Paper 97. Washington: Center for Global Development and the World Bank (www.cgdev.org/content/publications/detail/9815 [August 1996]).

Fischer, Ronald, Rodrigo Gutiérrez, and Pablo Serra. 2005. "The Effects of Privatization on Firms: The Chilean Case." In *Privatization in Latin America: Myths and Reality,* edited by Alberto Chong and Florencio López-de-Silanes. Inter-American Development Bank and Stanford University Press.

Fiszbein, Ariel, ed. 2005. *Citizens, Politicians, and Providers: The Latin American Experience with Service Delivery Reform.* Washington: World Bank.

Freedom House. 2007. *Freedom of the Press 2007: A Global Survey of Media Independence.* Lanham, Md.: Rowman and Littlefield Publishers.

Fuentes, Juan Alberto. 2006. "Retos de la Política Fiscal en América Central." Mexico City: United Nations, Economic Commission for Latin America and the Caribbean (ECLAC) and Instituto Centroamericano de Estudios Fiscales.

Fundación para el Desarrollo de la Libertad Ciudadana. 2003. *Informe Anual del Capítulo Panameño de Transparencia Internacional 2002–2003*. Ciudad de Panamá: Transparencia Internacional–Panamá.

Galasso, Emanuela. 2006. "With Their Effort and One Opportunity: Alleviating Extreme Poverty in Chile." Paper presented at the policy seminar "Evaluation Results of Chile Solidario: With Their Effort and One Opportunity." Washington, Inter-American Development Bank, February 20.

Galasso, Emanuela, and Martin Ravallion. 2004. "Social Protection in a Crisis: Argentina's Plan Jefes y Jefas." *World Bank Economic Review* 18, no.3: 367–99.

Galiani, Sebastian, Paul Gertler, and Ernesto Schargrodsky. 2005. "Water for Life: The Impact of the Privatization of Water Services on Child Mortality." *Journal of Political Economy* 113, no.1: 83–120.

Galiani, Sebastian, and Ernesto Schargrodsky. 2004. "Effects of Land Titling on Child Health." Research Network Working Paper R-491. Washington: Inter-American Development Bank.

———. 2007. "Property Rights for the Poor: Effects of Land Titling." Working Paper, January 12. Presented at the Oliver E. Williamson Seminar on Institutional Analysis, University of California, Berkeley, Haas School of Business, Institute of Management, Innovation and Organization, Berkeley, April 19.

Garces, Eliana, Duncan Thomas, and Janet Currie. 2000. "Longer-Term Effects of Head Start." Working Paper 8054. Cambridge, Mass.: National Bureau of Economic Research.

Garcia Aracil, Adela, and Donald R. Winkler. 2004. "Educación y Etnicidad en Ecuador." In *Etnicidad, Raza, Género, y Educación en América Latina*, edited by Donald R. Winkler and Santiago Cueto. Washington and Santiago, Chile: Partnership for Educational Revitalization in the Americas (PREAL).

Gargarella, Roberto. 2002. "Too Far Removed from the People: Access to Justice for the Poor, the Case of Latin America." Paper presented at the Bergen Seminar Series 2002–2003, "Accountability and Responsiveness Workshop," organized by the United Nations Development Program (UNDP) and Chr. Michelsen Institute (CMI). Bergen, Norway, November 18–19.

Gelos, R. Gaston. 2006. "Banking Spreads in Latin America." Working Paper 06/44. Washington: International Monetary Fund.

General Accounting Office (GAO). 2000. "Sugar Program: Supporting Sugar Prices Has Increased Users' Costs While Benefiting Producers." GAO/RCED-00-126.

Gertler, Paul. 2004. "Do Conditional Cash Transfers Improve Child Health? Evidence from Progresa's Control Randomized Experiment." *American Economic Review* 94, no. 2: 336–41.

Gertler, Paul, Sebastian Martinez, and Marta Rubio-Codina. 2006. "Investing Cash Transfers to Raise Long-Term Living Standards." Policy Research Working Paper 3994. Washington: World Bank.

Gershberg, Alec Ian. 2004. "Empowering Parents While Making Them Pay: Autonomous Schools and Education Reform Processes in Nicaragua." In *Crucial Needs, Weak Incentives: Social Sector Reform, Democratization, and Globalization in Latin America*, edited by Robert R. Kaufman and Joan M. Nelson. Woodrow Wilson Center Press and Johns Hopkins University Press.

Gilardi, Fabrizio, Jacint Jordana, and David Levi-Faur. 2006. "Regulation in the Age of Globalization: The Diffusion of Regulatory Agencies across Europe and Latin

America." In *Privatization and Market Development: Global Movements in Public Policy Ideas,* edited by Graene Hodge. Cheltenham, U.K. and Northampton, Mass.: Edward Elgar Publishing.

Gill, Indermit, Truman Packard, and Juan Yermo. 2005. *Keeping the Promise of Social Security in Latin America.* Stanford University Press.

Global Integrity. 2007. *2006 Global Integrity Report.* Washington (www.globalintegrity.org [May 2007])

Glomm, Gerhard, Juergen Jung, and Chung Tran. 2006. "Macroeconomic Implications of Early Retirement in the Public Sector: The Case of Brazil." CAEPR Working Paper 2006-008. Indiana University, Economics Department, Center for Applied Economics and Policy Research (CAEPR).

Glomm, Gerhard, and others. 2005. "Public Pensions and Capital Accumulation: The Case of Brazil." CESifo Working Paper 1539. Munich, Germany: Center for Economic Studies and Ifo Institute for Economic Research (CESifo).

Goel, Rajeev K., and Michael A. Nelson. 1998. "Corruption and Government Size: A Disaggregated Analysis." *Public Choice* 97, no. 1–2: 107–20.

Goldmark, Lara. 2006. "Beyond Finance: Microfinance and Business Development Services." In *An Inside View of Latin American Microfinance,* edited by Marguerite Berger, Lara Goldmark and Tomás Miller-Sanabria. Washington: Inter-American Development Bank, Multilateral Investment Fund.

Goldstein, Morris, and Philip Turner. 2004. *Controlling Currency Mismatches in Emerging Markets.* Washington: Institute for International Economics.

Gomes, Raquel. 2006. "Upgrading without Exclusion: Lessons from SMEs in Fresh Fruit Producing Clusters in Brazil." In *Upgrading to Compete: Global Value Chains, Clusters, and SMEs in Latin America,* edited by Carlo Pietrobelli and Roberta Rabellotti. Washington: Inter-American Development Bank and Harvard University, David Rockefeller Center for Latin American Studies.

Goñi, Edwin, J. Humberto López, and Luis Servén. 2006. "Fiscal Reform for Social Equity in Latin America." Paper prepared for the conference "Políticas Económicas para un Nuevo Pacto Social en América Latina." World Bank. Barcelona, Spain, October 6–7, 2006.

Gonzalez-Eiras, Martín, and Martín A. Rossi. 2007. "The Impact of Electricity Sector Privatization on Public Health." Research Network Working Paper 524. Washington: Inter-American Development Bank.

Graham, Carol. 1998. *Private Markets for Public Goods: Raising the Stakes in Economic Reform.* Brookings.

———. 2002. "Crafting Sustainable Social Contracts in Latin America: Political Economy, Public Attitudes, and Social Policy." Working Paper 29. Center on Social and Economic Dynamics, Brookings Institution.

Grantham-McGregor, Sally, and others. 1991. "Nutritional Supplementation, Psychosocial Stimulation, and Mental Development of Stunted Children: The Jamaican Study." *Lancet* 338, no. 8758: 1–5.

———. 2007. "Developmental Potential in the First 5 Years for Children in Developing Countries." *Lancet* 369, no. 9555: 60–70.

Grindle, Meredith. 2004. *Despite the Odds: The Contentious Politics of Education Reform.* Princeton University Press.

Grosh, Margaret, John Blomquist, and Yisgedullish Amde. 2002. "When the Present Is at Stake." *Spectrum* 1 (Winter): 5–7.

Grubb, Norton, and others. 2006. "Thematic Review of Tertiary Education: Korea." Country Note. Organization for Economic Co-operation and Development (OECD).

Guarcello, Lorenzo, Fabrizia Mealli, and Furio Rosati. 2003. "Household Vulnerability and Child Labor: The Effect of Shocks, Credit Rationing, and Insurance." UCW Working Paper. Understanding Children's Work (UCW) Project. Rome: World Bank, International Labor Organization, and United Nations Children's Fund–UNICEF.

Guasch, José Luis. 2004. *Granting and Renegotiating Infrastructure Concessions: Doing It Right.* World Bank Institute Development Studies. Washington: World Bank.

Guasch, José Luis, and Joseph Kogan. 2005. "Inventories and Logistic Costs in Developing Countries: Levels and Determinants, a Red Flag on Competitiveness and Growth." *Revista de la Competencia y la Propiedad Intelectual* 1, no. 1: 5–29.

Guasch, José Luis, and Stéphane Straub. 2006. "Renegotiation of Infrastructure Concessions: An Overview." *Annals of Public and Cooperative Economics* 77, no. 4: 479–93.

Gupta, Sanjeev, Hamid R. Davoodi, and Erwin R. Tiongson. 2001. "Corruption and the Provision of Health Care and Education Services." In *The Political Economy of Corruption,* edited by Arvind K. Jain. London: Routledge.

Gupta, Sanjeev, Hamid Davoodi and Rosa Alonso-Terme. 2002. "Does Corruption Affect Income Inequality and Poverty?" *Economics of Governance* 3, no. 1: 23–45.

Gurgur, Tugrul, and Anwar Shah. 2005. "Localization and Corruption: Panacea or Pandora's Box?" Policy Research Working Paper 3486. Washington: World Bank.

Haber, Stephen. 2006. "Why Banks Don't Lend: The Mexican Financial System." Draft. Stanford University.

Hagerstrom, Mark. 2006. "Basic Education." In *Decentralized Service Delivery for the Poor.* Vol. 2, *Background Papers.* Mexico City: World Bank.

Halac, Marina, and Sergio L. Schmukler. 2004. "Distributional Effects Crises: The Financial Channel." *Economía* 5, no. 1: 1–51.

Hall, Guillette, and Christopher Humphrey. 2003. "Mexico: Southern States Development Strategy." Working Paper 31116. Washington: World Bank.

Hall, Guillette, and Harry A. Patrinos, eds. 2006. *Indigenous Peoples, Poverty, and Human Development in Latin America: 1994–2004.* New York: Palgrave Macmillan.

Hallman, Kelly, and others. 2007. "Indigenous Girls in Guatemala: Poverty and Location." In *Exclusion, Gender, and Education: Case Studies from the Development World,* edited by Maureen Lewis and Marlaine Lockheed (Washington: Center for Global Development).

Handa, Sudhanshu, and Benjamin Davis. 2006. "The Experience of Conditional Cash Transfers in Latin America and the Caribbean." *Development Policy Review* 24, no. 5: 513–36.

Hanushek, Eric A., and Dennis D. Kimko. 2000. "Schooling, Labor Force Quality, and the Growth of Nations." *American Economic Review* 90, no. 5: 1184–208.

Hanushek, Eric A., and Ludger Wößmann. 2007. "The Role of Education Quality in Economic Growth." Policy Research Working Paper 4122. Washington: World Bank.

Harasic, Davor. 2007. "Chile's Partial Success." In *Transparency International, Global Corruption Report 2007: Corruption in Judicial Systems.* Cambridge University Press

Hardy, Daniel, Paul Holden, and Vassili Prokopenko. 2003. "Microfinance Institutions and Public Policy." *Journal of Policy Reform* 6, no. 3: 147–58.

Harris Clive. 2003. "Private Participation in Infrastructure in Developing Countries: Trends, Impacts, and Policy Lessons." Working Paper 5. Washington: World Bank.

Hausmann, Ricardo, and Michael Gavin. 1998. "Growth with Equity: The Volatility Connection." In *Beyond Trade-Offs: Market Reforms and Equitable Growth in Latin America,* edited by Nancy Birdsall, Carol Graham, and Richard Sabot. Brookings and Inter-American Development Bank.

Hausmann, Ricardo, Ugo Panizza, and Ernesto Stein. 2000. "Why Do Countries Float the Way They Float?" Working Paper 418. Washington: Inter-American Development Bank, Research Department.

Hazell, Peter, and others. 2006. "The Future of Small Farms: Synthesis Paper." Background paper for the World Development Report 2008 "Agriculture for Development." Santiago, Chile: Rimisp–Centro Latinoamericano para el Desarrollo Rural/Latin American Center for Rural Development.

Heckman, James J., and Dimitriy V. Masterov. 2007. "The Productivity Argument for Investing in Young Children." Working Paper 13016. Cambridge, Mass.: National Bureau of Economic Research.

Heckman, James J., and Carmen Pagés. 2000. "The Cost of Job Security Regulation: Evidence from Latin American Labor Markets." *Economía* 1, no. 1: 109-144.

———, eds. 2004. *Law and Employment: Lessons from Latin America and the Caribbean.* University of Chicago Press.

Heinemann, Alessandra, and Dorte Verner. 2006. "Crime and Violence in Development: A Literature Review of Latin America and the Caribbean." Policy Research Working Paper 4041. Washington: World Bank.

Henriques, Ricardo. 2002. *Raça e Gênero no Sistema de Ensino: Os Limites das Políticas Universalistas na Educação.* Brasília: United Nations Educational, Scientific and Cultural Organization (UNESCO).

Henson, Spencer. 2007. "New Markets and Their Supporting Institutions: Opportunities and Constraints for Demand Growth." Background paper for the World Development Report 2008 "Agriculture for Development." Santiago, Chile: Rimisp–Centro Latinoamericano para el Desarrollo Rural/Latin American Center for Rural Development.

Herrera, Javier, and François Roubaud. 2004. "Poverty and Corruption in Peru." In Transparency International, *Global Corruption Report 2004: Political Corruption.* London and Ann Arbor, Mich.: Pluto Press.

Hewings, Geoffrey. 2004. "Overview of Regional Development Issues." Paper presented at the Tenth Annual World Bank Conference on Development in Latin America and the Caribbean. San José, Costa Rica, November 3.

Hicks, Norman, and Quentin Wodon. 2001. "Social Protection for the Poor in Latin America." *CEPAL Review* 73 (April): 93–113.

Hnatkovska, Viktoria V., and Norman Loayza. 2004. "Volatility and Growth." Policy Research Working Paper 3184. Washington: World Bank.

Hofbauer, Helena. 2006. "'Citizens' Audit' in Mexico Reveals Paper Trail of Corruption." In Transparency International, *Global Corruption Report 2006: Corruption and Health.* London and Ann Arbor, Mich.: Pluto Press.

Holm-Nielsen, Lauritz B., and others. 2005. "Regional and International Challenges to Higher Education in Latin America." In *Higher Education in Latin America: The*

International Dimension, edited by Hans de Wit, Isabel C. Jaramillo, and Jocelyne Garcel-Avila. Washington: World Bank.

Hummels, David. 2006. "The Role of Geography and Size." Occasional Paper 35. Buenos Aires: Inter-American Development Bank, Institute for the Integration of Latin America and the Caribbean (INTAL).

Hunt, Jennifer. 2006. "Why Are Some Public Officials More Corrupt Than Others?" In *International Handbook on the Economics of Corruption,* edited by Susan Rose-Ackerman. Northampton, Mass.: Edward Elgar Publishing.

Huther, Jeff, and Anwar Shah. 2000. "Anti-Corruption Policies and Programs: A Framework Policy Evaluation." Policy Research Working Paper 2501. Washington: World Bank.

Htun, Mala. 2003. "Women and Democracy." In *Constructing Democratic Governance in Latin America,* edited by Jorge Dominguez and Michael Shifter. Johns Hopkins University Press.

Ideas for Development in the Americas (IDEA). 2007. "Fiscal Pacts in Latin America," vol. 12, January-April. Washington: Inter-American Development Bank.

Instituto Federal de Acceso a la Información Pública (IFAI). 2004. *Transparency: Access to Information and Personal Data: Regulatory Framework.* Mexico City: IFAI.

Instituto Libertad y Democracia/Institute for Liberty and Democracy (ILD). 2006a. "Evaluación Preliminar de la Economía Extralegal en 12 Países de Latinoamérica y el Caribe: Reporte de la Investigación en Argentina." Lima.

———. 2006b. "Evaluación Preliminar de la Economía Extralegal en 12 Países de Latinoamérica y el Caribe: Reporte de la Investigación en Guatemala." Lima.

———. 2006c. "Evaluación Preliminar de la Economía Extralegal en 12 Países de Latinoamérica y el Caribe: Reporte de la Investigación en México." Lima.

———. 2006d. "Evaluación Preliminar de la Economía Extralegal en 12 Países de Latinoamérica y el Caribe: Reporte de la Investigación en Perú." Lima.

———. 2006e. "Evaluación Preliminar de la Economía Extralegal en 12 Países de Latinoamérica y el Caribe: Reporte de la Investigación en Colombia." Lima.

Inter-Agency Consultation on Race in Latin America (IAC). 2003. *Race Report 2003.* Washington: Inter-American Dialogue.

Inter-American Development Bank (IDB). 1995. *Overcoming Volatility.* Economic and Social Progress in Latin America, 1995 report. Washington.

———. 1997. *Latin America after a Decade of Reforms.* Economic and Social Progress in Latin America, 1997 report. Washington.

———. 1999. *Facing Up to Inequality in Latin America.* Economic and Social Progress in Latin America, 1998–99 report. Washington.

———. 2001. *Competitiveness: The Business of Growth.* Economic and Social Progress in Latin America, 2001 report. Washington.

———. 2003a. "A New Generation of Social Programs." *IDEA* 1 (2nd quarter 2003).

———. 2003b. "MIF Evaluation: Support of Private Participation in Infrastructure." MIF/GN-78-9. Washington: Inter-American Development Bank, Office of Evaluation and Oversight.

———. 2004a. *Good Jobs Wanted.* Economic and Social Progress in Latin America, 2004 report. Washington.

———. 2004b. "Evaluation of MIF Projects: Market Functioning: Promotion of Competition and Consumer Protection." MIF/GN-78-14. Washington: Inter-American Development Bank, Office of Evaluation and Oversight.

————. 2005. *Unlocking Credit: The Quest for Deep and Stable Bank Lending*. Economic and Social Progress in Latin America, 2005 report. Washington.

————. 2006. *Living with Debt: How to Limit the Risks of Sovereign Finance*. Economic and Social Progress in Latin America, 2007 report. Inter-American Development Bank and Harvard University, David Rockefeller Center for Latin American Studies.

Inter-American Dialogue. 2003. *Access to Information in the Americas*. Washington: Inter-American Dialogue.

————. 2004. *All in the Family: Latin America's Most Important International Financial Flow*. Report of the Inter-American Dialogue Task Force on Remittances. Washington.

International Commission of Jurists (ICJ). 2005. *La Justicia en Guatemala: Un Largo Camino por Recorrer*. Geneva.

International Finance Corporation (IFC). 2006. *Doing Business in Brazil*. Washington: World Bank and International Finance Corporation.

International Labor Organization (ILO). 1999. *World Employment Report 1998–99*. Geneva.

————. 2003. *Panorama Laboral de América Latina y el Caribe 2003*. Lima: International Labor Organization, Regional Office for Latin America and the Caribbean.

————. 2006. *Panorama Laboral de América Latina y el Caribe 2006*. Lima: International Labor Organization, Regional Office for Latin America and the Caribbean.

International Monetary Fund (IMF). 2003a. *World Economic Outlook, September 2003: Public Debt in Emerging Markets*. Washington.

————. 2003b. "Fiscal Adjustment in IMF-Supported Programs." Evaluation Report, Independent Evaluation Office. Washington.

————. 2006a. *Regional Economic Outlook, November 2006: Western Hemisphere*. Washington.

————. 2006b. *World Economic Outlook, April 2006: Globalization and Inflation*. Washington.

————. 2006c. "Panama: Selected Issues and Statistical Appendix." Country Report 06/3. Washington.

————. 2007 (forthcoming). *Promoting Fiscal Discipline over the Business Cycle*. Washington.

————. 2007a. World Economic Outlook database, April (www.imf.org/external/pubs/ft/weo/2007/01/data/index.aspx [April 2007]).

————. 2007b. *World Economic Outlook, April 2007: Spillovers and Cycles in the Global Economy*. Washington.

————. 2007c. *Regional Economic Outlook, April 2007: Western Hemisphere*. Washington.

————. 2007d. "Mexico: Financial Sector Assessment Program Update: Technical Note: Financing of the Private Sector." Country Report 07/170. Washington.

International Organization for Migration (IOM). 2005. *World Migration 2005: Costs and Benefits of International Migration*. IOM World Migration Report Series, vol. 3. Geneva.

Jalan, Jyotsna, and Martin Ravallion. 2003. "Estimating the Benefit Incidence of an Antipoverty Program by Propensity Score Matching." *Journal of Business and Economic Statistics* 21, no. 1: 19–30.

James, Estelle, Guillermo Martinez, and Augusto Iglesias. 2006. "The Payout Stage in Chile: Who Annuitizes and Why?" *Journal of Pension Economics and Finance* 5, no. 2: 121–54.

Kapur, Devesh, and John McHale. 2005. *Give Us Your Best and Brightest: The Global Hunt for Talent and Its Impact on the Developing World.* Washington: Center for Global Development.

Kariuki, Mukami, and Jordan Schwartz. 2005. "Small-Scale Private Service Providers of Water Supply and Electricity: A Review of Incidence, Structure, Pricing, and Operating Characteristics." Policy Research Working Paper 3727. Washington: World Bank.

Karl, Terry L. 2001. "The Vicious Cycle of Inequality in Latin America." In *The Politics of Injustice in Latin America,* edited by Susan E. Eckstein and Timothy P. Wickham-Crowley. University of California Press.

Kaufman, Robert R., and Joan M. Nelson, eds. 2004. *Crucial Needs, Weak Incentives: Social Sector Reform, Democratization, and Globalization in Latin America.* Woodrow Wilson Center Press and Johns Hopkins University Press.

Kaufmann, Daniel. 2003. "Rethinking Governance: Empirical Lessons Challenge Orthodoxy." Discussion draft, March 11. Washington: World Bank.

———. 2005. "Myths and Realities of Governance and Corruption." In *Global Competitiveness Report 2005–2006: Policies Underpinning Rising Prosperity,* edited by Augusto Lopez-Claros, Michael Porter, and Klaus Schwab. Palgrave Macmillan and World Economic Forum.

Kaufmann, Daniel, and Art Kraay. 2002. "Growth without Governance." *Economía* 3, no.1: 169–215.

Kaufmann, Daniel, Art Kraay, and Massimo Mastruzzi. 2006. "Governance Matters V: Aggregate and Individual Governance Indicators for 1996–2005." Policy Research Working Paper 4012. Washington: World Bank.

Kaufmann, Daniel, Judit Montoriol-Garriga, and Francesca Recanatini. 2005. "How Does Bribery Affect Public Service Delivery? Micro-Evidence from Service Users and Public Officials in Peru." Discussion draft, November 21. Washington: World Bank Institute.

Kay, Stephen J., and Milko Matijascic. 2006. "Social Security at the Crossroads: Toward Effective Pension Reform in Latin America." *International Social Security Review* 59, no. 1: 3–26.

Kay, Stephen J., and Tapen Sinha, eds. 2007. *Lessons from Pension Reform in the Americas.* Oxford University Press.

Keefer, Philip, and Stephen Knack. 1995. "Institutions and Economic Performance: Cross-Country Tests Using Alternative Institutional Measures." *Economics and Politics* 7, no. 3: 207-27.

———. 2007 (forthcoming). "Boondoggles, Rent-Seeking, and Political Checks and Balances: Public Investment under Unaccountable Governments." *Review of Economics and Statistics* 89.

Kessler, Gabriel, and María Cecilia Roggi. 2005. "Programas de Superación de la Pobreza y Capital Social: La Experiencia Argentina." In *Aprender de la Experiencia: El Capital Social en la Superación de la Pobreza,* edited by Irma Arriagada. Santiago, Chile: United Nations, Economic Commission for Latin America and the Caribbean.

Kirilenko, Andrei, and Victoria Perry. 2004. "On the Financial Disintermediation of Bank Transaction Taxes." International Monetary Fund, Fiscal Affairs Department.

Kirilenko, Andrei, and Victoria Summers. 2003. "Bank Debit Taxes: Yield versus Disintermediation." In *Taxation of Financial Intermediation: Theory and Practice for Emerging Economies,* edited by Patrick Honohan. Washington: World Bank.

Klapper, Leora F. 2006. "The Role of Factoring for Financing Small and Medium Enterprises." *Journal of Banking and Finance* 30, no. 11: 3111–30.

Kohl, Benjamin. 2004. "Privatization Bolivian Style: A Cautionary Tale." *International Journal of Urban and Regional Research* 28, no. 4: 893–908.

Komives, Kristin, and others. 2006. "The Distributional Incidence of Residential Water and Electricity Subsidies." Policy Research Working Paper 3878. Washington: World Bank.

Krueger, Alan B., and Mikael Lindahl. 2001. "Education for Growth: Why and for Whom?" *Journal of Economic Literature* 39, no. 4: 1101–36.

Krugman, Paul. 1994. *The Age of Diminished Expectations.* 4th ed. MIT Press.

Kuczynski, Pedro-Pablo, and John Williamson, eds. 2003. *After the Washington Consensus: Restarting Growth and Reform in Latin America.* Washington: Institute for International Economics.

Lambsdorff, J. 2005. "Determining Trends for Perceived Levels of Corruption." Discussion Paper V-38-05. Germany: University of Passau.

Larraín Ríos, Guillermo. 2005. "Enhancing the Success of the Chilean Pension System: The Addition of Multiple Funds and Annuities." In *A Quarter Century of Pension Reform in Latin America and the Caribbean: Lessons Learned and Next Steps,* edited by Carolin A. Crabbe. Washington: Inter-American Development Bank.

Latin-American Shadow Financial Regulatory Committee. 2004. "Improving Access to Financial Services in Latin America: What Works and What Doesn't?" Statement 11 (September 8). Washington.

Latinobarómetro. 1995–2006. Data files. Santiago, Chile: Corporación Latinobarómetro.

Lavadenz, Isabel, and Klaus Deininger. 2003. "Land Policies." In *Colombia: The Economic Foundation of Peace,* edited by Marcelo M. Giugale, Olivier Lafourcade, and Connie Luff. Washington: World Bank.

Le Fort, Guillermo. 2006. "Política Fiscal con Meta Estructural en la Experiencia Chilena." Paper presented at the Second Annual Meeting of the Group of Latin American and Caribbean Public Debt Management Specialists (LAC Debt Group), sponsored by the Inter-American Development Bank. Cartagena, Colombia, April 20–21.

Levy, Santiago. 2006a. *Progress against Poverty: Sustaining Mexico's Progresa-Oportunidades Program.* Brookings.

———. 2006b. "Social Security Reform in Mexico: For Whom?" Paper prepared for the World Bank conference "Equity and Competitiveness in Mexico." Mexico City, November 27–28.

Levy-Yeyati, Eduardo. 2004. "Dollar, Debts, and the IFIs: Dedollarizing Multilateral Credit." Preliminary draft. Presented at the conference "Dollars, Debt, and Deficits—60 Years after Bretton Woods." Banco de España and the International Monetary Fund, Madrid, Spain, June 14–15.

Levy-Yeyati, Eduardo, Alejandro Micco, and Ugo Panizza. 2007 (forthcoming). "State Owned Banks: Do They Promote or Depress Financial Development and Economic Growth?" *Economía* 7, no. 2.

Lewis, Maureen A. 2006. "Governance and Corruption in Public Health Care Systems." Working Paper 78. Washington: Center for Global Development.

Lewis, Maureen A., and Marlaine E. Lockheed. 2006. *Inexcusable Absence: Why 60 Million Girls Still Aren't in School and What to Do about It.* Washington: Center for Global Development.

Limão, Nuno, and Anthony Venables. 2001. "Infrastructure, Geographical Disadvantage, Transport Costs, and Trade." *World Bank Economic Review* 15, no. 3: 451–79.

Lindert, Kathy, Emmanuel Skoufias, and Joseph Shapiro. 2006. "Redistributing Income to the Poor and the Rich: Public Transfers in Latin America and the Caribbean." Social Protection Discussion Paper 0605. Washington: World Bank.

Lindert, Kathy, and others. 2007. "The Nuts and Bolts of Brazil's Bolsa Família Program: Implementing Conditional Cash Transfers in a Decentralized Context." Social Protection Discussion Paper 0709. Washington: World Bank.

Llisterri, Juan José. 2006. "Credit Guarantee Systems in Latin America: Taking Stock." *Microenterprise Development Review* 9, no. 2: 9–16.

Llisterri, Juan José, and others. 2006. *Sistemas de Garantía de Crédito en América Latina: Orientaciones Operativas.* Washington: Inter-American Development Bank.

Loayza, Norman, Pablo Fajnzylber, and Cesar Calderón. 2005. *Economic Growth in Latin America and the Caribbean: Stylized Facts, Explanations, and Forecasts.* Washington: World Bank.

Loayza, Norman, Ana Maria Oviedo, and Luis Servén. 2005. "The Impact of Regulation on Growth and Informality: Cross-Country Evidence." Policy Research Working Paper 3623. Washington: World Bank.

Londoño, Juan Luis, and Rodrigo Guerrero. 1999. "Violence in Latin America: Epidemiology and Costs." Research Network Working Paper R-375. Washington: Inter-American Development Bank.

López, Ramón. 1996. "Land Titles and Farm Productivity in Honduras." In *Land Tenure Insecurity and Farm Productivity in Latin America: The Case of Honduras and Paraguay,* edited by Derek Byerlee and Alberto Valdés. Washington: World Bank.

———. 2005. "Why Governments Should Stop Non-Social Subsidies: Measuring Their Consequences for Rural Latin America." Policy Research Working Paper 3609. Washington: World Bank.

López, Ramón, and Alberto Valdés. 2001. "Fighting Rural Poverty in Latin America: New Evidence and Policy." In *Rural Poverty in Latin America,* edited by Ramón López and Alberto Valdés. London: Palgrave Macmillan.

Lopez-Acevedo, Gladys, and Hong Tan. 2005. "Evaluating Training Programs for Small and Medium Enterprises: Lessons from Mexico." Policy Research Working Paper 3760. Washington: World Bank.

Lopez-Claros, Augusto, and others, eds. 2006. *Global Competitiveness Report 2006–2007: Creating an Improved Business Environment.* Palgrave Macmillan and World Economic Forum.

López-Córdova, Jose E. 2006. "Globalization, Migration and Development: The Role of Mexican Migrant Remittances." Working Paper 20. Buenos Aires: Inter-American

Development Bank, Institute for the Integration of Latin America and the Caribbean (INTAL).

Lora, Eduardo. 2001. "Structural Reforms in Latin America: What Has Been Reformed and How to Measure It." Working Paper 466. Washington: Inter-American Development Bank, Research Department.

———. 2004. "A Decade after the Great Wave of Structural Reforms: What Have We Learned?" PowerPoint Presentation. Washington: Inter-American Development Bank, Research Department.

———. 2007. "Should Latin America Fear China?" Working Paper 531. Washington: Inter-American Development Bank, Research Department.

Lora, Eduardo, and Mauricio Olivera. 2005. "The Electoral Consequences of the Washington Consensus." Working Paper 530. Washington: Inter-American Development Bank, Research Department.

Lora, Eduardo, and Ugo Panizza. 2002. "Structural Reforms in Latin America under Scrutiny." Working Paper 470. Washington: Inter-American Development Bank, Research Department.

Love, Inessa, and Nataliya Mylenko. 2003. "Credit Reporting and Financing Constraints." Policy Research Working Paper 3142. Washington: World Bank.

Lucchetti, Leonardo, and Rafael Rofman. 2006. "Pension Systems in Latin America: Concepts and Measurements of Coverage." Social Protection Discussion Paper 616. Washington: World Bank.

Lundy, Mark. 2006. "New Forms of Collective Action by Small-Scale Growers." Santiago, Chile: Rimisp–Centro Latinoamericano para el Desarrollo Rural/Latin American Center for Rural Development.

Lustig, Nora. 2000. "Crises and the Poor: Socially Responsible Macroeconomics." *Economia* 1, no.1: 1–30.

Lustig, Nora, and Omar Arias. 2000. "Poverty Reduction." *Finance and Development* 37, no. 1.

Macedo, Roberto. 2000. "Privatization and the Distribution of Assets in Brazil." Working Paper 14. Washington: Carnegie Endowment for International Peace.

———. 2005. "Distribution of Assets and Income in Brazil: New Evidence." In *Reality Check: The Distributional Impact of Privatization in Developing Countries,* edited by Nancy Birdsall and John Nellis. Washington: Center for Global Development.

Macours, Karen, Alain de Janvry, and Elizabeth Sadoulet. 2004. "Insecurity of Property Rights and Matching in the Tenancy Market." Working Paper 992. University of California, Berkeley, Department of Agriculture and Resource Economics.

Maggi Campos, Claudio. 2006. "The Salmon Farming and Processing Cluster in Southern Chile." In *Upgrading to Compete: Global Value Chains, Clusters, and SMEs in Latin America,* edited by Carlo Pietrobelli and Roberta Rabellotti. Washington: Inter-American Development Bank and Harvard University, David Rockefeller Center for Latin American Studies.

Maldonado, Patricio, and others. 2004. "Political-Party Finance in Argentina, Chile, Costa Rica, and Mexico: Lessons for Latin America." America's Accountability Anti-Corruption Project. U.S. Agency for International Development (USAID) and Casals and Associates, Alexandria, Va.

Malhotra, Mohini, and others. 2006. *Expanding Access to Finance: Good Practices and Policies for Micro, Small, and Medium Enterprises.* Washington: World Bank Institute.

Malkin, Daniel. 2006. *Education, Science, and Technology in Latin America and the Caribbean: A Statistical Compendium of Indicators.* Washington: Inter-American Development Bank.

Maloney, William. 2004. "Informality Revisited." *World Development* 32, no. 7: 1159–78.

Marcel, Mario. 2006. "Reforming Chile's Pension Reform." Presentation at the seminar "Reforming Pension Reform." Inter-American Development Bank, Washington, November 27.

Martinez-Vazquez, Jorge. 2001. "The Impact of Budgets on the Poor: Tax and Benefit Incidence." Working Paper Series. Atlanta: Georgia State University, International Studies Program.

Martner, Ricardo, and Eduardo Aldunate. 2006. "Política Fiscal y Protección Social." Serie Gestión Pública 53. Santiago, Chile: United Nations, Economic Commission for Latin America and the Caribbean (ECLAC).

Mauro, Paolo. 1995. "Corruption and Growth." *Quarterly Journal of Economics* 110, no. 3: 681–712.

———. 1997. "The Effects of Corruption on Growth, Investment, and Government Expenditure: A Cross-Country Analysis." In *Corruption and the Global Economy,* edited by Kimberly Ann Elliott. Washington: Institute for International Economics.

———. 1998. "Corruption and the Composition of Government Expenditure." *Journal of Public Economics* 69, no. 2: 263–79.

———. 2004. "The Persistence of Corruption and Slow Economic Growth." *IMF Staff Papers* 51, no. 1: 1–18.

May, Ernesto, and others, eds. 2006. *Towards the Institutionalization of Monitoring and Evaluation Systems in Latin America and the Caribbean: Proceedings of a World Bank/Inter-American Development Bank Conference.* Lima: World Bank.

McEwan, Patrick J. 2004. "La Brecha de Puntajes Obtenidos en las Pruebas por los Niños Indígenas en Sudamérica." In *Etnicidad, Raza, Género, y Educación en América Latina,* edited by Donald R. Winkler and Santiago Cueto. Washington and Santiago, Chile: Partnership for Educational Revitalization in the Americas (PREAL).

McEwan, Patrick J., and Marisol Trowbridge. 2007. "The Achievement of Indigenous Students in Guatemalan Primary Schools." *International Journal of Educational Development* 27 (2007): 61–76.

McKenzie, David, and Dilip Mookherjee. 2005. "Paradox and Perception: Evidence from Four Latin American Countries." In *Reality Check: The Distributional Impact of Privatization in Developing Countries,* edited by Nancy Birdsall and John Nellis. Washington: Center for Global Development.

Melgar Peña, Carlos. 2007. "Judicial Corruption and the Military Legacy in Guatemala." In Transparency International, *Global Corruption Report 2007: Corruption in Judicial Systems.* Cambridge University Press.

Mello, Luiz. 2006. "Fiscal Responsibility Legislation and Fiscal Adjustment: The Case of Brazilian Local Governments." Policy Research Working Paper 3812. Washington: World Bank.

Mesa-Lago, Carmelo. 2005. "Evaluation of a Quarter Century of Structural Pension Reforms in Latin America." In *A Quarter Century of Pension Reform in Latin America and the Caribbean: Lessons Learned and Next Steps,* edited by Carolin A. Crabbe. Washington: Inter-American Development Bank.

Mesquita Moreira, Mauricio. 2007. "Fear of China: Is There a Future for Manufacturing in Latin America?" *World Development* 35, no. 3: 355–76.

México, Secretaría de Desarrollo Social (México-SEDESOL). 2007. *Oportunidades: Un Programa de Resultados.* Mexico City: SEDESOL, Programa de Desarrollo Humano Oportunidades.

Miller, Margaret, and Dina Rojas. 2005. "Improving Access to Credit for SMEs: An Empirical Analysis of the Feasibility of Pooled Data Small Business Credit Scoring Models in Colombia and Mexico." Working Paper. Washington: World Bank.

Mocan, Naci. 2004. "What Determines Corruption? International Evidence from Micro Data." Working Paper 10460. Cambridge, Mass.: National Bureau of Economic Research.

Morán, Ricardo, ed. 2003. *Escaping the Poverty Trap: Investing in Children in Latin America.* Washington: Inter-American Development Bank.

Morley, Samuel, and David Coady. 2003. *From Social Assistance to Social Development: Targeted Education Subsidies in Developing Countries.* Washington: Center for Global Development and the International Food Policy Research Institute.

Moura Castro, Claudio. 2002. "Education in the Information Age: Promises and Frustrations." In *Making Technology Work for Education in Latin America and the Caribbean: Notes on Issues, Policies, and Innovations,* edited by Juan Carlos Navarro, Norma García, and Laurence Wolff. Washington: Inter-American Development Bank.

Navajas, Sergio, and Luis Tejerina. 2006. "Microfinance in Latin America and the Caribbean: Connecting Supply and Demand." Working Paper. Washington: Inter-American Development Bank.

Navarro, Juan C. 2005. "Two Kinds of Education Politics." In *The Politics of Policies: Economic and Social Progress in Latin America 2006 Report.* Inter-American Development Bank and Harvard University.

Nellis, John. 2003. "Privatization in Latin America." Working Paper. Washington: Center for Global Development and Inter-American Dialogue.

Nellis, John, and Nancy Birdsall, eds. 2005. *Reality Check: The Distributional Impact of Privatization in Developing Countries.* Washington: Center for Global Development.

Nellis, John, Rachel Menezes, and Sarah Lucas. 2004. "Privatization in Latin America: The Rapid Rise, Recent Fall, and Continuing Puzzle of a Contentious Economic Policy." Policy Brief. Washington: Center for Global Development and Inter-American Dialogue.

Nickson, Andrew, and Claudia Vargas. 2002. "The Limitations of Water Regulation: The Failure of the Cochabamba Concession in Bolivia." *Bulletin of Latin American Research* 21, no. 1: 99–120.

Ñopo, Hugo, Jaime Saavedra, and Maximo Torero. 2004. "Ethnicity and Earnings in Urban Peru." Discussion Paper 980. Bonn, Germany: Institute for the Study of Labor (IZA).

Ocampo, José Antonio. 2002. "Rethinking the Development Agenda." *Cambridge Journal of Economics* 26, no. 3: 393–407.

———. 2004. "Latin America's Growth and Equity Frustrations during Structural Reforms." *Journal of Economic Perspectives* 18, no. 2: 67–88.

Oldsman, Eric. 2000. "Making Business Development Work: Lessons from the Enterprise Development Center in Rafaela, Argentina." Best Practices Series. Washington: Inter-American Development Bank, Sustainable Development Department.

Organization for Economic Cooperation and Development (OECD). 2003. *White Paper on Corporate Governance in Latin America*. Paris.

———. 2004. *Global Corruption Report 2004: Political Corruption*. London and Ann Arbor, Mich.: Pluto Press.

———. 2005a. *Revenue Statistics 1965–2004*, 2005 ed. Paris.

———. 2005b. *Agricultural Policies in OECD Countries: Monitoring and Evaluation 2005*. Paris.

Orozco, Manuel. 2006a. "International Flows of Remittances: Cost, Competition, and Financial Access in Latin America and the Caribbean—Toward an Industry Scorecard." Washington: Inter-American Dialogue.

———. 2006b. "Diasporas, Philanthropy, and Hometown Associations: The Central American Experience." Washington: Inter-American Development Bank, Multilateral Investment Fund.

Paiva, Angela R., ed. 2004. *Ação Afirmativa na Universidade: Reflexão sobre Experiências Concretas Brasil–Estados Unidos*. Rio de Janeiro: Desiderata and Pontifícia Universidade Católica do Rio de Janeiro (PUC/RJ).

Palma, Julieta, and Raúl Urzúa. 2005. "Anti-Poverty Policies and Citizenry: The Chile Solidario Experience." Policy Paper 12. Paris: UN Educational, Scientific, and Cultural Organization (UNESCO).

Palmade, Vincent, and Andrea Anayiotos. 2005. "Rising Informality: Reversing the Tide." *Public Policy Journal* 298 (August).

Pan-American Health Organization (PAHO). 2002. "Cultural Diversity and Disaggregation of Statistical Health Information." Final report, Experts' Workshop. Quito, Ecuador, June 4–5, 2002.

Panizza, Ugo, and Mónica Yañez. 2006. "Why Are Latin Americans So Unhappy about Reforms?" Working Paper 567. Washington: Inter-American Development Bank, Research Department.

Panizza, Ugo, and others. 2006. "CLYPS Dataset on Public Debt Level and Composition in Latin America." Washington: Inter-American Development Bank.

Papademetriou, Demetrios, and others. 2003. "NAFTA's Promise and Reality: Lessons from Mexico and the Hemisphere." Carnegie Endowment Report. Washington: Carnegie Endowment for International Peace.

Paredes, Ricardo. 2005. "Evaluación del Programa de Capacitación Laboral Chile Joven." Documento de Trabajo 172. Santiago, Chile: Pontificia Universidad Católica de Chile, Departamento de Ingeniería Industrial y de Sistemas.

Parker, Norma, and others. 2004. "Corruption in Latin America: A Desk Assessment." Americas' Accountability Anti-Corruption Project. U.S. Agency for International Development (USAID) and Casals and Associates, Alexandria, Va.

Partnership for Educational Revitalization in the Americas (PREAL). 2001. *Lagging Behind: A Report Card on Education in Latin America*. Washington and Santiago, Chile.

———. 2006. *Quantity without Quality: A Report Card on Education in Latin America*. Washington and Santiago, Chile.

Patrinos, Harry Anthony, and Emmanuel Skoufias. 2007. *Economic Opportunities for Indigenous Peoples in Latin America*. Washington: World Bank.

Paxson, Christina, and Norbert Schady. 2007. "Cognitive Development among Young Children in Ecuador: The Roles of Wealth, Health, and Parenting." *Journal of Human Resources* 42, no. 1: 49–84.

Peltier-Thiberge, Nicolas. 2006. "Infraestructura Rural." In *Perú–La Oportunidad de un País Diferente: Próspero, Equitativo, y Gobernable,* edited by Marcelo M. Giugale, Vicente Fretes-Cibils, and John L. Newman. Lima: World Bank.

Perry, Guillermo, and others. 2006. *Poverty Reduction and Growth: Virtuous and Vicious Circles.* Washington: World Bank.

———. 2007a. *Latin America and the Caribbean's Response to the Growth of China and India: Overview of Research Findings and Policy Implications.* Washington: World Bank.

———. 2007b. *Informality: Exit and Exclusion.* Washington: World Bank, Latin American and the Caribbean Studies.

Perú, Ministerio de Trabajo y Promoción del Empleo (Perú-MTPE). 2005. *Elaboración de Estadísticas de la Micro y Pequeña Empresa.* Lima: Ministerio de Trabajo y Promoción del Empleo, Dirección Nacional de la Micro y Pequeña Empresa.

———. 2006. *Plan Nacional de Promoción y Formalización para la Competitividad y Desarrollo de la Micro y Pequeña Empresa 2005–2009.* Lima: Ministerio de Trabajo y Promoción del Empleo, Dirección Nacional de la Micro y Pequeña Empresa.

Pessino, Carola. 2001. "La Convertibilidad y El Mercado Laboral." Paper presented at the conference "La Primera Década de la Convertibilidad." Central Bank of the Republic of Argentina.

Pessino, Carola, and Ricardo Fenochietto. 2007 (forthcoming). "Efficiency and Equity of the Tax Structure in Argentina, Brazil, and Chile: Analysis and Policy Considerations." Working Paper. Washington: Center for Global Development and Inter-American Dialogue.

Pietrobelli, Carlo, and Roberta Rabellotti. 2006. "Supporting Enterprise Upgrading in Clusters and Value Chains in Latin America." In *Upgrading to Compete: Global Value Chains, Clusters, and SMEs in Latin America,* edited by Carlo Pietrobelli and Roberta Rabellotti. Washington: Inter-American Development Bank and Harvard University, David Rockefeller Center for Latin American Studies.

Pietrobelli, Carlo, Roberta Rabellotti, and Elisa Giuliani. 2006. "Upgrading in Global Value Chains: Lessons from Latin American Clusters." In *Upgrading to Compete: Global Value Chains, Clusters, and SMEs in Latin America,* edited by Carlo Pietrobelli and Roberta Rabellotti. Washington: Inter-American Development Bank and Harvard University, David Rockefeller Center for Latin American Studies.

Popkin, Margaret. 2004. "Access to Justice, Good Governance, and Civil Society." Revised version of paper presented at the Third Regional Conference on Justice and Development. Inter-American Development Bank and Justice Studies Center of the Americas. Quito, Ecuador, July 24–26, 2003.

Pritchett, Lant. 2005. "The Political Economy of Targeted Safety Nets." Social Protection Discussion Paper 0501. Washington: World Bank.

———. 2006. *Let Their People Come: Breaking the Gridlock on Global Labor Market Mobility.* Washington: Center for Global Development.

Proética. 2006. *Informe del Estado de la Lucha Anticorrupción en el Perú: 2002–2004.* Lima: Proética– Consejo Nacional para la Ética Pública.

Quapper, Klaudio D., and Rodrigo F. Valenzuela. 2005. "Análisis de las Juventudes en Chile Preguntando desde la Educación y la Empleabilidad: Chile Califica–GTZ e InterJoven." Buenos Aires: redEtis, Instituto de Desarrollo Económico y Social.

Rajan, Ragurham G., and Luigi Zingales. 2004. *Saving Capitalism from the Capitalists: Unleashing the Power of Financial Markets to Create Wealth and Spread Opportunity.* New York: Crown Business.

Ramey, Garey, and Valerie A. Ramey. 1995. "Cross-Country Evidence on the Link between Volatility and Growth." *American Economic Review* 85, no. 5: 1138–51.

Ravallion, Martin. 2000. "Monitoring Targeting Performance: When Decentralized Allocations to the Poor Are Unobserved." *World Bank Economic Review* 14, no. 2: 331–45.

Rawlings, Laura B. 2005. "A New Approach to Social Assistance: Latin America's Experience with Conditional Cash Transfer Programs." *International Social Security Review* 58, no. 2–3: 133–61.

Rawlings, Laura B., and Gloria M. Rubio. 2005. "Evaluating the Impact of Conditional Cash Transfer Programs." *World Bank Research Observer* 20, no. 1: 29–55.

Reardon, Thomas. 2006. "The Rapid Rise of Supermarkets and the Use of Private Standards in Their Food Product Procurement Systems in Developing Countries." In *Agro-Food Chains and Networks for Development,* edited by Ruerd Ruben, Maja Slingerland, and Hans Nijhoff. Wageningen, Netherlands: Springer.

Reardon, Thomas, and Julio A. Berdegué. 2002. "The Rapid Rise of Supermarkets in Latin America: Challenges and Opportunities for Development." *Development Policy Review* 20, no. 4: 371–88.

———. 2006. "The Retail-Led Transformation of Agrifood Systems and Its Implications for Development Policies." Background paper for the World Development Report 2008 "Agriculture for Development." Santiago, Chile: Rimisp–Centro Latinoamericano para el Desarrollo Rural/Latin American Center for Rural Development.

———. 2007. "WDR Background Paper on Retail-Led Transformation of Agrifood Systems: Box Focusing on Whether the Rise of Supermarkets Excludes Small Farmers." Short background paper for the World Development Report 2008 "Agriculture for Development." Santiago, Chile: Rimisp–Centro Latinoamericano para el Desarrollo Rural/Latin American Center for Rural Development.

Recart, Maria Olivia. 2005. "Fundación Chile: 29 Years Fostering Innovative Business Development in Key Chilean Clusters." Paper discussed at the World Bank workshop "Generating and Sustaining Growth without Picking Winners: Case Studies of New Industrial Policy Organizations." Santiago, Chile, June 13.

Reinhart, Carmen M., Kenneth S. Rogoff, and Miguel A. Savastano. 2003. "Debt Intolerance." *Brookings Papers on Economic Activity,* no. 1: 1–74.

Reis, Jose Guilherme, with Tito Yepes and Fernando Lecaros. 2007. "The Infrastructure Agenda for Competitiveness: Sequence Matters." In *Colombia 2006-2010: A Window of Opportunity.* Bogotá: World Bank.

Reydon, Bastiaan Philip, and Francisca Neide M. Cornélio, eds. 2006. *Mercado de Terras no Brasil: Estrutura e Dinâmica.* Brasília: Ministério do Desenvolvimento Agrário, Núcleo de Estudos Agrários e Desenvolvimento Rural (NEAD).

Reydon, Bastiaan Philip, and Ludwig A. Plata. 2002. "Evolução Recente do Preço da Terra Rural no Brasil e os Impactos do Programa da Cédula da Terra." Série Estudos NEAD. Brasília: Ministério do Desenvolvimento Agrário, Núcleo de Estudos Agrários e Desenvolvimento Rural (NEAD).

Riveros, Hernando, and Pilar Santacoloma. 2004. "Alternatives to Improve Negotiation and Market Access Capabilities of Small-Scale Rural Entrepreneurs in Latin America." AGSF Working Document 4. Rome: United Nations Food and Agriculture Organization (FAO), Agricultural Management, Marketing, and Finance Service (AGSF).

Rodríguez, Jorge, Carla Tokman, and Alejandra Vega. 2006. "Política de Balance Estructural: Resultados y Desafíos tras Seis Años de Aplicación en Chile." Estudios de Finanzas Públicas. Santiago, Chile: Ministerio de Hacienda, Dirección de Presupuestos.

Rodrik, Dani. 1997. *Has Globalization Gone Too Far?* Washington: Institute for International Economics.

———. 2005. "Growth Strategies." In *Handbook of Economic Growth*, vol. 1, edited by Philippe Aghion and Steven Durlauf, pp. 967–1014. Elsevier.

———. 2006. "Goodbye Washington Consensus, Hello Washington Confusion? A Review of the World Bank's *Economic Growth in the 1990s: Learning from a Decade of Reform.*" *Journal of Economic Literature* 44, no. 4: 973–87.

Rojas-Suarez, Liliana, and Simon Johnson, eds. 2008 (forthcoming). *Helping Reforms Deliver Growth in Latin America*. Washington: Center for Global Development.

Roodman, David. 2005. "Production-Weighted Estimates of Aggregate Protection in Rich Countries toward Developing Countries." Working Paper 66. Washington: Center for Global Development.

Roodman, David, and Uzma Qureshi. 2006. "Microfinance as Business." Working Paper 101. Washington: Center for Global Development.

Rosemberg, Fulvia. 2004. "Desigualidades de Raza y Género en el Sistema Educacional Brasileño." In *Etnicidad, Raza, Género, y Educación en América Latina*, edited by Donald R. Winkler and Santiago Cueto. Washington and Santiago, Chile: Partnership for Educational Revitalization in the Americas (PREAL).

Rucci, Graciana. 2004. "Macro Shocks and Schooling Decisions: The Case of Argentina." Paper presented at the Population Association of America's 2004 Annual Meeting, Boston, April 1–3, hosted by Princeton University, Office of Population Research and Center for Research on Child Well-Being.

Rutter, Michael, Henri Giller, and Ann Hagell. 2000. *Antisocial Behavior by Young People*. Cambridge University Press.

Saavedra, Jaime 2003. "Labor Markets during the 1990s." In *After the Washington Consensus: Restarting Growth and Reform in Latin America*, edited by John Williamson and Pedro-Pablo Kuczynski. Washington: Institute for International Economics.

Sahay, Ratna, and Rishi Goyal. 2006. "Volatility and Growth in Latin America: An Episodic Approach." Working Paper 06/287. Washington: International Monetary Fund.

Salazar, Daniel G., and others. 2003. "Credit Scoring." IT Innovation Series. Washington: Consultative Group to Assist the Poor (CGAP).

Salazar, Katya, and Jacqueline de Gramont. 2007. "Civil Society's Role in Combating Judicial Corruption in Central America." In Transparency International, *Global Corruption Report 2007: Corruption in Judicial Systems*. Cambridge University Press.

Salazar, Roxana, and José Pablo Ramos. 2007. "Increased Transparency Helps Curb Corruption in Costa Rica." In Transparency International, *Global Corruption Report 2007: Corruption in Judicial Systems*. Cambridge University Press.

Sánchez-Páramo, Carolina, and Norbert Schady. 2003. "Off and Running? Technology, Trade, and the Rising Demand for Skilled Workers in Latin America." Policy Research Working Paper 3015. Washington: World Bank.

Santiago Consultores Asociados. 1999. "Evaluación Ex-Post Programa Chile Joven II." Preliminary final report presented at the seminar Modelos de Evaluación para Programas de Capacitación de Jóvenes. International Labor Organization, Inter-American Research and Documentation Center on Vocational Training (CINTERFOR). Medellín, Colombia, July 17–18.

Santiso, Carlos. 2006. "Improving Fiscal Governance and Curbing Corruption: How Relevant Are Autonomous Audit Agencies?" *International Public Management Review* 7, no. 2: 97–09.

Savedoff, William D., Ruth Levine, and Nancy Birdsall. 2006. "When Will We Ever Learn? Improving Lives through Impact Evaluation." Report of the Evaluation Gap Working Group. Washington: Center for Global Development (www.cgdev.org/content/publications/detail/7973 [May 2006]).

Schady, Norbert R. 2006. "Early Childhood Development in Latin America and the Caribbean." *Economía* 6, no. 2: 185–225.

Schmitt, John. 2005. "Is It Time to Export the U.S. Tax Model to Latin America?" *Challenge* 48, no. 3: 84–108.

Schott, Peter K. 2006. "The Relative Revealed Competitiveness of China's Exports to the United States vis-à-vis Other Countries in Asia, the Caribbean, Latin America, and the OECD." Occasional Paper 39. Buenos Aires: Inter-American Development Bank, Institute for the Integration of Latin America and the Caribbean (INTAL).

Schreiner, Mark. 2003. "Scoring: The Next Breakthrough in Microcredit?" Occasional Paper 7. Washington: Consultative Group to Assist the Poor (CGAP).

Schultz, Paul T. 2004. "School Subsidies for the Poor: Evaluating the Mexican Progresa Poverty Program." *Journal of Development Economics* 74, no.1: 199–250.

Schumpeter, Joseph A. 1975. *Capitalism, Socialism, and Democracy.* Originally published in 1942. New York: Harper and Row.

Schwartzman, Simon. 2003. "Higher Education and the Demands of the New Economy in Latin America." Flagship Study Background Paper, Latin American and Caribbean Studies. Washington: World Bank.

Sehnbruch, Kirsten. 2006. "Unemployment Insurance or Individual Savings Accounts: Can Chile's New Scheme Serve as a Model for Other Developing Countries?" *International Social Security Review* 59, no. 1: 27–48.

Seligson, Mitchell A. 2006. "The Measurement and Impact of Corruption Victimization: Survey Evidence from Latin America." *World Development* 34, no. 2: 381–404.

Serrano, Guillermo P. 2006. "Bolivia." Country report in Transparency International, *Global Corruption Report 2006: Corruption and Health.* London and Ann Arbor, Mich.: Pluto Press.

Serviço Brasileiro de Apoio às Micro e Pequenas Empresas (SEBRAE). 2004. "Fatores Condicionantes e Taxa de Mortalidade de Empresas no Brasil." Relatório de Pesquisa. Brasília: SEBRAE.

———. 2006. "Onde Estão as Micro e Pequenas Empresas no Brasil." Observatório das MPEs. São Paulo: SEBRAE-SP.

Shah, Anwar, and Mark Schacter. 2004. "Combating Corruption: Look Before You Leap." *Finance and Development* 41, no. 4.

Silva, Nelson do Vale. 2000. "Extent and Nature of Racial Inequalities in Brazil." In *Beyond Racism: Embracing an Independent Future.* Atlanta: Southern Education Foundation.

Singh, Anoop. 2006. "Macroeconomic Volatility: The Policy Lessons from Latin America." Working Paper 06/166. Washington: International Monetary Fund.

Singh, Anoop, and others. 2005. "Stabilization and Reform in Latin America: A Macroeconomic Perspective of the Experience since the 1990s." Occasional Paper 238. Washington: International Monetary Fund.

Sislen, David, and others. 2007. "Cutting Red Tape in Lima: How Municipal Simplification Improves Investment Climate." *En Breve* 99 (January).

Skoufias, Emmanuel. 2000. "Is Progresa Working? Summary of the Results of an Evaluation by IFPRI." Synthesis Evaluation Report. Washington: International Food Policy Research Institute (IFPRI).

———. 2005. *Progresa and Its Impacts on the Welfare of Rural Households in Mexico.* Research Report 139. Washington: International Food Policy Research Institute (IFPRI).

Skoufias, Emmanuel, and W. Susan Parker. 2001. "Conditional Cash Transfers and Their Impact on Child Work and Schooling: Evidence from the Progresa Program in Mexico." *Economia* 2, no. 1: 45–86.

———. 2006. "Job Loss and Family Adjustments in Work and Schooling during the Mexican Peso Crisis." *Journal of Population Economics* 19, no. 1: 163–81.

Soares, Fabio V., and others. 2006. "Cash Transfer Programs in Brazil: Impacts on Inequality and Poverty." Working Paper 21. Brasília: United Nations Development Program, International Poverty Center.

Sobel, David L., and others. 2006. "The Federal Institute for Access to Public Information in Mexico and a Culture of Transparency." Report for the William and Flora Hewlett Foundation. University of Pennsylvania, Annenberg School for Communication.

Solo, Tova Maria. 2003. *Independent Water Entrepreneurs in Latin America: The Other Private Sector in Water Services.* Washington: World Bank.

Speck, Bruno W. 2004. "Campaign Finance Reform: Is Latin America on the Road to Transparency?" In Transparency International, *Global Corruption Report 2004: Political Corruption.* London and Ann Arbor, Mich.: Pluto Press.

Stotsky, Janet G., and Asegedech WoldeMariam. 2002. "Central American Tax Reform: Trends and Possibilities." Working Paper 02/227. Washington: International Monetary Fund.

Stubbs, Josefina. 2007. "Afro-Colombian and Indigenous Peoples: Issues, Progress, and Remaining Challenges." In *Colombia 2006–2010: A Window of Opportunity.* Bogotá: World Bank.

Subbarao, Kalanidhi. 1997. "Public Works as an Anti-Poverty Program: An Overview of Cross-Country Experience." *American Journal of Agricultural Economics* 79, no. 2: 678–83.

———. 2003. "Systemic Shocks and Social Protection: Role and Effectiveness of Public Works Programs." Social Protection Discussion Paper 0302. Washington: World Bank.

Svensson, Jakob. 2005. "Eight Questions about Corruption." *Journal of Economic Perspectives* 19, no. 3: 19–42.

Székely, Miguel, 1999. "Volatility: Children Pay the Price." *Latin American Economic Policies* 8 (Third Quarter): 3–4.

————. 2001. "The 1990s in Latin America: Another Decade of Persistent Inequality, but with Somewhat Lower Poverty." Working Paper 454. Washington: Inter-American Development Bank, Research Department.

Székely, Miguel, and Marianne Hilgert. 2001. "What Drives Differences in Inequality across Countries?" Working Paper 439. Washington: Inter-American Development Bank.

Tanzi, Vito. 1998a. "Corruption around the World: Causes, Consequences, Scope, and Cures." *IMF Staff Papers* 45, no. 4: 559–94.

————. 1998b. "Corruption and the Budget: Problems and Solutions." In *Economics of Corruption,* edited by Arvind K. Jain. Boston: Kluwer Academic Publishers.

Tanzi, Vito, and Hamid R. Davoodi. 1998a. "Corruption, Public Investment, and Growth." In *The Welfare State, Public Investment, and Growth,* edited by Hirofumi Shibata and Toshihiro Ihori. Tokyo: Springer Verlag.

————. 1998b. "Roads to Nowhere: How Corruption in Public Investment Hurts Growth." Economic Issues 12. Washington: International Monetary Fund.

————. 2001. "Corruption, Growth, and Public Finances." In *The Political Economy of Corruption,* edited by Arvind K. Jain. London: Routledge.

Tanzi, Vito, and Howell H. Zee. 2000. "Tax Policy for Emerging Markets: Developing Countries." Working Paper 00/35. Washington: International Monetary Fund.

Tejo, Pedro. 2003. *Mercados de Tierras Agrícolas en América Latina y el Caribe: Una Realidad Incompleta.* Santiago, Chile: Economic Commission for Latin America and the Caribbean (ECLAC).

Thomas, Vinod, Yan Wang, and Xibo Fan. 2003. "Measuring Education Inequality: Gini Coefficients of Education for 140 countries, 1960–2000." *Journal of Education Planning and Administration* 17, no. 1: 5–33.

Thorn, Kristian, Lauritz Holm-Nielsen, and Jette Samuel Jeppesen. 2004. "Approaches to Results-Based Funding in Tertiary Education: Identifying Finance Reform Options for Chile." Policy Research Working Paper 3436. Washington: World Bank.

Traa, Bob, and Alina Carare. 2007. "A Government's Net Worth." *Finance and Development* 44, no. 2.

Transparency International. 2003. *Global Corruption Report 2003: Access to Information.* London: Profile Books.

————. 2006a. Corruption Perceptions Index (CPI) 2006 (www.transparency.org/surveys/#cpi [November 2006]).

————. 2006b. "Corruption and Governance Measurement Tools in Latin American Countries." Working Paper. Transparency International, Policy and Research Department, and United Nations Development Program (UNDP).

————. 2006c. *Global Corruption Report 2006: Corruption and Health.* London and Ann Arbor, Mich.: Pluto Press.

————. 2007. *Global Corruption Report 2007: Corruption in Judicial Systems.* Cambridge University Press.

Transparencia Mexicana. 2006. *Índice Nacional de Corrupción y Buen Gobierno 2005.* Resultados 2001, 2003, y 2005. Mexico City: Transparencia Internacional–México.

Transparencia por Colombia. 2005. *Índice de Integridad de las Entidades Públicas Nacionales 2003–2004.* Colección Documentos Observatorio de Integridad 4. Bogotá.

————. 2006. "Integrity Index for Public Institutions: Evaluating Colombia's Health Sector." In Transparency International, *Global Corruption Report 2006: Corruption and Health,* London and Ann Arbor, Mich.: Pluto Press.

Treisman, Daniel. 2000. "The Causes of Corruption: A Cross-National Study." *Journal of Public Economics* 76, no. 3: 399–457.

Trémolet, Sophie, and Catherine Hunt. 2006. "Taking Account of the Poor in Water Sector Regulation." Water Supply and Sanitation Working Note 11. Washington: World Bank.

United Nations. 2007. "Crime and Development in Central America: Caught in the Crossfire." New York: Office of Drugs and Crime, United Nations.

Universidad de Chile. 2006. "Evaluación de Impacto del Programa de Formación en Oficios para Jóvenes de Escasos Recursos: Informe Final." Santiago: Universidad de Chile, Departamento de Economía, Centro de Microdatos.

Urizar, Alejandro. 2006. "Guatemala." Country report in Transparency International, *Global Corruption Report 2006: Corruption and Health.* London and Ann Arbor, Mich.: Pluto Press.

Urrea, Fernando. 2006. "Consideraciones sobre Raza y Condiciones Socioeconómicas de las Poblaciones Afrodescendientes en América Latina y el Caribe." Paper presented at "Conference to Establish a Policy Agenda for Racial Equality in the Americas." Inter-American Dialogue, World Bank, Inter-American Development Bank, Canadian Foundation for the Americas, and Inter-America Foundation. Washington, February 28.

U.S. General Social Survey. 2001. The National Data Program for the Sciences. National Opinion Research Center. University of Chicago.

Vaitsman, Jeni, and Rômulo Paes-Sousa, eds. 2007. *Avaliação de Políticas e Programas do MDS–Resultados.* Vol. 2, *Bolsa Família e Assistência Social.* Brasília: Ministério do Desenvolvimento Social, Secretaria de Avaliação e Gestão da Informação.

Valdez, José A. 1998. "Capitalization: Privatization Bolivian Style." The Lessons of Privatization, *Economic Reform Today,* no. 1. Center for International Private Enterprise.

Velasco, Andrés, and others. 2007. "Compromisos Fiscales y la Meta de Superávit Estructural." Estudios de Finanzas Públicas 9. Santiago, Chile: Ministerio de Hacienda, Dirección de Presupuestos.

Vélez, Carlos Eduardo, Ricardo Paes de Barros, and Francisco H. G. Ferreira. 2004. "Policy Report." In World Bank, *Inequality and Economic Development in Brazil.* Washington.

Ventura, Juan Pablo. 2001. "Política de Apoyo a las Pequeñas y Medianas Empresas: Análisis del Programa de Reconversión Empresarial para las Exportaciones." Serie Estudios y Perspectivas (Oficina Buenos Aires). Santiago, Chile: United Nations, Economic Commission for Latin America and the Caribbean (ECLAC).

————. 2003. "Institucionalidad de Apoyo a la Pequeña Empresa en Argentina." Background Paper. Washington: Inter-American Development Bank, Micro, Small, and Medium Enterprise Unit.

Vial, Joaquin, and Peter K. Cornelius. 2002. "The Latin American Competitiveness Report 2001–2002" (World Economic Forum). Oxford University Press.

Villanueva, E. 2003. "Social Participation and Access to Public Information in Latin America." Background Paper, Access to Information in the Americas Project. Washington: Inter-American Dialogue.

Villatoro, Pablo. 2005a. "Los Programas de Protección Social Asistencial en América Latina y sus Impactos en las Familias: Algunas Reflexiones." Paper presented at the meeting "Políticas hacia las Familias, Protección e Inclusión Sociales." Economic Commission for Latin America and the Caribbean (ECLAC). Santiago, Chile, June 28–29.

———. 2005b. "Programas de Transferencias Monetarias Condicionadas: Experiencias en América Latina." *Revista de la CEPAL* 86 (August): 87–101.

Walecki, Marcin. 2004. "Political Finance and Political Corruption." In Transparency International, *Global Corruption Report 2004: Political Corruption.* London and Ann Arbor, Mich.: Pluto Press.

Wei, Shang-Jin. 2000. "How Taxing Is Corruption on International Investors?" *Review of Economics and Statistics* 82, no. 1: 1–11.

Williamson, John. 1990. "What Washington Means by Policy Reform." In *Latin American Adjustment: How Much Has Happened?* edited by John Williamson. Washington: Institute for International Economics.

———. 2000. *Exchange Rate Regimes for Emerging Markets: Reviving the Intermediate Option.* Washington: Institute for International Economics.

———. 2005. *Curbing the Boom-Bust Cycle: Stabilizing Capital Flows to Emerging Markets.* Policy Analyses in International Economics 75. Washington: Institute for International Economics.

World Bank. 2007a. "Brazil: Improving Fiscal Circumstances for Growth." Vol. 2, "Main Report." Report 36595. Washington.

———. 2007b. "Colombia Gender Review." Report 39335. Washington.

———. 2007c. "Brazil: How to Revitalize Infrastructure Investments in Brazil: Public Policies for Better Private Participation. Vol. 2, "Background Report." Report 36624. Washington.

———. 2006a. *Doing Business 2007: How to Reform.* Washington: World Bank and International Finance Corporation.

———. 2006b. "Brazil: Interest Rates and Intermediation Spreads." Report 36628. Washington.

———. 2006c. "Doing Business in Mexico 2007." Report 39325. México City: World Bank and International Finance Corporation.

———. 2006d. "Mexico: Mexico's Competitiveness: Reaching Its Potential." Report 35388. Washington.

———. 2006e. "Country Assistance Strategy for the Argentine Republic 2006–2008." Report 34015. Washington.

———. 2005a. *Global Economic Prospects 2006: Economic Implications of Remittances and Migration.* Washington.

———. 2005b. "Brazil: Programmatic Fiscal Reform Loan: Social Security Reform Project." Report 32226. Washington.

———. 2005c. *World Development Report 2006: Equity and Development.* Washington.

———. 2005d. "Ecuador: Investment Climate Assessment." Report 31900. Washington.

———. 2005e. "Brazil: Investment Climate Assessment." Vol. 2, "Background Documents." Washington: World Bank and International Finance Corporation.

———. 2004a. "Argentina: Economic Recovery Support Structural Adjustment Loan Project." Report 27271. Washington.

————. 2004b. *World Development Report 2005: A Better Investment Climate for Everyone.* Oxford University Press.

————. 2003a. *Challenges and Opportunities for Gender Equality in Latin America and the Caribbean.* Washington.

————. 2003b. *World Development Report 2004: Making Services Work for Poor People.* Washington.

————. 2002a. *Constructing Knowledge Societies: New Challenges for Tertiary Education.* Washington.

————. 2002b. "Brazil Gender Review: Issues and Recommendations." Report 23442. Washington.

————. 1993. *The East Asian Miracle: Economic Growth and Public Policy.* Oxford University Press and World Bank.

World Development Indicators (WDI). 2006. CD-ROM. Washington: World Bank.

Zaltsman, Ariel. 2006. "Desarrollo de la Capacidad de Evaluación: Experiencia con la Institucionalización de Sistemas de Monitoreo y Evaluación en Cinco Países Latinoamericanos." ECD Working Paper Series 16. Washington: World Bank

Zervos, Sara. 2004. "The Transaction Costs of Primary Market Issuance: The Case of Brazil, Chile, and Mexico." Policy Research Working Paper 3424. Washington: World Bank.

Zettelmeyer, Jeromin. 2006. "Growth and Reforms in Latin America: A Survey of Facts and Arguments." Working Paper 06/210. Washington: International Monetary Fund.

Index

Africa, 12, 111n2

Agricultural issues: Asian economic growth and, 101–02; employment, 101; low productivity, 104; property rights and, 104–05, 107; research and development, 108–10; rural markets, 101–03; supermarkets, 103; trade, 103n9, 162n5; infrastructure, 105–06, 108. *See also* Repairing rural markets

Argentina: agricultural issues in, 102n5, 103n7; business issues in, 78n8, 85n24, 87n28, 88–89; corruption in, 111, 112, 116b, 118n19, 121, 152n13; economic crises in, 1–2, 22, 23; educational issues in, 123n1, 124nn4–5, 134n25; employment issues in, 95, 96; financial transaction tax in, 37; international repo facility of, 48n13; media in, 115n15; race, gender, and ethnicity in, 142; pension system in, 69, 73; privatization in, 151nn9–10, 152, 153n18; property rights in, 109; poverty in, 157–58; public protests in, 27; public services in, 157–58; social safety nets in, 51; tax administration in, 65nn14–16; taxes in, 59, 60n6, 60n7, 61. *See also* Latin America

Asia: agricultural research in, 109; business issues in, 75; educational issues in, 123, 124, 134n27; as an emerging economy, 1, 2; growth in, 11, 12; property rights in, 107n23; public services and infrastructure in, 146, 148

Assets. *See* Economic issues

Autonomous Schools Program (Nicaragua), 131

Banco do Brasil, 122

Banking issues: collateral, 84; counter-cyclical requirements, 47–48; credit bureaus, 79, 81, 82; credit scoring, 79, 81, 82; development banks, 86; e-banking, 79; entry of foreign banks, 48; microfinance, 79n11; prudential standards, 47; public banks, 82–83; risk management, 81, 82; scoring technologies, 81; securities markets, 84b; SME lending, 82, 84b; subsidies, 86. *See also* Financing issues

Bolivia: aid to, 161; corruption in, 111, 115–16; economic issues in, 155b; educational issues in, 127n12, 139; employment issues in, 139; health issues in, 140, 152n12; media in, 115n15; privatization in, 151n9, 152n12, 153,